**LABOR AND EMPLOYMENT
RELATIONS ASSOCIATION SERIES**

A Racial Reckoning in Industrial Relations: Storytelling as Revolution from Within

Edited by

Tamara L. Lee
Sheri Davis-Faulkner
Naomi R Williams
Maite Tapia

Cover design and illustration: Mary Cha

First Edition
ISBN 978-0-913447-24-6
Price: $34.95

LABOR AND EMPLOYMENT RELATIONS ASSOCIATION SERIES

LERA *Proceedings of the Annual Meeting* (published online annually, in the fall)

LERA *Annual Research Volume* (published annually, in the summer/fall)

LERA Online Membership Directory (updated daily, member/subscriber access only)

LERA *Labor and Employment Law News* (published online each quarter)

LERA *Perspectives on Work* (published annually, in the fall)

Information regarding membership, subscriptions, meetings, publications, and general affairs
of the LERA can be found at the Association website at www.leraweb.org. Members can make
changes to their member records, including contact information, affiliations, and preferences,
by accessing the online directory at the website or by contacting the LERA national office.

LABOR AND EMPLOYMENT RELATIONS ASSOCIATION
University of Illinois at Urbana-Champaign
School of Labor and Employment Relations
121 Labor and Employment Relations Building
504 East Armory Ave., MC-504
Champaign, IL 61820
Telephone: 217/333-0072   Fax: 217/265-5130
Website: www.leraweb.org
E-mail: LERAoffice@illinois.edu

Contents

CHAPTER 1

Introduction

TAMARA L. LEE
Rutgers University
Department of Labor Studies and Employment Relations

MAITE TAPIA
Michigan State University
School of Human Resources and Labor Relations

SHERI DAVIS-FAULKNER
Rutgers University
Center for Innovation in Worker Organization
and Department of Labor Studies and Employment Relations

NAOMI R WILLIAMS
Rutgers University
Department of Labor Studies and Employment Relations

The field of [industrial relations] has created a body of knowledge whose class-centered vocabulary (workers) speaks only to the conditions of marginalized workers on specialized occasion, despite the fact that inequity permeates and is at work in every system we study.

To put it bluntly, we are engaged in "separate, but equal" knowledge production. Indeed, it is a radical analogy to a dark period in US society—a long-held, normalized societal framework that was resistant to change, vigorously defended, and generally accepted as the controlling narrative.

That being said, developing a canon of critical industrial relations is an opportunity for IR scholars to more fully incorporate the counter-narratives of non-privileged identities of workers in our analysis as well as acknowledge the historically contextualized nature of our labor market institutions.

—Lee and Tapia (2021: 657)

We have previously written that as gatekeepers of knowledge regarding the world of work, the field of industrial relations owes theoretical reparations for pervasive and persistent systemic bias in our literature (Lee and Tapia 2021). Industrial relations theories of organizing, employment relations, and economic democracy are cloaked in the language of color-blindness, with conceptualizations of justice and class identity traditionally viewed through the lens of dominant social identity groups (Kelly 1998; McAlevey 2016). Moreover, our literature mostly fails to recognize and address the saliency and ubiquity of anti-Blackness and other oppressive systems of white supremacy in the labor and employment context. This has led to distorted and underinformed notions of worker justice that reinforce and perpetuate systemic discrimination (Block and Sachs 2020; Flynn, Holmberg, Warren, and Wong 2016).

Instead, we embrace the traditions and tenets of critical race theory and intersectionality (CRT/I) to acknowledge and deconstruct the false realities that thrive in traditional color-blind approaches to understanding social systems and the relationships among their actors (Crenshaw 1989; Matsuda 1987). By providing tools for deep, socio-structural examinations of race and other socially constructed identities, CRT/I helps industrial relations theory name and acknowledge the overlapping oppressions that disproportionately impact Black and other marginalized workers.

In this edited volume, we confront white-dominant constructions through the counternarratives of our contributors—a collection of experts from outside and within the field of labor and employment. We provide a platform for "special voices" from below (Matsuda 1987) to share their experience and provide relevant historical and political context that should work in tandem with our knowledge creation around issues of labor and employment in and outside of the enterprise. To do so, we convened thematic working groups over the course of a year that served as community writing spaces as well as circle groups for sharing the pain, suffering, joy, and accolades we were simultaneously experiencing as a result of racial uprisings; a global pandemic; and attacks on voting, reproductive, and LGBTQIA+ rights. We are proud of our collection that encompasses artists, activists, union organizers, and scholars and are grateful for the connections we made throughout this journey. That we thrived in these conditions is an ancestral testament.

The collective voices assembled here are meant to be disruptive and radical, reflecting a deep connection to the principles and best practices of CRT/I. Specifically, these principles, together with feminist ideology, center Afrocentric ways of community-based knowledge building and networking. We therefore go beyond the traditional way of knowledge production in academia, acknowledging and uplifting the diversity of voices and possibilities of storytelling. Building bridges and deeper connections among scholars, activists, practitioners, and artists is a necessary departure from our academic silos, yet it is often discouraged. This volume was created with intention and includes traditional chapters, commentary pieces, dialogues between practitioners and scholar-activists, and implications for on-the-ground mobilizations, as well as art and graphic illustrations. Our cover art, for example, represents a series of dialogues between the editors and Vicko Alvarez, a Tejana movement–based artist and educator, in which we explored the promise of an intersectional labor movement for social justice rooted in historical struggles against white supremacy and its comforts. The resulting image tells a story of racial reckoning and theorizes a path forward. Such collaborations build bridges and deeper connections among scholars, activists, practitioners, and artists is a necessary departure from our academic silos, yet it is often discouraged. This volume, we hope, becomes a testament to the possibilities of knowledge creation that can arise when working in expansive dialogic spaces.

OVERVIEW OF THE VOLUME

Scholar-activists, folks engaged in theoretical and practical knowledge production with an aim of social justice, provide the narrative for the Introduction and Part I of this racial reckoning in industrial relations. Their contributions answer Lee and Tapia's (2021) call for the development of a canon of critical industrial relations, as well as set forth a blueprint for how industrial relations scholars can and should engage critical labor history, racial capitalism, and CRT/I in the examination of labor and employment relations. In "Labor Tales of Critical Race Theory," Sheri Davis-Faulkner dives deep into the foundational CRT/I texts such as Matsuda's "Looking to the Bottom" to demonstrate how the use of "counterstories" and other tenets provide opportunity for industrial relations theorists, particularly during contemporary political, social, and labor contestation. Naomi R Williams' chapter on the shared origins and theoretical divergences in industrial relations and labor history could very well have been titled "What to the Labor Historian Is Critical Race Theory?" Williams provides historical context for existing analytical fissures despite our "Commons root." Danielle Phillips-Cunningham, with the clarity and power customary in her scholarship, grounds our understanding of contemporary organizing for systemic equity in the early theory and praxis of Black women organizers, leaving us to reflect on the intentionality that underlies the erasure of their contributions and the potential harm that flows from the disregard of their vital narratives.

Part I's historical and political context for racial reckoning also confronts deficits in existing industrial relations frameworks for understanding racial (in)justice in the US political economy. For example, Austin McCoy delivers a historical intervention into our failed understandings of abolitionist politics of Black worker collectives in the long fight against violent policing. He provides a mechanism for reframing contemporary Black anti-policing uprisings as Black worker uprisings and forces us to confront traditional conceptualizations of antifascist and abolitionist praxis as outside the gates of the labor movement. Sanjay Pinto, in his chapter on racial capitalism at work, brings racial capitalism frameworks to more deeply probe systemic inequities born by Black and Latine communities during the COVID-19 pandemic. By outlining the core mechanisms of racial capitalism, Pinto provides industrial relations scholars with additional frameworks for contemplating the future of work and worker organizing in the context of macro struggles for racial and economic justice. Salil Sapre and Maite Tapia's timely examination of labor militancy shuns traditional color-blind industrial relations frameworks in favor of a CRT/I approach that centers the Black repertoire of resistance, frequently overlooked or erased by both labor scholars and some activists. Their findings lead to an alternative understanding of a mainstream labor movement in long decline—and implications for its revival. Tamara Lee and Nicole Burrowes allow readers to eavesdrop on an intimate and radical conversation between Black scholars across disciplines who reckon with imperialism, colonialism, and issues of social identity in their research in the Caribbean and Global South. Through shared storytelling, they engage in annotated circle work that delves into the complexities of intersectional identities for both researcher and subject. The footnotes and in-text citations are ripe with mature fruit for the hungry comparative scholar and those engaged in the study of systems not their own. Closing out Part I, Erica Smiley anchors readers in the historic framework of Radical Reconstruction, arguing that "strategies to combat white supremacy are central to democratizing employment and other economic relationships." In addition, Smiley calls for greater investment in "new southern worker organizing strategies" to advance the multiracial democracy our ancestors laid the groundwork for with the 13th, 14th, and 15th Amendments to the Constitution.

In Part II, we reorient the lens of expertise to the activists and practitioners engaged in theory building from below and within. In "Intersectionality of Liberation," the voices of a diverse array of young activists take on the construction of intersectionality and its meaning for the liberation of the various identity groups engaged in liberation struggle. Their conversation is a model for counter-storytelling, as they radically confront tensions and opportunities in the places where race, ethnicity, gender identity, sexual orientation, disability, and national origin converge in the fights against global white supremacy, patriarchy, transphobia, ableism, and other systems of oppression. Moderator Tahira Benjamin explicitly defines their lexicon ("We are going to use the term 'community role' because we're reimagining and redefining what the capitalist world of 'work' is.") and then leads the panelists in an exploration and reimagination of justice from below and on the front lines of broader working-class social movements. In another powerful conversation between scholar-activists engaged in work at the intersections of labor and environmental justice, J. Mijin Cha and Larry Williams, Jr., moderated by Maite Tapia, discuss "just transition" with a racial lens and in relation to their personal stories. The discussion is testimony to the experiences of scholar-activists of color doing justice work in predominantly white spaces, uncovering systemic barriers in social justice praxis.

We end the volume with Part III, which gives first-hand accounts from labor movement leaders. In "The Strategy Is Love," WILL (Women Innovating Labor Leadership) Empower hosts a powerhouse collection of labor movement leaders from unions, worker centers, community organizations, and foundations in a worker-centered discussion responding to questions posed by their peers nationwide. It is an exercise in intersectional organizing from the lens of an inclusive set of women and nonbinary labor leaders long engaged in bargaining for a common good and equitable society. In an autobiographical account, Javier Morillo provides an insightful narrative of what it takes to lead a union in its efforts to match its strategic organizing to its vision: "We All Deserve to Live Lives of Joy." In seeking to transform "what they deserved" into "what they had the power to win," Morillo takes us on a passionate journey that involves navigating micro-aggressions institutionally normalized in traditional collective bargaining. Finally, long-time labor activist Valery Alzaga and political educator Harmony Goldberg, in conversation with Maite Tapia, talk about using the framework of racial capitalism as part of the political education for labor and community organizations. They explain how this framework is meant to create a transformational space where members of unions and other organizations don't just become better critics—but better organizers and activists.

We present this volume as both a blueprint and a call to action for industrial relations scholars. We must diversify our approaches, reckon with racial injustice within our field and scholarship, and welcome new voices into our field. We offer this volume as a path forward.

ENDNOTE

1. There are conversations occurring across and within the diaspora as to the appropriate language to express gender neutrality. Here, we follow James Lee's construction as he outlines in "Call Me Latine" (https://callmelatine.com/faq).

REFERENCES

Block, Sharon, and Benjamin Sachs. 2020. "Clean Slate for Worker Power: Building a Just Economy and Democracy." Report of the Labor and Worklife Program, Harvard Law School. https://bit.ly/3CSes5j

Crenshaw, Kimberlé. 1989. "Demarginalizing the Intersection of Race and Sex: A Black Feminist Critique of Antidiscrimination Doctrine, Feminist Theory and Antiractist Politics." *University of Chicago Legal Forum* 1989 (1): 139–167. https://bit.ly/3qeS5Sv

Flynn, Andrea, Susan Holmberg, Dorian Warren, and Felicia Wong. 2016. "Rewrite the Racial Rules: Building an Inclusive American Economy." Roosevelt Institute Report. https://bit.ly/3CSeQAN

Kelly, John. 1998. *Rethinking Industrial Relations: Mobilisation, Collectivism and Long Waves.* London: Routledge.

Lee, Tamara L., and Maite Tapia. 2021. "Confronting Race and Other Social Identity Erasures: The Case for Critical Industrial Relations Theory." *ILR Review* 74 (3): 637–662.

RACIAL RECKONING IN INDUSTRIAL RELATIONS

Matsuda, Mari J. 1987. "Looking to the Bottom: Critical Legal Studies and Reparations Minority Critiques of the Critical Legal Studies Movement." *Harvard Civil Right–Civil Liberties Law Review* 22 (2): 323–400.

McAlevey, Jane. F. 2016. *No Shortcuts: Organizing for Power in the New Gilded Age.* New York: Oxford University Press.

CHAPTER 2

Labor Tales of Critical Race Theory: Disrupting Normative in Search of the Transformative

SHERI DAVIS-FAULKNER
Rutgers University
Center for Innovation in Worker Organization
and Department of Labor Studies and Employment Relations

Abstract

Labor counterstories in critical race theory have been hiding in plain sight for nearly three decades. In this chapter, I argue that foundational critical race theory texts provide useful tenets for advancing labor scholarship and movement building, especially during this time-critical moment of disruption. I assert that Mari Matsuda's seminal piece, "Looking to the Bottom," provides a blueprint for academic and movement power brokers (gatekeepers) to resolve issues of abstraction undergirded by a predominantly class-first "universal" worker narrative. This blueprint is broken into three parts. First, recognize that voices from the bottom can and do offer a "special voice" rooted in historical and contemporary experiences of discrimination and oppression. Second, contextualize labor issues using the lens of those at the bottom and the historical and political context illuminating their lived experiences. Third, make a commitment to align future scholarship and activism with the broader justice and reparations projects envisioned by those on the bottom who are working to transforms systems that are rooted in white supremacy and patriarchy.

Those on the bottom who speak out against the odds for their vision of justice, often become powerful people in the popular mind. The critical scholar can invoke Sojourner Truth, as she silenced a hostile crowd with the power of her slave experience; Cesar Chavez, as he fasted for the forgotten farm workers; Minoru Yasui, who like Homer Plessy before him, orchestrated his own arrest to bring to the highest court in the land a case that revealed the poverty of the American legal system; and Rosa Parks, who dared to imagine that a black woman could remain seated on a Montgomery bus while a white man stood. . . . By joining these crusaders, [critical scholars] can derive the authority to say, "We are on their side, we are right, and we will prevail." Alliance with the bottom lends moral force to the project of critical scholarship and helps complete the utopian vision.

—Mari Matsuda (1987)

INTRODUCTION

A year ago today, I, along with the rest of the nation and the world, watched as Trump's supporters and white supremacist groups, including entire families, breeched the barriers surrounding the Capitol steps; attacked the few police officers charged with protecting the building; and stormed the congressional floor and the offices of members of Congress in a violent attempt to overturn the 2020 election results. They effectively held congressional members, staffers, and journalists hostage for hours. When they were tired and satisfied, they picked up their loot and went home, having desecrated, even defecated in, the halls of Congress. While many white people were shocked and stunned that this kind of violent behavior could occur in the nation's capital, people of color had seen it coming. And we found ourselves more disturbed by how little resistance the traitors faced, having originally assumed we'd see the insurrectionists get a little taste of their own police brutality medicine. Not surprised, but disappointed, people of color witnessed yet another deadly episode of unchecked white supremacist violence.

The predominantly white participants of the January 6 insurrection are *currently* military officers, police officers, firefighters, nurses, retail workers, teachers, and other public sector workers; they are youth, elders, neighbors, elected leaders, religious leaders, church members, landlords, small-business owners, employers, and trade unionists. The insurrection, and violent armed confrontations by Trump-supporting supremacists leading up to it in states across the nation, is evidence of the resurgence of overt racism and open practice of white supremacy, which is also coursing through the veins of the labor movement. If the goal of organized labor over the past four decades was to win the "hearts and minds" of predominantly white workers to embrace a class solidarity agenda that disrupts inequality, then the insurrection indicates that this largely white-centric/colorblind project has failed. Seeing their humanity and ceding to white supremacist nostalgic ideology are not the same; the risks for POCs and women is too great to conflate them.

The long tail of the insurrection is evident at town hall and school board meetings, where mask mandates and critical race theory (CRT) are targeted as bogeymen threatening the nation. It is also visible in state legislation with Jim Crow–like voting restrictions and gerrymandered district maps meant to dilute the voting power of BIPOC communities. It is showing up as a refusal to take precautions to prevent the spread of COVID-19, which disproportionately causes death in Black and Indigenous communities. Like the 2020 public lynching of George Floyd by Darren Wilson and the bystanders of the unionized Minneapolis Police Department, the events of January 6, 2021, cannot be unseen. Scholarly inquiry about labor, class, work, and poverty cannot and should never have been separated from race and gender categories, much less the racism and sexism employed to police the boundaries of the exclusive rights granted to a privileged few through white supremacy and patriarchy. To stay relevant, to win against late-stage capitalism and the authoritarian right-wing movement, labor relations scholarship needs to apply a CRT framework to fully recognize and comprehend the dynamics in place. Continuing to ignore it will not protect workers, especially workers and women of color.

In this chapter, I argue that part of this failure is due to the absence of a real racial reckoning in the field of labor studies, employment relations, industrial relations, and many sectors of organized labor. It serves as a primer for understanding key CRT tenets that will be referenced and engaged within the chapters of this volume. My intent is to briefly introduce concepts by amplifying a few of the stories about labor, work, and class struggle from each seminal CRT text, including stories that undergird the tenets. I am also challenging organized labor in general and labor relations in academia, to apply critical race approaches to curricula, discourse, and personnel practices. This not an exhaustive chronicle of all the CRT concepts and tenets; my hope is that readers will see alignment of their interests (both activism and research) with the marginalized people/laborers centered in the CRT texts and even further within the chapters of this volume. As a matter of practice, I always begin with the story; here is a part of my story.

In the four short years that I have worked in a labor studies department, attended professional conferences, and read the literature, I have been disheartened by the mainstream acceptance of scholarship that lacks a basic analysis of race and racism and barely attempts engagement with the now advanced stages of intersectional scholarship. The impending "browning of America" means the "browning of labor," so my initial expectation was that labor scholars and labor scholarship would be much more inclusive of people of color, at the very least. My next hope was that the predominantly white labor scholars were engaging with (meaning reading, citing, and in dialogue with) the comprehensive bodies of scholarship by people of color. However, I have found that in this moment when workers, especially workers at the bottom of the wage ladder, are noticeably people of color, there seems to be little to no effort to hear their voices, listen to their voices, incorporate their voices into theory-making or move methodologically toward an expansive reparatory praxis. Instead, I see comfort with the status quo of colorblindness, neutrality, and a myth of universal workers.

In my effort to disrupt the status quo, I have written articles independently and collaboratively for popular and academic labor journals. I incorporated critical race theory into my assessment of labor struggles in the academy and economic justice movements. I also organized a seminar for faculty, students, and staff in my department, inviting Professor Mari Matsuda, founding CRT legal scholar, to give a review of labor struggles with a CRT lens.

Matsuda and other founding CRT scholars such as Derrick Bell, Charles Lawrence III, Richard Delgado, Kimberlé Crenshaw, and Cheryl Harris provide a body of critical legal scholarship dating from the late 1980s that shape the key CRT tenets of counternarrative, interest convergence, whiteness as property, looking to the bottom, and intersectionality—to name a few. Taken collectively, they provide a rough blueprint for doing critical scholarship that attends to the history of race and racism, which is necessarily intertwined with a plethora of labor struggles and stories. CRT also presents methodological practices congruent with an expansive liberatory project, and it is high time more scholars thinking about the future of labor and workers engage with it.

My colleagues and co-editors, Tami Lee and Maite Tapia, are leading the charge for an intervention in industrial relations scholarship and praxis with their recent publication, "Confronting Race and Other Social Identity Erasures: The Case for Critical Industrial Relations Theory." Lee and Tapia argue the following:

> The field of industrial relations ... has a philosophical problem: the dominance of white and privileged-group narratives in the questions we ask, the theory we build, the research we publish, and the manner in which we explain labor and employment phenomena. While the real world of industrial relations is embedded in identity-conscious social systems of oppression, such as white supremacy and patriarchy, our leading scholarship routinely uses identity-neutral theoretical frames. ... The result is a canon of knowledge that defaults to white and privileged-group narratives as the standard lens through which we understand all workers and workplace issues. (Lee and Tapia 2021)

Beginning with my first Labor and Employment Relations Association conference in 2018, I have been commenting on the lack of racial diversity of both panelists and attendees. In response, various participants, including colleagues, named the same one Black woman tenured in the field and one Black woman doctoral student as examples of diversity. Black women do not represent all diversity; however, these numbers do signal the presence of barriers and exclusionary practices, like a canary in the coal mine kind of trouble. In 2018, LERA was hosted in Baltimore, a majority Black city that had recently been rocked by the court's refusal to prosecute union police officers for the murder of Freddy Gray. The tensions brewing related to worker justice and racial justice were not discussed in general conference spaces, even though Dorcas Gilmore, attorney and leader of the Baltimore Black Worker Center (BBWC), was a panelist.

The weekend of the conference, the BBWC hosted a "know your rights training." Seeking connection with Black workers and the city, my colleague and I attended the worker center training, visited the factory of a Black woman–owned business with national distribution, and briefly attended the Baltimore Pride Parade. Seven months prior, I attended the National Women's Studies Association (NWSA) conference, at the same hotel as LERA, celebrating the 40th anniversary of the Combahee River Collective, "a group of Black lesbian feminists whose iconic statement [highlighted] the negligence of the white-dominated feminist movement and the male-dominated Black liberation movement toward Black women's issues and the need for an understanding of interlocking systems of oppression."

My experience of the NWSA and LERA conferences was radically different in terms of the diversity of attendees, panelists, and topics—one had recognized the shifting demographics of their constituency and the other had not. And as a Black woman anchored in both, that was disappointing. To be fair, my criticism of labor relations scholarship as white-washed is not new. In 1977, Combahee's Black Feminist Statement spoke directly to the challenges of this moment, as if no time had passed.

> We have arrived at the necessity for developing an understanding of class relationships that takes into account the specific class position of Black women who are generally marginal in the labor force, while at this particular time some of us are temporarily viewed as doubly desirable tokens at white-collar and professional levels. *We need to articulate the real class situation of persons who are not merely raceless, sexless workers, but for whom racial and sexual oppression are significant determinants in their working/economic lives.* Although we are in essential agreement with Marx's theory as it applied to the very specific economic relationships he analyzed, we know that his analysis must be extended further in order for us to understand our specific economic situation as Black women.

The Combahee statement also attends to action, practice, and projects:

> The inclusiveness of our politics makes us concerned with any situation that impinges upon the lives of women, Third World, and working people. We are of course particularly committed to working on those struggles in which race, sex, and class are simultaneous factors in oppression. We might, for example, become involved in workplace organizing at a factory that employs Third World women or picket a hospital that is cutting back on already inadequate health care to a Third World community, or set up a rape crisis center in a Black neighborhood. Organizing around welfare and daycare concerns might also be a focus. (Combahee River Collective 1995)

Neither the contemporary experience of Black workers in Baltimore nor the intersectional analysis made possible by more than 40 years of the Combahee River Collective's groundbreaking Black Feminist Statement seemed to have a place in the LERA space, except during a panel that was majority women of color—a panel scheduled for the last day, during the latest time slot on Father's Day; when the conference tables were broken down and the LERA signs removed; and most of the participants were gone, except for the incoming LERA president who was present and seemingly "looking to the bottom."

The primary framing for this chapter is Matsuda's seminal work, "Looking to the Bottom: Critical Legal Studies and Reparations," where she argues for critical scholars to "look to" and try to "see from" the perspectives of those situated at the bottom, rather than relying on imagination of POC experiences, to craft roadmaps to justice and reparations. Matsuda goes on to say that choosing to align with reparation projects advanced by those with lived experience of racial and other forms of discrimination and oppression presents more opportunities for a reconstruction that is not exploitative and rooted in white supremacy.

LABOR STORIES AND CRT TENETS
Intersectionality, Praxis, Scholar-Activism

In [DeGraffenreid v. General Motors], five Black women brought suit against General Motors, alleging that the employer's seniority system perpetuated the effects of past discrimination against Black women. Evidence adduced at trial revealed that General Motors simply did not hire Black women prior to 1964 and that all of the Black women hired after 1970 lost their jobs in a seniority-based layoff during a subsequent recession. The district court granted summary judgment for the defendant, rejecting the plaintiffs' attempt to bring a suit not on behalf of Blacks or women, but specifically on behalf of Black women.

—Kimberlé Crenshaw (1989)

A Story of "Intersectionality"

I was introduced to Kimberlé Crenshaw's work during my "Intro to Feminist Theory" undergraduate course,[1] where I learned the importance of scholar-activism and praxis. My major, psychology, felt off to me because I felt the need to pretend to be "objective." I knew then what I know now: Humans, especially US-trained academics, tend to inquire about what they are interested in knowing. Intersectionality, praxis, and scholar-activism allowed me to be honest with myself and others about why I study Black people, and Black women in particular. I am part of a lineage of feminist scholar-activists who began a project to write Black women into existence and in ways that recognize our humanity, resilience, and resistance practices in a cruel and unjust US system and culture. Praxis is, to me, the more honest "way of knowing" that requires me to be explicit about my positionality and biases, to not only study and observe but also to act to change unjust systems, and to reflect on what I do in community and with accountability to the communities I seek to serve and whose circumstances I want to improve.

Crenshaw, a self-described scholar-activist, modeled praxis when she coined the term "intersectionality" to illuminate the flaws of the legal system through a three-part counterstory about Black women workers. First, Black women workers had been excluded from jobs with General Motors when white women and Black men were hired for very specific labor roles, including performing front office administrative duties and menial janitorial work, respectively. Second, since Black women workers were the last to be hired, when a recession triggered layoffs, the collectively bargained seniority system was activated; therefore, Black women were the first workers fired. Third, when Black women workers sought a legal (not union) remedy to sex discrimination *and* race discrimination, the judicial system would not recognize them as representatives of an injured group who deserved a hearing, much less remedy.

Black women workers were not recognized as *women* who were injured because General Motors hired white women—no sex discrimination. Black women workers were not recognized as representative of Black workers because General Motors hired Black men—no race discrimination. When Black women workers tried to represent themselves as Black women, Judge Harris Kenneth Wangelin (*DeGraffenreid v. General Motors 1976*)—white and male—rejected their claim. However, Crenshaw indicates in her footnotes that when white men brought "reversed discrimination" claims, they were not required to meet the same burden of proving race and sex discrimination.

There is a primary project and a meta-project in "Demarginalizing the Intersection of Race and Sex." Crenshaw asserts that there is a problem with Title VII antidiscrimination laws recognizing Black women plaintiffs. Black women are not central subjects in legal framing, only propertied white men are; therefore, Black women's narratives are illegible. Crenshaw further explains that since there was no name for this particular problem of invisibility, the claims brought by Black women could not be remedied. She coined the term "intersectionality" to make the lived experiences of Black women visible so that their injuries would also be visible for remedy. Crenshaw worked to demonstrate how the interlocking oppressions caused by white supremacy, patriarchy, and capitalism worked to keep Black women unemployed and poor through no fault of their own.

General Motors in the 1970s was unionized; however, UAW has a history of functioning as a violent actor when it comes to women workers. Much like the company with their exclusive hiring practices and the judicial system refusing to protect Black women, the union has also been inaccessible to provide remedies for its own injured members. According to Ana Avendaño's New Labor Forum essay, "#MeToo Inside the Labor Movement":

> A shocking *New York Times* exposé of brutal conditions endured by United Auto Workers (UAW) women at two Chicago auto plants published in December 2017 puts into question whether unions have evolved when it comes to addressing sexual harassment. Women told the *New York Times* that "bosses and fellow laborers treated them as property or prey. Men crudely commented on their breasts and buttocks; graffiti of

> penises was carved into tables, spray-painted onto floors, and
> scribbled onto walls. They groped women, pressed against
> them, simulated sex acts and punished those who refused."
>
> Harassers include managers and co-workers, and most recent-
> ly, the UAW bargaining committee chairman, Allen Millender.
> Save for the failed efforts of one steward, the union took no
> steps to protect the women yet went out of its way to protect
> the accused harasser. When Millender received a two-week
> suspension following a company investigation, the union
> grieved the case to arbitration. … In the early 1990s, the union
> faced public scrutiny when it failed to protect its female mem-
> bers from harassment at the very same plants featured in the
> *New York Times* exposé. (Avendaño 2019)

Centering the narratives of women workers of color illuminates the racist *and* sexist histories of unions, corporations, and the judicial system. These stories point to the cultural and structural exclusion that have caused the economic limitations which lead to the gender and racial wage gaps that we struggle to close now. These stories have deep resonance for me as the daughter of a UAW retiree: My father's union job provided financial security and stability, health insurance, and the college education that led me to study feminism and to join the labor movement. Now, after three decades of debates lamenting "identity-based" scholarship, "intersectionality" has finally become a mainstream theoretical and methodological approach in multiple disciplines and only recently considered in labor studies.

Putting Intersectionality to Work

Through #MeToo and racial reckonings, movement activists have had the platform to reclaim intersectionality for disrupting dominant narratives and norms that center propertied heterosexual white men (and those in proximity) over the rights of everyone else. An example of advancing an intersectional approach in movement work is Mississippi Resisté's response to ICE raids in 2020, during the height of COVID-19. An intersectional approach in labor scholarship would recognize the complexity of the 2020 ICE raid of a chicken processing plant, where the Trump administration targeted the plant in retaliation for immigrant/migrant and documented and undocumented workers successfully winning a significant lawsuit challenging race and sex discrimination and other forms of employment discrimination in the plant:

> On August 7, [2020] hundreds of immigration officials de-
> scended upon seven food processing plants in Mississippi and
> arrested about 680 people suspected of living and working
> in the country without permission. It was the largest immi-
> gration operation of its kind in more than a decade, and the

largest single-state raid ever, officials said. The seven plants targeted by immigration officials were owned by four companies spread across six towns. They were Peco Foods Inc., with plants in Bay Springs, Canton, and Sebastopol; *Koch Foods Inc., with a plant in Morton; PH Food Inc. in Morton;* MP Food Inc. in Pelahatchie; and Pearl River Foods Inc. in Carthage. MP Food and PH Food are associated with A&B Inc. (Zhu and Gates 2009)

The raid alone is cause for concern, however, when put into a historical and political context *with* a race- and gender-conscious analysis, we see a much more egregious abuse of power—white male power to be exact. Koch Foods is estimated to be a $3 billion dollar corporation that supplies chicken for Walmart, Burger King, Kroger, and Aldi's. It is believed to be predominantly owned by one individual, Joseph Grendys, worth $2.3 billion dollars (Harris 2014). However, the EEOC lawsuit paints a different picture:

Koch Foods, one of the largest poultry suppliers in the world, will pay $3,750,000 and furnish other relief to settle a class employment discrimination lawsuit filed by the US Equal Employment Opportunity Commission (EEOC), the federal agency announced [August 1, 2018]. The EEOC charged the company with *sexual harassment, national origin and race discrimination, [and] retaliation against a class of Hispanic workers at Koch's Morton, Mississippi, chicken processing plant.*

According to the EEOC's lawsuit, Koch subjected individual plaintiff/intervenors and classes of Hispanic employees and female employees to a hostile work environment and disparate treatment based on their race/national origin (Hispanic) and sex (female), and further retaliated against those who engaged in protected activity. EEOC alleges that supervisors touched and/or made sexually suggestive comments to female Hispanic employees, hit Hispanic employees, and charged many of them money for normal everyday work activities. Further, a class of Hispanic employees was subject to retaliation in the form of discharge and other adverse actions after complaining.

All this alleged conduct violates Title VII of the Civil Rights Act of 1964 (US Equal Opportunity Employment Commission 2018).

Intersectionality is the reason that the "female Hispanic employee" claims could be seen fully for remedy. An intersectional labor scholarship would amplify this victory and celebrate the Latino-led Mississippi Resisté, as innovative strategists, when they organized the communities of the detained workers after the Koch Foods plant happened to be raided by ICE. Rather than calling for charity, organizers saw the raid as a community organizing opportunity to build long-term power. On August 10, 2019, they created a Facebook profile and began to promote posts like the following: "A todas las familias afectadas por las redadas en Mississippi por favor llamen al línea comunitaria" ["To all the families affected by the raids in Mississippi, please call the community hotline"]. They partnered with local organizations and organizers throughout the South to provide the impacted families with multi-sited access to attorneys, food and supply pantries, and even virtual "know your rights" trainings. One such example is the following:

> Forest! Los invitamos a que participen en un taller para que la comunidad aprenda más acerca de sus derechos laborales. Va a ser un espacio para crear solidaridad, compartir nuestras experiencias con otros trabajadores, y aprender más de todos los derechos laborales que tenemos sin importar estatus migratorio. Vengan el sábado a las 10:00am o a las 5:30pm de la tarde!

> *Forest! We invite you to participate in a workshop so the commu-nity can learn more about their labor rights. It will be a space to create solidarity, share our experiences with other workers, and learn more about all the labor rights we have, regardless of migra-tion status. Join us Saturday at 10:00am or 5:30pm!* [2]

I learned of this "call for organizers" from Denise Diaz, Central Florida Jobs With Justice co-director, who explained to me that she had just returned from working with the group in Mississippi. They recruited seasoned Black and brown *southern* organizers to Mississippi to help mobilize workers and community members to challenge the detention and deportation and to assess the care needs of children and families left behind. They turned the spotlight on unjust public and private detention center systems as well, consistently amplifying the fact that these workers, who are identified as Latina/Latino/Latinx/Chicano/Hispanic workers, were detained during the height of the spread of COVID-19, and their children were left behind to fend for themselves. This example shows that labor could be a race- and gender-conscious site for worker struggle that attends to the needs of womxn and nonbinary workers of color.

(Counter)Storytelling: Race Consciousness and Oppositional Voice

I am certain that my kindergarten teacher was not intentionally racist in choosing Little Black Sambo. I knew even then, from a child's intuitive sense, that she was a good, well-meaning person. A less benign combination of racial mockery and profit motivated the white men who produced the radio show and played the roles of Amos and Andy. But we who had joined their conspiracy by our laughter had not intended to demean our race. ... To be thought of as a Negro is to be thought of less than human. We were all victims of our culture's racism. We had all grown up on Little Black Sambo and Amos and Andy.

Americans share a common historical and cultural heritage in which racism has played and still plays a dominant role. Because of this shared experience, we also inevitably share many ideas, attitudes, and beliefs that attach significance to an individual's race and induce negative feelings and opinions about nonwhites. To the extent that this cultural belief system has influenced all of us, we are all racists. At the same time, most of us are unaware of our racism. We do not recognize the ways in which our cultural experience has influenced our beliefs about race or the occasions on which those beliefs affect our actions. In other words, a large part of the behavior that produces racial discrimination is influenced by unconscious racial motivation.

—Charles Lawrence III (1987)

Everyone has been writing stories these days. ... Derrick Bell has been writing "Chronicles," and in the Harvard Law Review *at that. Many others have been daring to become more personal in their writing, to inject narrative, perspective, and feeling how it was "for me"— into their otherwise scholarly, footnoted articles and, in the case of the truly brave, into their teaching. Many, but by no means all, who have been telling legal stories are members of what could be loosely described as **outgroups, groups whose marginality defines the boundaries of the mainstream,** whose voice and perspective—whose consciousness—has been suppressed, devalued, and abnormalized. The attraction of stories for these groups should come as no surprise. **For stories create their own bonds, represent cohesion, shared understandings, and meanings**. The cohesiveness that stories bring is part of the strength of the outgroup. An outgroup creates its own stories, which circulate within the group as a kind of counter-reality. ... The dominant group creates its own stories, as well. The stories or narratives told |by the ingroup remind it of its identity in relation to outgroups, and provide it with a form of shared reality in which its own superior position is seen as natural. ... **The stories of outgroups aim to subvert that ingroup reality***

—Richard Delgado (1989)

Bell, Delgado, and Lawrence set the stage for the use of storytelling in legal scholarship as a core part of critical race theory practice. Storytelling is one of the few ways that people of color speak themselves into existence in arenas where their voices and experiences are often excluded or muted. Too often their experiences are taken out of context, listed as bullet points beneath an already constructed argument that is situated in a narrow historical frame. Stacy Davis-Gates, part of a recent wave of women of color elected as labor leaders, speaks about having to maintain a dual or multiple consciousness (Matsuda 1989: 1–2, 5, 10) in terms of being accountable to union members and to the communities of color she comes from and/or serves. She sees bargaining as the way to "practice unionism when you educate children in spaces that ain't never loved them." She goes on to say, "We lost two moms that are at an elementary school in the west side of Chicago [which is a predominantly Black community] that had 11 classes out of 17 classes in quarantine. An elementary school!" (WILL Empower 2021).

The practice of storytelling allows me to put this Black educator/labor leader's experience in dialogue with that of white union educator/occupational therapist, Christine Priola, who was photographed in the Senate chambers standing next to the Senate President's chair on January 6 during the insurrection. Upon her return, Priola submitted a resignation letter stating that "she refused to take the coronavirus vaccine to return to classes and did not agree with union dues 'which help fund people and groups that support the killing of unborn children'" (Caniglia 2015).

Storytelling—counterstorytelling—a key instrument in critical race theory, makes lived experiences in the real world visible so that we can better illuminate the tensions and challenges to class and worker solidarity, whereas the universal worker narrative often leaves race and racism uninterrogated. For instance, the way Priola shows up as a worker is an individual issue; it is a choice to be unvaccinated against coronavirus and to work with children who cannot be vaccinated against coronavirus but are required to attend school in person. Choosing to be an unvaccinated educator has consequences for children, their families, and their communities. Statistics have consistently shown that there are racial disparities regarding those groups more likely to die from complications related to COVID-19; they are Black, Latinx, and Indigenous people (Artiga, Hill, and Ndugga 2021).

Furthermore, POC labor leaders represent and protect Priola's interests as a union member, regardless of how she feels about unions and dues. However, they still recognize the history of educators, who are majority white women in public schools (National Center for Education Statistics 2021), perpetuating racist behaviors and practices, whether consciously or unconsciously, since desegregation laws put Black and brown children in their care. Lawrence's story at the beginning of this section speaks directly to this as a long-standing cultural issue, but I argue that it is also a labor issue given Priola's trade unionist status.

Finally, Priola's ability to leave D.C. after being involved in a violent effort to overturn a national election and to return home to her job is a structural and systemic issue. When I employ a non-neutral and race-conscious assessment putting the January 6 insurrection in historical and political context, there is a much more disturbing narrative revealed by the treatment of Christine Priola. Kyle Rittenhouse, the Illinois white male teenager who killed two Black protesters and injured a third in Kenosha, Wisconsin—like Priola, he "returned to his residence in Illinois shortly after the shootings." Not only were police present at the protest in Kenosha, but they were later sued for effectively "deputizing" armed white nationalist counterprotesters like Rittenhouse (Helmore 2021). In contrast, Priola's participation in the violent insurrection in Washington, D.C., does not match the experience of police engagement with mostly Black protesters in D.C. after the murder of George Floyd. "[Thousands] of law enforcement officials, armed with tear gas, rubber bullets and firearms were deployed to protect the city … [and more] than 300 were arrested on June 1, 2020." Priola was arrested in Ohio and accused of "knowingly entering or remaining in a restricted building; violent entry; and unlawful activities on Capitol grounds," and she was released on bond (BostonGlobe.com, no date). Rittenhouse, having murdered two Black people, was released on a $2 million dollar cash-bail, and was later acquitted. Numerous #BlackLivesMatter protesters are in jail facing felony charges (Orellano 2021).

My style of writing may seem confrontational; it is meant to be oppositional (Calmore 1992: 1, 4–9). All too often stories about race and racism are told passively to maintain the "right to comfort" (White Supremacy Culture 2021) of predominantly white audiences. "Someone was a victim of racism" or "someone was oppressed"; when the focus is race or racism, then it is about someone who is Black or "nonwhite." "Black" has functioned as the counterpart, the negation, or the antithesis of white. Being a Black woman writing about race, white supremacy, and Blackness, while also naming white perpetrators of racism and oppression in an active voice might be off-putting. However, oppositional storytelling (Delgado 1989: 2, 9) is in fact necessary to create space for diverse authentic voices and perspectives when the goal is transformation, even when it is uncomfortable for the majority audience to hear.

"Whiteness as Property": Exclusion, Gatekeeping, Privilege of Obliviousness

Every day my grandmother rose from her bed in her house in a Black enclave on the south side of Chicago, sent her children off to a Black school, boarded a bus full of Black passengers, and rode to work. No one at her job ever asked if she was Black; the question was unthinkable. By virtue of the employment practices of the "fine [retail] establishment" in which she worked, she could not have been. Catering to the upper-middle class, understated tastes required that Blacks not be allowed. She quietly went about her clerical worked discuss their worries—their children's illnesses, their husbands' disappointments, their boyfriends' infidelities—all of the mundane yet critical things that made up their lives. She came to know them, but they did not know her, for my grandmother occupied a completely different place. That place—where white supremacy and economic domination meet—was unknown turf to her white co-workers. They remained oblivious to the worlds within worlds that existed just beyond the edge of their awareness and yet were present in their very midst.

Each evening, my grandmother, tired and worn, retraced her steps home, laid aside her mask, and reentered herself.

—Cheryl Harris (1993)

"Black" has been legally and culturally imbued with meaning: (1) labor that can be exploited and (2) laborers concentrated in manual low-wage/unpaid work. Cheryl Harris begins her exploration of "whiteness as property" by writing about her grandmother who concealed her Blackness in the 1930s to gain employment in a high-end Chicago department store. Having migrated from the South (where she was known as Black) to the North (where she had anonymity) "[Harris's grandmother] could thus enter the white world, albeit on a false passport, not merely passing, but *tres*passing" because white people, white owners, had the legal "right to exclude."

Consider this. If there was an organizing drive at Harris's grandmother's workplace, what is the likelihood that she would get involved considering the risk? This question could be applied to immigrant/migrant workers who are *passing* as citizens, or LGBTQ workers whose home life is kept private, or workers with disabilities that are not visible. Even if these workers know their rights, there is no guarantee that their fellow co-workers, the union, or antidiscrimination laws will protect them and their livelihood—*and* yet we still resist.

If inclusive organizing is important, then understanding the interior lives of workers—a call for more involvement of humanities in labor studies—means not just relying on (1) the part that is visible in the workplace, (2) the narrative that fits into an already constructed dominant labor story, or (3) the "trauma porn" of extreme poverty, most likely caused by racism and sexism, that might trump the bosses' campaign to seem humane. Harris writes that "[day] in and day out, [her grandmother] made herself invisible, then visible again, for a price too inconsequential to do more than barely sustain her family and at a cost too precious to conceive."

Labor counterstories in critical race theory have been hiding in plain sight for nearly three decades. Literary scholars try to unpack the experiences of people of color who *pass* for white, but Harris digs much deeper than the individual level inquiry to attend to the historical and political context of a worker passing for white to earn enough to provide for her family as a single Black woman. Patricia Williams's powerful book *The Alchemy of Race and Rights* presents the phrase "spirit murder" to explain the impact of daily micro-aggressions and full-on aggressions that Black people experience from retail workers, transit workers, co-workers, and anyone else we encounter in the workplace, the marketplace, and the consumer spaces of our everyday experience being recognizably Black. Unlike literary scholars, Harris focuses on the "white supremacist capitalist patriarchy" that bell hooks explicitly named, to spotlight the collective and interlocking oppressive systems that likely motivated Harris's grandmother to journey into whiteness for work and then to "[re-enter] herself" and live in a Black segregated community.

> [Harris examines] the emergence of whiteness as property and [traces] the evolution of whiteness from color to race to status to property as a progression historically rooted in white supremacy and economic hegemony over Black and Native American peoples. The origins of whiteness as property lie in the parallel systems of domination of Black and Native American peoples out of which were created racially contingent forms of property and property rights. [She] further [argues] that whiteness shares the critical characteristics of property even as the meaning of property has changed over time. In particular, whiteness and property share a common premise—a conceptual nucleus—of *a right to exclude*. This conceptual nucleus has proven to be a powerful center around which whiteness as property has taken shape. Following the period of slavery and conquest, white identity became the basis of racialized privilege that was ratified and legitimated in law as a type of status property. (Harris 1993)

In *An Indigenous People's History of the United States*, Indigenous scholar, Roxanne Dunbar-Ortiz explains the following:

> The burgeoning of the corporation brought about a new era of attacks on Indigenous governments, lands, and resources. After the military power and resistance of Indigenous nations and communities were stifled by the growing US military machine following the Civil War, compliance on the part of Indigenous leaders became necessary for survival. ... Industrialized civilization justified exploitation and destruction of whole societies and expansion without regard for the sovereignty of peoples; it promoted individualism, competition, and selfishness as righteous character traits. The means by which the US government assured corporate freedom to intrude in Indigenous territories was federal trusteeship, the very instrument that was mandated to protect them (Dunbar-Ortiz 2015).

Ortiz, like Harris, attends to the drivers of exploitation that are legally sanctioned and too often protected, like corporations. Under a broad lens, the labor "market" and the property/real estate "market" are designed and governed by rules and regulations established to protect owners. The brutal history of slavery and colonization are American legacies that provide rich context for current-day income inequality, labor exploitation, wage suppression, and (re)gentrification— the removal of entire communities of color and working-class people from "prime real estate" for the benefit of wealthy white owners. The deeds of the finance sector, which underwrites public and private employers as well as public and private landlords/property owners, are mostly invisible.

Innovative campaigns such as Bargaining for the Common Good center the lived experiences of people of color in unions and community organizations. When researchers use an intersectional (i.e., race and gender conscious) lens to put the spotlight on the top of the ownership ladder, the financial actors controlling workplaces and communities tend to be wealthy, white, and male—as they have been historically. Labor scholars and powerful movement actors tend to treat workplace issues and community issues as separate fights, but organizations like Action Center on Race and the Economy (acrecampaigns.org) and coalitions like Take on Wall Street (takeonwallst.org) reveal common owner/owner groups profiting on the exploitation of workers at work and residents at home. These are points that scholars and organizers of color have been making.

"I don't want to discuss inclusion until we interrogate the exclusionary decision makers, policies, and practices that got us to this point." This is my mantra in faculty meetings, diversity trainings, diversity committee meetings, and conference presentations. "Whiteness as property" spotlights the systems beneath workers choosing to pass for better economic opportunities and also how workers assimilate and take on the culture of the "ingroup." Coded discussions about scholars of color not being "collegial" or "rigorous" when they do not regularly attend majority white departmental events or when they foreground an analysis of race and racism in their work are examples of common pressures to assimilate. The "whiteness as property" CRT tenet calls on organizations to do their pre-work to understand how "the right to exclude" shapes policies, practices, and procedures before engaging people of color (workers/members, organizers/activists, faculty/staff) in diversity, inclusion, and belonging activities.

Begin by interrogating the persistence of white supremacist heteropatriarchal culture and structures in the organization. Then demonstrate ongoing transparent disruptions to those systems. Finally, invest real resources in repairing past harms and presenting rigorous and enforceable remedies for future injuries. This is simply a down payment toward a multiracial reconstructed system that does not privilege whiteness.

Looking to the Bottom: A Blueprint and Reparations

The abundance of material comforts in this nation results in part from the labor of the nonwhite workers who have been relegated to some of the hardest, most dangerous, and least compensated work. This list includes black slaves, Chinese railroad workers, Chicano miners, and legions of today's undocumented toilers in factory and field. One cannot be detached from privilege while enjoying the benefits of this country's high standard of living; in that sense, we are all part of the beneficiary class.

—Mari Matsuda (1987)

Returning to the work of Mari Matsuda, I argue that "Looking to the Bottom" provides a blueprint for academic and movement power brokers (gatekeepers) to resolve issues of abstraction undergirded by a predominantly class-first "universal worker" narrative. First, recognize that voices from the bottom do offer a "special voice" rooted in historical and contemporary experiences of discrimination and oppression. Second, contextualize labor issues using the lens of those at the bottom and the historical and political context illuminating their lived experiences. Third, make a commitment to align future scholarship and activism with the broader justice and reparations projects envisioned by those on the bottom who are working to transform systems rooted in white supremacy and patriarchy. In this section, I review the practices of *ILR Review* and LERA for the purposes of laying out opportunities for taking steps in an alternate direction—both in terms of scholarship and responses to movements in real time.

In 2011, Rutgers University Press published *Opportunity Denied: Limiting Black Women to Devalued Work* by Enobong Hanna Branch. The disciplines associated with *Opportunity Denied* include women's studies, African American studies, and sociology (Rutgers University Press 2012). This prompts the question "Why not labor studies?" Rutgers University boasts one of the largest and most well-known departments for labor studies and employment relations, and the text is clearly about labor. Either Branch did not see the work within the labor studies framing or those who actively shape the contours of labor studies did not recognize her work as an important part of the field.

A cursory look at the book review section of *ILR Review*, the premier peer-reviewed journal for industrial relations, indicates that *Opportunity Denied* was not engaged or cited within the journal in 2011 or 2012. It was reviewed in peer-reviewed journals for American studies, sociology, and gender and society, with *Labour/Le Travail*[3] being the only explicit labor journal I could locate that reviewed the book. During 2012, *ILR Review* published a book review by a white (presenting) woman scholar reviewing the work of a white (presenting) woman scholar who wrote about the care work of home health aides (Leana 2012), who are predominately women of color. There was also a contribution titled "The

Decreasing Effects of Skin Tone on Women's Full-Time Employment," where the abstract is as follows:

Using the Coronary Artery Risk in Young Adults (CARDIA) survey for the period spanning 1985 to 2000, which includes both African American and white young adults, as well as an *objective* measure of skin tone from a light spectrometer and a self-reported measure of race, they find that the effect of skin tone on employment diminished over time. These results hold across both samples as well as within the African American subsample. Further investigation indicates that all the labor market gains can be attributed to *African American women*, whose outcomes converged with those of their white counterparts by 2000. Similarly, within the subsample, the employment outcomes of darker-toned women converged with those of lighter-toned women. ... The expansion of full-time employment opportunities occurred primarily in the low-skilled service occupation. (Akee and Yuksel 2021)

As a "lighter-toned woman," I feel so seen now that the "objective measure of skin tone from a light spectrometer" provided results that the gap between me and white women vying for full-time work was closed in 2000, so long as I, and women like me, am concentrated in "low-skilled service occupations." It is important to contrast Randall Akee and Mutlu Yuksel's abstract of this "skin tone" study led by two men about women and labor (lacking any historical or political context) with that of Branch's *Opportunity Denied*, written by a Black woman about Black women. The description is as follows:

Blacks and Whites. Men and Women. Historically, each group has held very different types of jobs. The divide between these jobs was stark—clean or dirty, steady or inconsistent, skilled or unskilled. In such a rigidly segregated occupational landscape, race and gender radically limited labor opportunities, relegating Black women to the least desirable jobs. *Opportunity Denied* is the first comprehensive look at changes in race, gender, and women's work across time, comparing the labor force experiences of Black women to White women, Black men and White men. Enobong Hannah Branch *merges empirical data with rich historical detail*, offering an original overview of the evolution of Black women's work.

From free Black women in 1860 to Black women in 2008, the experience of discrimination in seeking and keeping a job has been determinedly constant. Branch focuses on occupational segregation before 1970 and situates the findings of contemporary studies in a broad historical context, illustrating how inequality can grow and become entrenched over time through the institution of work. (Branch 2011)

Having so few scholars of color who identify or have shared experiences with the workers they study—who identify their labor-focused work with labor and industrial relations—is in fact a problem. A chicken and egg problem. As it stands, graduate students, particularly students of color, would have to search beyond the field to access work relevant to their interests if they want to explore more comprehensive race- and gender-conscious theoretical and methodological approaches. I can guarantee that graduate students are checking the websites and the publications to determine whether they can live and thrive in certain disciplines. This is but one example why there must be a concerted effort to recruit labor scholars who are affiliated with other disciplines to identify with labor studies— while at the same time recruiting more students of color, particularly working-class students, to labor studies as a pathway for their scholarship. That means that the field would have to signal a sharp and radical turn.

CONCLUSION
Interest Convergence: Historical and Political Context

[Prior] to [Brown v. Board of Education of Topeka, Kansas], black claims that segregated public schools were inferior had been met by orders requiring merely that facilities be made equal. What accounted, then, for the sudden shift in 1954 away from the separate but equal doctrine and towards a commitment to desegregation?... [There] were whites who realized that the South could make the transition from a rural, plantation society to the sunbelt with all its potential and profit only when it ended its struggle to remain divided by state-sponsored segregation. Thus, segregation was viewed as a barrier to further industrialization in the South ... [and] for those whites who sought an end to desegregation on moral grounds or for the pragmatic reasons, ... Brown appeared to be a welcome break with the past. When segregation was finally condemned by the Supreme Court, however, the outcry was nevertheless great, especially among poorer whites who feared loss of control over their public schools and other facilities. Their fear of loss was intensified by the sense that they had been betrayed. They relied, as had generations before them, on the expectation that white elites would maintain lower class whites in a societal status superior to that designated for blacks. In fact, there is evidence that segregated schools and facilities were initially established by legislatures at the insistence of the white working class. [The] convergence of black and white interests that led to Brown in 1954 and influenced the character of its enforcement has begun to fade.

—Derrick Bell (1980: 1, 3, 8)

Return to the opening paragraph about the insurrection with a reframe as "the outcry ... among "poorer whites who feared loss of control" that was "intensified by the sense that they have been betrayed" by white elites: This violent behavior is not new; it is merely a recent display of the stranglehold that white supremacy has on this nation's progress toward equality. Interest convergence explains why people of color remain skeptical when suddenly approached to assist those in power with addressing racial discrimination.

I joined the chorus of those questioning the lack of attention to race and racism within the Labor and Employment Relations Association in 2018. I helped my colleague, Lisa Schur, organize a panel on diversity for the 2019 conference. The rallying cry #BlackLivesMatter was coined July 13, 2013, via Twitter ("8 Years Strong" 2021), and since the murder of Trayvon Martin, there has been a steady trail of videos depicting mostly white and unionized police officers shooting and killing Black people. However, it was not until the public lynching of George Floyd in May 2020, the subsequent revelation of Ahmaud Arbery's and Breonna Taylor's murders, and the global uprising against police murder that LERA issued the following statement:

> Since its founding in 1947, LERA has promoted the exchange of ideas and open dialogue. Today, we must speak out and condemn the systemic, institutional racism that routinely deprives people of color in the United States their freedom of expression—and their very lives. Over and over in recent years, we have seen unarmed Black men and women killed by police officers and vigilantes. Tragically, the use of lethal force against our minority communities has a long history in the United States; George Floyd, Ahmaud Arbery, and Breonna Taylor are simply the latest victims. Black Lives Matter. It is the most egregious example of discrimination in our society but not the only. LERA stands with everyone across the country and around the world calling for change, demanding justice and equality for all. (Labor and Employment Relations Association, no date)

CRT scholars would describe this as a moment of "interest convergence." A collective response to #BLM statements by Black and other people of color has been that statements should be blueprints for the way that an organization, association, corporation, or institution intends to conduct itself moving forward. Absent that commitment, a "statement" is simply following a dominant or newly acceptable trend. If this statement is indeed a "blueprint" that LERA is committed to then "[condemning] systemic, institutional racism," affirming that "Black lives matter," and "calling for change and demanding justice and equality for all" is in alignment with those voices on the bottom and requires intentional action.

Matsuda offers the following:

> Critical scholars condemn racism, support affirmative action, and generally adopt the causes of oppressed people throughout

the world. It is time to consider extending those commitments to the practice of critical scholarship and the development of theory. Such an extension requires deliberate efforts to *read and cite the work of minority scholars* within and without the law, to consider the intellectual history of nonwhite America, and to learn about the life experiences of people of color. In short, what is needed now is an expanded method of inquiry, akin to feminist consciousness raising.

Recruiting a multiracial team, including three Black scholar-activists, to co-edit a volume about a racial reckoning in labor is a start. However, establishing criteria for how the series continues to attend to race and racism moving forward demonstrates a commitment to change. Identifying the problem with the lack of diversity at LERA conferences is a start. Doing an assessment of the demographics of conference participants to have some empirical data and then setting goals and investing resources in achieving those goals is a commitment to ending one layer of institutional racism. Offering scholarships to help with registration to help diversify attendees is a start. Addressing the cultural and systemic barriers that "ingroup" privilege obscures by doing targeted outreach for panelists who are scholars of color doing labor in other disciplines, as well as paid invitations for more labor leaders, organizers, activists, and workers of color to help shape the program and to present at LERA annually is a concrete shift. This volume represents a start but is by no means exhaustive or representative of the lived experiences of all people of color. The editors assert, however, that there will be no transformation without a blueprint and a commitment to a full reconstruction.

ENDNOTES

1. Comparative Women's Studies & Women's Resource Center at Spelman College (a Historically Black College and University).

2. Mississippi Resisté Facebook page, August 21, 2020 (with Facebook translation).

3. *Labour/Le Travail* is the official, semi-annual publication of the Canadian Committee on Labour History.

REFERENCES

"8 Years Strong." 2021. Black Lives Matter. July 13. https://bit.ly/3Jkvn2L

Akee, Randall, and Mutlu Yuksel. 2012. "The Decreasing Effect of Skin Tone on Women's Full-Time Employment." *ILR Review* 65 (2): 398–426.

Artiga, Samantha, Latoya Hill, and Nambi Ndugga. 2021. "Racial Disparities in COVID-19 Impacts and Vaccinations for Children." Kaiser Family Foundation. September 16. https://bit.ly/36gSfl8

Avendaño, Ana. 2019. "#MeToo Inside the Labor Movement." New Labor Forum. January 24. https://bit.ly/3KRwLKN

Bell, Derrick A. Jr. 1980. "Comment: *Brown v. Board of Education* and the Interest-Convergence Dilemma." *Harvard Law Review* 93 (3): 518–533.

BostonGlobe.com. No date. "How Arrests in the Capitol Riot Compare to That of Black Lives Matter Protests." https://bit.ly/3L3AHbt

Branch, Enobong Hannah. 2011. *Opportunity Denied: Limiting Black Women to Devalued Work.* New Brunswick, NJ: Rutgers University Press.

Calmore, John O. 1992. *Critical Race Theory, Archie Shepp, and Fire Music: Securing an Authentic Intellectual Life in a Multicultural World.* Los Angeles: University of Southern California Press.

Caniglia, John. 2021. "Former Cleveland Schools' Therapist Arrested on Federal Charges Involving Attack at U.S. Capitol." Cleveland.com. January 14. https://bit.ly/3tdcj0H

Combahee River Collective. 1995. "A Black Feminist Statement." In *Words of Fire: An Anthology of African-American Feminist Thought*, 231–240. New York: The New Press.

Crenshaw, Kimberlé. 1989. "Demarginalizing the Intersection of Race and Sex: A Black Feminist Critique of Antidiscrimination Doctrine, Feminist Theory and Antiracist Politics." *University of Chicago Legal Forum* 1989 (1): Article 8.

DeGraffenreid v. General Motors Assembly Div., Etc. 1976. 413 F. Supp. 142 (E.D. Mo. 1976). Justia Law. https://bit.ly/3wa7mI6

Delgado, Richard. 1989. "Storytelling for Oppositionists and Others: A Plea for Narrative." *Michigan Law Review* 87 (8): 2411–2441.

Dunbar-Ortiz, Roxanne. 2015. *An Indigenous Peoples' History of the United States.* Boston: Beacon Press.

Harris, Cheryl I. 1993. "Whiteness as Property." *Harvard Law Review* 106 (8): 1710–1791.

Harris, Melissa. 2014. "Inside Billionaire Joe Grendys' Chicken Empire." *Chicago Tribune.* October 24. https://bit.ly/3CMYJoc

Helmore, Edward. 2021. "Kenosha Police Accused of 'Deputizing' Militia Vigilantes During Jacob Blake Protests." *The Guardian.* October 17. https://bit.ly/37y4wSW

Labor and Employment Relations Association. No date. "Black Lives Matter Statement." https://bit.ly/3MVa2ze

Lawrence, Charles R. III. 1987. "The Id, the Ego, and Equal Protection: Reckoning with Unconscious Racism." *Stanford Law Review* 39 (2): 317–388.

Leana, Carrie R. 2012. "Review: *The Caring Self: The Work Experiences of Home Care Aides*, by Clare L. Stacey." *ILR Review* 65 (3): 740–741.

Lee, Tamara L., and Maite Tapia. 2021. "Confronting Race and Other Social Identity Erasures: The Case for Critical Industrial Relations Theory." *ILR Review* 74 (3): 637–762.

Matsuda, Mari J. 1987. "Looking to the Bottom: Critical Legal Studies and Reparations Minority Critiques of the Critical Legal Studies Movement." *Harvard Civil Right–Civil Liberties Law Review* 22 (2): 323–400.

Matsuda, Mari J. 1989. "When the First Quail Calls: Multiple Consciousness as Jurisprudential Method." *Women's Rights Law Reporter* 11 (1): 7–10.

National Center for Education Statistics. 2021. "Characteristics of Public School Teachers." https://bit.ly/36kFCFQ

Orellano, Iveliz. 2021. "Black Lives Matter Protesters Are Still Facing Felony Charges." Teen Vogue. November 4. https://bit.ly/3MSVrV2

Rutgers University Press. 2022. "Opportunity Denied: Limiting Black Women to Devalued Work." Catalog Entry. https://bit.ly/3KKUaxo

US Equal Employment Opportunity Commission. 2018. "Koch Foods Settles EEOC Harassment, National Origin and Race Bias Suit." Press Release. https://bit.ly/3KKTmZo

White Supremacy Culture. 2021. "Right to Comfort: Power Hoarding & Fear of Conflict." May. https://bit.ly/3qb3qmr

WILL Empower. 2021. "Leading for Innovative Strategies in Unprecedented Times." YouTube. November 3. https://bit.ly/35VkPc6

Zhu, Alissa, and Jimmie E. Gates. 2019. "Chicken Plant Workers Reportedly Fired After MS ICE Raid." Clarion-Ledger. August 14. https://bit.ly/3KPfm55

PART I

HISTORY AND
POLITICAL CONTEXT

Chapter 3

Origin Stories:
Labor History and Industrial Relations

Naomi R Williams
Rutgers University
Department of Labor Studies and Employment Relations

Abstract

This chapter details the origin of industrial relations and labor history as academic fields. It examines the development of both from John R. Commons' work on institutional economics and traces scholars' efforts to find practical solutions to US labor problems. Examining a period of divergence in the fields, when labor history scholars engaged with critical theories such as critical race theory, identity formation, and intersectionality, it details innovations in historical theories and methodologies that produced a subfield of critical labor history.

These critical research interventions have reshaped how scholars tell labor history and interpret the past. By highlighting two recent monographs, author Naomi R Williams argues that industrial relations should engage with critical labor history and invite more labor historians in the Labor and Employment Relations Association.

My first experience at a LERA conference was disconcerting. As a historian of the working class, I had made my academic professional home in the Labor and Working-Class History Association. When I joined the Labor Studies and Employment Relations Department at Rutgers in 2018, it seemed like a perfect opportunity to become a member of LERA. I of course knew of the organization and worked closely with LERA members in scholar-activist and practitioner spaces. Yet there were very few historians in the association, and the panels seemed narrowly focused on particular aspects of the employment relationship and policy matters that governed the employment relationship. As a scholar focused on expanding economic democracy and mobilizing and supporting workers' efforts for building a just economy, I felt out of place. Part of my discomfort harkened back to a long-standing critique offered by George W. Brooks and Maurice Neufeld at the 1961 Industrial Relations Research Association convention. They both suggested that labor history was irrelevant to scholars across disciplines (Brody 1989).

Although labor history and industrial relations have the same origin story in the United States, a look at the development and transformation of industrial relations over the 20th century, as well as at the institutional home of LERA, has highlighted a divergence between the fields. All academic fields transform over time, on the basis of perceived moments of crisis, theoretical advancements, critical analyses, and changing social norms. Labor history grew out of industrial relations, and over time, scholars in both fields stopped engaging with scholarship from the other. This divergence, just when labor history was transformed as a result of new critical theoretical insights, represented a lost opportunity for industrial relations scholars to deepen their understanding of how social identities were, do, and will remain critical to full understanding of working-class conditions. Specifically, since the 1980s, the field of labor history has embraced historical analyses that have demonstrated the ways class, race, gender, and other social categories "remain axes of domination determining how social, economic, and political power is distributed, enforced, and institutionalized" in the United States (Phillips-Cunningham 2020). By contrast, in failing to integrate these historical contexts of systemic oppressions into their research and to historicize research questions, industrial relations scholars produce research that reinforces inequality and fails to represent the true diversity of workers and types of work in the United States (Lee and Tapia 2021).[1]

While not a state of the field narrative, this chapter seeks to understand the ways critical analyses in labor history reshaped the field and discuss how a reconnection between these shared academic lineages will provide much-needed vitalization moving forward. Beginning in the 1970s, scholars introduced several overlapping critical theories within labor history, including worker agency, identity (race, class, community, etc.), gender and race as analytic tools, intersectionality (interlocking systemic oppressions), and racial capitalism.[2] These critical research interventions have reshaped how scholars tell labor history and interpret the past. This chapter begins with the joint origin story of industrial relations and labor history and maps the divergence that occurred during the mid to late 20th century. It will then look at a series of critical theoretical interventions within the field of labor history, providing a brief overview of new scholarship and implications. Finally, the chapter ends with an invitation for LERA to re-create spaces for labor historians and critical historical analysis within the field of industrial relations. It argues that to address both the identity crisis that has been described within LERA and to keep industrial relations relevant for economic justice as well as bring in new scholars, we must consciously integrate labor history into the field of industrial relations and historians into LERA.

JOINT ORIGINS

Industrial relations and labor history both trace, in part, their origins to John R. Commons and his students. It started as a debate within the field of economics. Commons and his like-minded associates split from orthodox labor economics. This new area of institutional economics and the scholars that Commons trained helped develop what we now know as the fields of industrial relations and labor history. This section is not intended to be an overview of the broad theoretical shifts within the fields. Instead, the focus here will be on the shared theoretical origins of industrial relations and labor history. Bruce Kaufman expertly lays out the historical origins of industrial relations in his 2010 essay on the founding of industrial relations theory. He links to Commons and his contemporaries and the focus on institutional economics and points to efforts to address the "labor problem" in the late 19th century. Kaufman explains, "The [industrial relations] solution was a pragmatic, incremental but cumulatively substantial reform, reengineering and re-balancing of the institutions of capitalism in order to bring more stability, efficiency, justice, and human values to the employment relationship" (2010: 76). Tracing the work of these mostly labor economists, Kaufman concludes that "one principle stands out as the foundation upon which the [industrial relations] field, in both its positive and normative aspects, is based: … that *labor is embodied in human beings*" (2010: 79; emphasis in original).

This founding principle has taken different shapes and trajectories throughout the 100-year history of industrial relations. Kaufman argues that the broadest conceptualization of industrial relations is the founding one but that in practice, research has focused more narrowly on unions and collectively organized employment relationships (2020). Following the trajectory of its origin story, institutionally focused labor economists make up the core of this multidisciplinary field. Joined with other social scientists from sociology, political science, labor law, and others, as well as practitioners from management, unions, and government, LERA—the academic home for these scholars—has shaped and reshaped the field from its founding in 1947 through today.

The coalition of industrial relations scholars fractured after 1950. Some groups of scholars left to form their own specializations, and public support for the labor movement started to decline. Into the 1960s, industrial relations scholarship narrowed "with its subject and practice domain shrinking to (mostly) unionized employment relationships and its value commitments similarly shifting to a more explicit union-favoring position" (Kaufman 2020: 49). In the 1990s, with the decline of union density and the rise of neoliberalism, there was discussion of an industrial relations crisis. Consequently, Thomas A. Kochan called on industrial relations scholars to apply research in new ways "to a rapidly changing set of issues to be relevant to today's labor markets" to address increased labor force diversity and other forces brought on by neoliberalism and to account for declining power of unions and collective bargaining to protect workers' rights (1998: 39). Much of the debate about the direction of industrial relations has been around developing some theory or collection of theories that shapes the field (Budd 2008; Kaufman 2010). Yet, while these debates examine the merits of organizational/institutional approaches and various ways to consider the employment relationship and worker voice, there has only recently been any discussion of critical engagement with social structures and the historical forces that shape employment relationships, labor markets, and labor as a social movement in the United States (Lee and Tapia 2021).

As with the industrial relations origin story, David Brody marks the origins of labor history to the work of John R. Commons at the University of Wisconsin as he gathered the data to compile the first two volumes of *The History of Labour in the United States*. George E. Barnett's seminars at Johns Hopkins came together with the Wisconsin School and helped form the basis for the field of labor history (Brody 1989). As Brody explains, labor historians were deeply influenced by economists who sought to resolve the "labor problem" through ethical concerns with working people, practical solutions to labor conflict, and attentiveness to social and institutional context. What became known as the Wisconsin School of Labor History (and later, Old Labor History) was led by the work of Commons and scholars such as Selig Perlman and Robert Taft. Based on labor history's origins within industrial relations, it was institutionalist in nature and embedded in the theory of practical solutions to labor conflict (Brody 1993). The New Labor History built on the ethical concerns for working people within the broader industrial relations field but shifted based on a generation of working-class graduate students who sought to better incorporate the lived experiences of workers into the field of labor history. These scholars, including Herbert Gutman and David Montgomery, would reshape labor history, move more squarely into the broader field of history, and focus on history from "the bottom up." Gutman brought working-class culture into the sphere of labor history, while Montgomery focused on shop-floor stories (Brody 1989). The 1970s saw a revolution in the study of the US working class as scholars followed Gutman and Montgomery and shifted the focus away from histories of unions to encompass all aspects of working-class life. And then in the 1980s, as with several other academic disciplines, a group of scholars called for deeper critical analysis along the intersections of race, class, and gender (Lewis 1995; Trotter 1994).

DIVERGENCE

Examining a period of divergence between labor history and industrial relations allows a review of the ways labor historians have called for and implemented such critical analyses within the field. This examination is useful to understand the benefits of bridging the gap between industrial relations and labor history. In the United States, the 1960s and 1970s represented a period of sustained social revolution. From the civil rights movement, women's liberation, gay rights, the Chicano movement, disability rights, and offspring of all these movements, questions of class, race, and gender inequality took on new meaning and expanded into all areas of American life. These social movements opened the door to ask new and better questions about societies, human agency, and justice. At the same time, post–World War II social spending programs created opportunities for more working-class students to attend college. While racism and sexism still limited opportunities, many formerly excluded groups of people sought out college and graduate studies. This group of scholars brought their lived experiences as survivors of racism, sexism, and other inequities into the classroom and demanded that their educations better reflect the reality of US society. The social activism and sustained critical study made clear that deeply entrenched social inequalities would not be fixed overnight. Within this context, some scholars—many of whom were women of color—began to introduce new tools of critical analysis, such as intersectionality, critical race theory, and others (Collins 2019).

While the New Labor History explored workers' lives, culture, and shop-floor experiences, most of those studies focused on white, male, industrial workers, and mostly those in the skilled trades. Black workers and race as a social category with a clear history were rarely explored. Women, and the gendered nature of work, were often overlooked. Early correctives produced monographs and articles that sought, with varying levels of success, to include the experiences of workers across different employment sectors, women workers, Black workers, and immigrant workers. By the mid-1980s, scholars started to challenge the field to approach these expansions with a more critical lens. For example, Ava Baron charged labor historians to make gender a "fundamental category of all historical analysis" (1991: 19). Earl Lewis, in his critique of the failure of historians to bring critical racial analysis to their studies, pointed to the ways labor historians had often framed research questions in terms of "race *or* class or race *and* class," yet "the conceptual design assumes that aspects of individual identity are simply additive or subtractive" (Lewis 1995: 784). These early correctives and critiques enriched labor history and have led to more relevant research questions, areas of focus, and expansion within the field.

Similarly, work on whiteness and new understandings of racial capitalisms have reshaped theoretical structures of labor history. David Roediger, Barbara Fields, Noel Ignatiev, and others produced groundbreaking scholarship historicizing whiteness, race, and race ideology. This body of literature has helped fuel historical analysis on the ways race plays an ever-shifting role in the history of the United States (Arnesen 1998; Fields 1990; Ignatiev 1995; Lewis 1995; Roediger 1991). The political theorist Cedric Robinson published *Black Marxism: The Making of the Black Radical Tradition* in 1983. Historians, always eager to integrate new theories into their narratives, found Robinson's critique of Marx's failure to recognize the racial character of capitalism, together with his illustration of the Black radical tradition into labor history, as useful in their revisionist histories of work and labor in the United States (Kelley 2017; Robinson 1983). These calls for critical analyses based on race and gender produced a new body of labor history that offers opportunities for industrial relations scholars today. New historiographies make more visible the labor problems that industrial relations scholars seek to address. New understandings of the diversity and complexity of workers, their organizations, and the implementation of social policy in the United States provide industrial relations scholars new opportunities to find practical solutions to today's labor problems. Incorporating critical labor history into industrial relations provides an "opportunity for scholars to challenge prevailing color-blind and singular, class-centered theories" (Lee and Tapia 2021: 650).

CRITICAL LABOR HISTORY

Scholars such as Tera W. Hunter and Joe Trotter Jr. led the way in introducing critical race studies to labor history in the 1980s and 1990s. Hunter's work on domestic workers brought into focus the workers often excluded from labor history and Black history. Her scholarship looking at domestic workers has fueled two generations of labor historians. She centers Black women and their efforts to reshape freedom in the late 19th century. In an early essay, she showcases the ways Black washerwomen fought against injustice and analyzes employer and public officials' responses to "reveal how structures of inequality were reproduced and challenged in daily interactions" (Hunter 1993: 207). As she explains, household labor had broad political and social implications that are often missed when these workers are treated as outside of mainstream labor. Trotter has led the way in developing research that rejects the victimization model regarding Black workers in urban settings. Like Hunter's, his scholarship has opened the door to a rich literature that better incorporates the Black experience in US labor history. Coming from the field of urban history, Trotter traces what he describes as the proletarianization of Black urban workers in his 1985 study, *Black Milwaukee*. He offers his monograph as a counternarrative to ghetto-formation studies that failed to consider the agency of the Black working class (Trotter 1994). These and similar works helped expand the meaning of "working class" and repositioned Black workers as "producers, givers, and assets" in the making of the United States (Trotter 2019: xv).

Bringing critical race theory to labor history launched several new directions of inquiry in the field. For example, the group of scholars doing work around the "Long Civil Rights" theory have benefited from critical racial analysis and revisionists' efforts to better incorporate the experiences of Black workers in US history. Historian Jacquelyn Dowd Hall shows why historians must dramatize "the hidden history of politics and institutions—the publicly sanctioned choices that continually shape and reshape the social landscape and yet are often invisible to citizens trained in not seeing and in thinking exclusively in ahistorical, personal terms" (2005: 1262–1263). Writing against historians who argued that race eclipsed class as the key feature of American liberalism, her synthesis of critical labor history highlighted a different story of the postwar period. What came out of the New Deal era was what Robert Korstad calls "civil rights unionism." It was the link between race and class, Hall argues, that helped Black activists on the left articulate the ways racism had been bound up with economic exploitation since the founding of the republic. And for civil rights unionists, "workplace democracy, union wages, and fair and full employment went hand in hand with open, affordable housing, political enfranchisement, educational equity, and an enhanced safety net, including health care for all" (Hall 2005: 1245–1246). The Long Civil Rights movement historians have illustrated how color-blind research fails to capture the vibrancy and diversity of worker organizing and misses opportunities to incorporate successful organizing and mobilizing strategies. Labor history scholars built on a generation of work that sought to bring agency to the working class to expand definitions of "working class" to be more inclusive of all working people. They incorporated identity formation theories and critical race theory, and they historicized racial capitalism. By engaging critical labor history narratives, industrial relations scholars can think creatively about expanding beyond union-centric and formal collective bargaining as they seek to explore today's labor problems and find practical solutions. Two recent monographs offer such examples.

Using women's own stories about their lives and work, Premilla Nadasen offers a great example of the ways recent labor histories have incorporated CRT/I into narratives of workers' efforts to expand economic democracy and create more just societies in her 2015 *Household Workers Unite: The Untold Story of African American Women Who Build a Movement*. Following the groundbreaking work of Tera Hunter, Nadasen offers this counternarrative to stories like the book and film, "The Help," told from the perspective of white employers, that reinforce stereotypes of household workers as helpless victims. *Household Workers Unite* covers the period from the 1950s to 1970s, detailing the history of domestic workers on the margins of the labor movement, who nonetheless built a mass movement for change. Centering on the women of color, mostly Black, who built and sustained this movement through the politics of storytelling, Nadasen shows "how the voices and analytical perspective of working-class [B]lack women, as understood through their stories, can help us rethink the basic contours of the postwar period" (2015: 3). This book adds to the growing literature within labor history that more accurately reflects the realities of Black women's labor and activism. Their collective efforts built a national labor movement through storytelling, political and economic alliances, and redefining domestic work in the larger US political economy. These women successfully claimed their rights as workers against employers' focus on domestic workers as "family" to reinforce low wages, hypersurveillance, and exploitation. They also adapted labor organizing tactics to better fit the working and living experiences of domestic workers. This entailed forgoing the "confrontational, zero-sum model guiding traditional labor organizing [and attempting] to cultivate support from employers" by leveraging their importance to the household (Nadasen 2015: 105). They used community-based, grassroots strategies to organize workers in public spaces. And they proved that domestic workers were not "unorganizable." Their efforts partially paid off with the 1974 amendments to the Fair Labor Standards Act that extended minimum wage benefits to some categories of domestic work. Nadasen successfully adds to the historiography of 20th-century labor activism by centering the voices of Black domestic workers. This reframing helps show the ways domestic workers themselves redefined the meaning of work, highlights the limits of the formal labor movement, and offers new models of worker organizing. These types of historical narratives, implementing CRT/I, provide much-needed correctives in labor history and offer key insights for industrial relations scholars seeking to solve the labor question in the 21st century by bringing the views and experiences of marginalized voices into academic spaces.

Eithne Quinn's 2019 *A Piece of the Action: Race and Labor in Post–Civil Rights Hollywood* provides another excellent example of how labor historians are integrating CRT/I theories into their narratives. *A Piece of the Action* builds on the work of critical race theorists and labor and cultural historians while also examining the ways racial capitalism played out in 1970s Hollywood productions. As she explains, "This eclectic method allows me to explore the interplay among economic, political, and cultural trends in understanding how film shaped and was shaped by the politics of race" (Quinn 2019: 6). Combining analyses of films with their production histories, Quinn demonstrates when, where, and how the white power structure came together to re-create narratives that upheld white supremacy. Centering the Black creatives who demanded more realistic showcases of the Black experience from 1972 to 1976, when the white Hollywood establishment's interests aligned with the need to prove themselves race liberals, is an example of "interest convergence" (Bell 1980). This period represents a window into the ways race, labor, and liberalism intersected in the Hollywood film industry. As Quinn argues, Black actors such as Sidney Poitier and Harry Belafonte demonstrated solidarity with Black writers, producers, and production crews to move beyond the stereotypical stories of the Black experience by using their box-office pull to help release films that portrayed people as complex characters with complicated story lines. Quinn provides an important counternarrative within the historical context of the immediate post–civil rights era that demonstrates how Hollywood was in lockstep with an emerging neoliberal understanding of equality. By providing lip service to access, opportunity, and inclusion, they maintained "insidious informal all-white Hollywood networks in which most decisions were made" (Phillips 2021: 146).

While centering Black creatives and their efforts to be active agents within Hollywood, Quinn provides a powerful analysis of the ways the all-white Hollywood establishment participated in creating a new cultural understanding of whiteness. As she illustrates, "White producers, directors, and writers guided films to narratives that were rooted in their own stereotypical assumptions" (Phillips 2021: 146). The Hollywood establishment produced films that "deployed racially meritocratic language at strategic moments to mask the industry's still starkly racialized political economy. Notwithstanding the existence of individual white progressives, the new limits-of-tolerance discourses … shielded the industry from both racial self-knowledge and lasting constructive change to its exclusionary job practices, financial arrangements, and persisting racist imagery" (Quinn 2019: 4). With *A Piece of the Action*, Quinn advances our understanding of the connection between neoliberalism and neoconservatism in late-20th century United States. Quinn's merging of cultural and political history highlights the ways a "soft white" cultural backlash helped contort the demands of civil rights activists for color blindness, invalidating demands for affirmative action, and severely hampering the effectiveness of the Equal Employment Opportunity Commission. This narrative provides key insights for industrial relations scholars seeking to offer practical policy proposals to better guarantee economic democracy for all workers and to dismantle white supremacy.

A REIMAGINING: CRITICAL INDUSTRIAL RELATIONS

In their call for a Critical Industrial Relations theory, Lee and Tapia detail how in the fields of legal studies, education, social movement studies, and others, calls for CRT/I analyses furthered those fields and led to new and exciting research getting at the root causes of systemic oppression in the United States (2021). Like the scholars of an earlier generation in labor history, they are asking industrial relations scholars to employ new methods of inquiry that confront racism within the field itself. They argue that there is an urgent need to integrate CRT/I theory into industrial relations to reverse trends of exclusion and the harms it creates. Failure to implement these analyses lead to race-neutral instead of race-conscious research. Failure to identify and interrogate intersecting systems of oppression produces research that does not reflect the whole range of worker experiences, and it does not provide reliable answers that lead to economic justice or practical solutions for the most vulnerable among the working classes.

And the time is now. The COVID-19 pandemic that started in 2020 and the economic crisis that continues to impact working people in the United States also brought racism and other interlocking forms of oppression to the center of the nation's attention. The racial and economic uprisings that started in the summer of 2020 and continue into 2022 highlight both the continued relevance of collective action and worker mobilization and the need for scholars and practitioners to ask better questions, provide practical solutions to finally dismantle systemic racism, and sustain democracy in the United States. Organizations and institutions issued statements (re)affirming their commitments to racial justice. Statements and performances of antiracism need to be coupled with actual work to dismantle systems of oppression. We need to further diversify our academic fields and weed out racism within our institutions.

Industrial relations scholars need to reconceptualize the working class and the labor movement more broadly. Engaging with and integrating critical labor history narratives into their research is a great way to do that. The scholar-activist Barbara Ransby reminds us: "Nothing is predetermined or dictated by history. However, historical conditions both create and limit possibilities for change. And all individual participants in this moment may not even be fully aware of the history on which they stand. Nevertheless, it is there. What is also there is an ever-shifting political reality" (2018: 11). As the above section highlighted, recent historiographies have offered key insights into the shifting political, social, and cultural landscape in the United States.

As I recently argued, reconceptualizing worker mobilizations in the 20th century by centering Black workers reshapes our understanding of who counts as a worker and what organizing strategies are most effective in both unionization efforts and in broader social justice campaigns. How we envision the working class in our research and policy work can impact better, more inclusive decision making. When we disrupt normative notions of a white, industrial, unionized working class, we can find new solutions to old problems (Williams and Davis-Faulkner 2021).

Industrial relations scholars must also expand their understanding of worker organizations. Too much focus on unionized workers and unions as the only source of collective worker voice misses valuable lessons from across the spectrum of the labor movement. For example, the SEIU-backed Fight for $15 movement has reshaped the political narrative around fair wages and increased minimum wages in states and localities across the nation (Williams and Davis-Faulkner 2021).

Industrial relations scholars need to expand diversity and inclusion efforts within LERA. As the chapters in this volume illustrate, scholars and practitioners across fields are doing research and work that fits within LERA's purview. Too many scholars, especially graduate students who are interested in today's labor problems, inequality, and producing scholarship that will disrupt intersecting systems of oppression, do not see LERA as their professional home. LERA is already doing this work: recruiting graduate students; diversifying leadership, conference panels, and publications; and establishing a new diversity policy and a new apprenticeship membership category for union members (Batt 2019). Bringing CRT/I theory into industrial relations scholarship—as Lee and Tapia have called for—will go a long way in recruiting new scholars and practitioners to LERA and industrial relations studies.

Industrial relations and labor history have joint origins in the efforts of economists to solve the labor problems of the late 19th and early 20th centuries. The fields both flourished in the postwar period as unions and collective bargaining seemed to offer solutions to workers' lived experiences of employer dominance and exploitation. The decline of union density and loss of worker voice in public debate caused moments of crises in both disciplines. Labor history benefited from critical studies and produced new histories that offer more robust understandings of racial capitalism in its shifting forms and the intersecting systems of race, gender, class, and other forms of oppression that embed social institutions and dictate how all people move through the world of work and in larger society. Labor history has returned to questions of institutions, politics, and power, and has developed more sophisticated ways to integrate human agency into these narratives. These insights offer key lessons for industrial relations scholars today.

ENDNOTES

1. Lee and Tapia describe industrial relations research that examines the importance of other social identities beyond class and illustrate how applying critical race theory/intersectionality (CRT/I) could reshape research questions, conclusions, and relevance.

2. For a discussion of the how this has been comparably absent from industrial relations, see Lee and Tapia (2021). In that article, the authors review advances in other social science fields and examine industrial relations scholarship as it pertains to worker organizing to illustrate the lack of a critical industrial relations theory.

REFERENCES

Arnesen, Eric. 1998. "Up from Exclusion: Black and White Workers, Race, and the State of Labor History." *Reviews in American History* 26 (1): 146–174.

Baron, Ava, ed. 1991. *Work Engendered: Toward a New History of American Labor*. Ithaca: Cornell University Press.

Batt, Rosemary. 2019. "LERA's Identity Crisis at 75." *Perspectives on Work* 23: 75–77.

Bell, Derrick A., Jr. 1980. "*Brown v. Board of Education* and the Interest-Convergence Dilemma." *Harvard Law Review* 93 (3): 518–533.

Brody, David. 1989. "Labor History, Industrial Relations, and the Crisis of American Labor." *ILR Review* 43 (1) 7–18.

Brody, David. 1993. "Reconciling the Old Labor History and the New." *Pacific Historical Review* 62 (1): 1–18.

Budd, John W. 2008. "A Meta-Paradigm for Revitalizing Industrial Relations." In *New Directions in the Study of Work and Employment: Revitalizing Industrial Relations as an Academic Field*. Charles J. Whalen, ed. Cheltenham: Edward Elgar.

Collins, Patricia Hill. 2019. *Intersectionality as Critical Social Theory*. Durham: Duke University Press.

Fields, Barbara Jeanne. 1990. "Slavery, Race and Ideology in the United States of America." *New Left Review* I (181): 95–118.

Hall, Jacquelyn Dowd Hall. 2005. "The Long Civil Rights Movement and the Political Uses of the Past." *Journal of American History* 91 (4): 1233–1263.

Hunter, Tera W. 1993 "Domination and Resistance: The Politics of Wage Household Labor in New South Atlanta." *Labor History* 34 (2–3): 205–220.

Ignatiev, Noel. 1995. *How the Irish Became White*. Oxfordshire: Routledge.

Kaufman, Bruce. 2010. "The Theoretical Foundation of Industrial Relations and Its Implications for Labor Economics and Human Resource Management." *Industrial & Labor Relations Review* 64 (1): 74–108.

Kaufman, Bruce. 2020. "The Founding of Industrial Relations and LERA: IR Celebrates 100 Years, LERA 73." *Perspectives on Work* 24: 46–53.

Kelley, Robin D.G. 2017 "What Did Cedric Robinson Mean by Racial Capitalism?" *Boston Review*. https://bit.ly/3G1n5KA

Kochan, Thomas A. 1998. "What Is Distinctive About Industrial Relations Research?" In *Researching the World of Work: Strategies and Methods in Studying Industrial Relations.* Keith Whitfield and George Strauss, eds. Ithaca: ILR Press.

Nadasen, Premilla. 2015. *Household Workers Unite: The Untold Story of African American Women Who Built a Movement.* Boston: Beacon Press.

Lee, Tamara L., and Maite Tapia. 2021. "Confronting Race and Other Social Identity Erasures: The Case for Critical Industrial Relations Theory." *Industrial & Labor Relations Review* 74 (3): 637–662.

Lewis, Earl. 1995. "To Turn as on a Pivot: Writing African Americans into a History of Overlapping Diasporas." *American Historical Review* 100 (3): 765–787.

Phillips, Lisa. 2021. "A Piece of the Action: Race and Labor in Post–Civil Rights Hollywood." Book Review. *Labor* 18 (4): 145–147.

Phillips-Cunningham, Danielle T. 2020. *Putting Their Hands on Race: Irish Immigrant and Southern Black Domestic Workers.* New Brunswick: Rutgers University Press.

Ransby, Barbara. 2018. *Making All Black Lives Matter: Reimagining Freedom in the 21st Century.* Oakland: University of California Press.

Robinson, Cedric J. 2020. *Black Marxism: The Making of The Black Radical Tradition,* revised and updated 3rd ed. Chapel Hill: University of North Carolina Press.

Roediger, David. 1991. *The Wages of Whiteness: Race and the Making of the American Working Class.* Brooklyn: Verso.

Quinn, Eithne. 2019. *A Piece of the Action: Race and Labor in Post–Civil Rights Hollywood.* New York: Columbia University Press.

Trotter Jr., Joe William. 1994. "African-American Workers: New Directions in U.S. Labor Historiography." *Labor History* 35 (4): 495–523.

Trotter Jr., Joe William. 2019. *Workers on Arrival: Black Labor in the Making of America.* Oakland: University of California Press.

Williams, Naomi R, and Sheri Davis-Faulkner. 2021. "Worker Mobilization and Political Engagement: A Historical Perspective." In *Revaluing Work(ers): Toward a Democratic and Sustainable Future.* Tobias Schulze-Cleven and Todd E. Vachon, eds. Champaign: Labor and Employment Relations Association.

CHAPTER 4

"The World Will Get a Correct Estimate of the Negro Woman": The Intellectual Work of Early Black Women Labor Organizers

DANIELLE PHILLIPS-CUNNINGHAM
Texas Woman's University
Multicultural Women's and Gender Studies

Abstract

Educator, labor organizer, and civil rights activist Nannie Helen Burroughs declared in 1915 that the "world was going to get a correct estimate of the Negro woman" when they could vote. While women were granted the right to vote in 1920, Black women would not have equal access to the ballot box until the passage of the Civil Rights Act of 1964 and the Voting Rights Act of 1965 because of Jim Crow laws. Voter suppression and the general exclusion of Black workers from white organized labor unions did not stop Black women from inserting their labor demands into politics. This chapter offers a genealogy of Black women's development of intersectional research methods and organizing strategies that led to unprecedented labor initiatives in the United States during the late nineteenth 19th and early twentieth 20th centuries. I argue that Black women's intellectual tradition of comprehensive labor organizing should be integral to how we conceptualize and teach about labor justice today.

INTRODUCTION

Southern Black women community organizers have become front and center in public discussions about the urgency of systemic change in the United States. Stacey Abrams, LaTosha Brown, and other Black women organizers, as well as organizations such as Care in Action of the National Domestic Workers Alliance, have been widely credited for changing the electoral map and helping elect the first Black person from Georgia to the US Senate since Reconstruction (11Alive Staff 2021; Bailey 2020; Kelly 2021; "Stacey Abrams Showed the Power" 2021). Recognizing the profound influence of Black women's community organizing on US politics is a new and long overdue phenomenon. Still, like their 19th- and 20th-century predecessors, Black women have not been acknowledged for their intellectual work that has been integral to their groundbreaking political organizing.

Black women have a long tradition of developing intersectional analytic frameworks and research methods that have guided their labor resistance and has been essential to their grassroots organizing since emancipation. The National Domestic Workers Alliance's We Dream in Black project captures the seamless and historical relationship between Black women's fight for voting and labor rights in their bold agenda statement:

"We are the proud legacies of village-making, dream-holding, voter registering, union building, road-marching, poetry-in-motion, this land is our land, stunting-on-all-y'all, Black domestic workers" (National Domestic Workers Alliance, no date). It is time that we all engage Black women's intersectional methods that drive the organizing so powerfully described by the We Dream in Black project—in our classrooms, policies, and community organizing—if we are to truly achieve labor justice for everyone.

Feminist legal scholar Kimberlé Crenshaw was the first to coin the term *intersectionality* as a framework needed to make visible and address forms of racial and gendered workplace discrimination that impact Black women. In her classic article, "Demarginalizing the Intersection of Race and Sex," Crenshaw traced the origins of intersectional theorizing to the activism of Black women suffragists who organized against systemic inequalities rooted in race, class, gender, sexuality, age, and other markers of difference (Crenshaw 1989: 139–140). As Crenshaw later explained in a 2016 TED Talk, intersectionality has and continues to matter in the 21st century because without a lens that allows us to "see how social problems impact all the members of a targeted group, many will fall through the cracks of our movements, left to suffer in virtual isolation" (Crenshaw 2016).

Labor organizing by Black women, I argue, is a promising pathway for building movements that bring people together across communities to address inequalities that impact the majority of workers. With a particular focus on southern Black women, this chapter offers a historic mapping of Black women's legacies of operationalizing intersectionality into innovative and comprehensive research methods and strategies for challenging labor exploitation.

Southern Black women across socioeconomic classes had to develop especially unique approaches to asserting their right to labor protections as those who fought against patriarchy and the legacies of slavery in its most blatant and brutal forms. As LaTosha Brown, founder of Black Voters Matter, explained, the South is a "space that has been the home for the Confederacy, the space that has been root for white supremacy and white nationalists" and it is where "the Southern strategy was born … that is being fueled and engineered by people of color, and Black folks are on the vanguard" (Kelly 2021).

While charting the intellectual work of southern Black women organizers, I also challenge the masculinized construct of who counts as a labor leader and strategist. Booker T. Washington and W.E.B. Du Bois are widely remembered as the two representative thinkers on the subjects of race and labor (Aiello 2016; BlackPast, no date; Frontline 1998). At the same time, Black women and Black female-led organizations are not widely considered labor leaders and thinkers. Contemporary activists are building on the work of these early women who laid the foundation for community mobilization that is shaking up the United States.

THE ATLANTA WASHING SOCIETY STRIKE: INTERSECTIONAL MAPPING AND COALITION BUILDING

The immediate years following the Civil War were full of great promise and hostile threats to racial progress and labor protections for Black people. In 1865, 1868, and 1870, Congress ratified the 13th, 14th, and 15th Amendments, respectively, to formally abolish slavery and involuntary servitude, except in cases of punishment for criminal offenses; grant citizenship to everyone born on US soil, including formerly enslaved Black people; and extend voting rights to Black men. Prior to the passage of the amendments, Congress had also established the Freedmen's Bureau, also known as the Bureau of Refugees, Freedmen, and Abandoned Lands, to provide Black people with resources such as shelter, medical services, and labor contract adjudication services, which were critical for Black survival and reintegration into the United States (Blight 2001: 45). The sheer determination of Black people to assert their freedom coupled with the Freedmen's Bureau and amendments paved the way for them to establish their own schools, stores, businesses, libraries, community theaters, social services, and political and labor organizations (Glenn 2001: 94).

Threatened by the advancements of Black people, President Andrew Johnson, Lincoln's successor and a staunch white supremacist, did everything he could to roll back their constitutional rights. Soon after assuming the presidential office, Johnson weakened the Freedmen's Bureau and 13th, 14th, and 15th Amendments by encouraging US southern governments to draft and implement the "Black Codes." This series of laws restricted the mobility of Black people in an effort to control their labor and mobility.

As historian Carol Anderson explained, "black economic independence was anathema to a power structure that depended on cheap, exploitable, rightless labor and required black subordination" (Anderson 2016: 20). Specifically, the codes effectively restricted Black people to household employment and sharecropping; made it illegal for Black people to seek new employment without approval from their previous employer; restored property ownership to former slaveholders; legalized the murders and arrests of Black people for minor infractions and crossing arbitrary neighborhood boundaries drawn by everyday white citizens and policemen; and denied Black people the right to serve on juries, vote, and testify against whites in court cases (Anderson 2016: 19).

Johnson's successor, President Rutherford B. Hayes, withdrew federal troops from the former Confederate states through the Compromise of 1877 before Black people could amass enough economic and political power to recover from the violence, physical destruction, and labor exploitation that the Black Codes imposed on their communities. Black people in the South were left to fend for themselves against the Ku Klux Klan (KKK) and ex-Confederate soldiers in local government and police departments for nearly a century. The KKK threatened to lynch Black people who exercised their 15th Amendment right to vote. Southern governments also imposed skin color tests and nearly unpassable reading tests that made it all but impossible for Black citizens to vote, and they passed a series of laws establishing racial segregation to assert political, social, and economic control (Anderson 2016: 44). White employers had legal cover to exploit Black workers. White landowners kept Black sharecroppers in perpetual debt—making it nearly impossible for them to make a decent living. Domestic service employers could physically abuse and call for the arrest of domestic workers who left their places of employment, protected themselves against sexual assault, verbally challenged them, or refused to adhere to their dictates. They also often paid domestic workers low wages, if any at all. With no labor protections, Black women and girls in household positions were subjected to and resisted labor exploitation in the homes of white families while navigating and challenging racial segregation, racism, and sexual harassment in their workplaces, not to mention limited educational opportunities and racialized gender violence.

As a collective group of workers, Black women were never silent about the glaring juridical and physical violence inflicted on their communities. Since the end of slavery, they had asserted their right to labor protections as workers who were US citizens and who provided services of immense value to the US economy. One of the hallmark campaigns of Black women after emancipation was their fight for labor rights in household employment. Their petitions and strikes were bold assertions of autonomy and citizenship against white supremacist legal, political, and social structures that legalized the exploitation of Black labor.

Washerwomen were among the first labor organizers to articulate and organize against intersecting inequalities in the US economy. Their approaches were what young people would describe today as "gangsta"—or unabashedly assertive and demanding. They often risked being jailed, lynched, and harassed by policemen and local KKK members, as well as losing their incomes to protest for labor protections and living wages for Black women.

With a keen awareness of the entangled webs of power that relegated them to low-wage work, washerwomen strategized and devised multiple resistance methods to pinpoint and challenge the very ideologies and institutions that stood in the way of their political and economic freedom during a time when southern white employers and lawmakers were eager to reinstate the social and economic order of slavery in every way except in name only.

Four years after the Compromise of 1877, Black washerwomen in Atlanta organized labor protests that captured public historical memory for several decades after historian Tera Hunter first documented the protests.[1] On July 19, 1881, twenty women laundry workers in Atlanta formed a labor organization called the Washing

Society that staged the state's largest and most resilient labor strike. They protested the refusal of white customers to pay them living wages and the threats on their trade posed by commercial laundries. The society developed intersectional approaches to organizing that simultaneously challenged ideologies and institutions of racism, patriarchy, and classism that were foundational to the systemic exploitation of most workers.

To build a diverse coalition of supporters, Washing Society members knocked on hundreds of doors across Atlanta, sought alliances with white workers, called out elected officials for their suppression tactics, and authored petitions to assert the urgent need for living and standardized wages.

The striking laundresses also held strategizing meetings at Wheat Street Baptist Church, a popular community organizing place where Black women had social and political influence as people who did critical work for the everyday maintenance and operation of the church.[2] The church was also a site that had offered social services and formal education courses to laborers in the city since its founding shortly after the Civil War (Schott-Bresler 2014).

Society members' speeches at the church identifying intersecting racial inequalities that impacted the laundry trade must have resonated with Black men, who had also experienced racial labor exploitation. While meeting at Wheat Street, the society attracted thousands of supporters that included both women and men (Hunter 1997: 93–94). They also used their knowledge of the routes that they traveled to pick up laundry orders to map out the racial and gendered geography of the city and design plans for canvassing in specific neighborhoods that would draw the most support for their planned strikes. Organization members petitioned in communities where Black and white washerwomen lived. Although white women made up only 1% to 2% of the laundresses in Atlanta, the Washing Society understood that labor exploitation relied on racial and gendered divisions between Black and white workers in the same occupations.

The laundresses often risked their own safety to canvas in white neighborhoods to garner support from poor white workers. They were successful at convincing a few white laundresses, who were probably Irish women, to join their strike (Hunter 1997: 89). Using an intersectional approach, they also made extraordinary use of the interconnectivity between networks within the Black community to recruit workers who were directly and indirectly impacted by the exploitation of laundresses. As Tera Hunter put it, "The washerwomen had exercised remarkable leverage in the face of class, gender, and racial hostility. Through the use of formal and informal community networks in which they shared work routines, work sites, living space, and social activity, the strikers organized thousands of women and men" (Hunter 1997: 97).

The Washing Society's nuanced canvassing and networking methods led to the growth of their trade organization from a membership of 20 people to 3,000 people within three weeks of its establishment. Along with a few Black male and Irish immigrant women allies, Matilda Crawford, Sallie Bell, Carrie Jones, Dora

Jones, Orphelia Turner, Sarah A. Collier, and the other members of the Washing Society demanded that the Atlanta city government standardize the wages of all washerwomen ("The Washerwomen's Strike" 1881). Establishing a potent coalition of workers, however, was far from easy and required a multilayered approach. Members targeted the local city government because they had a keen awareness of the power that institutions and laws played in creating and maintaining systemic inequalities. Their protest plans and public letters to city officials reflected a sophisticated analysis of capitalism and how much it relied on the exploitation of women's household labor.

Perhaps the Washing Society's most audacious and radical threat was to stage a second strike with domestic workers during the 1881 Atlanta Cotton Exposition. Their bold move demonstrated that Black women's laundry work was just as—if not more—essential to the local hospitality industry and everyday operations of white people's homes. The Washing Society knew that striking Black women laborers would disrupt the city's plans to unveil a false image of the "New South" as a prosperous region with harmonious race relations and the very practicality of accommodating thousands of visitors (Hunter 1997: 96–97).

Journalists and lawmakers panicked at the thought of a strike during the time of the exposition and attempted to halt the Washing Society's plans. The city council threatened the society by passing a resolution charging society members an annual business tax of $25. Tenant landlords also threatened to raise the rent of society members so that they would not be able to afford where they lived and worked. The society responded with an open letter to the mayor declaring that they would in turn raise the prices of washing to afford the tax. As they announced, "We, the members of our society, are determined to stand our pledge and make extra charges for washing, and we have agreed, and are willing to pay $25 or $50 for licenses as a protection so we can control the washing for the city." They also threatened, "Don't forget this … We mean business this week or no washing" (Hunter 1997: 93). While it is unknown from local news reports whether or not their demands were met, they had succeeded in exercising significant political and economic leverage. The fact that they did not wage a strike during the exposition meant that employers probably heeded their warnings, and it was not until 1910 when laundry companies would pose a serious threat to the employment of Black women in the city.

THE NATIONAL ASSOCIATION OF COLORED WOMEN'S CLUBS: A NETWORK OF INTERSECTIONAL RESEARCHERS AND UNION-BUILDING WOMEN

At the dawn of the 20th century, less than 50 years after emancipation and with Jim Crow laws in place across much of the country, Black girls and women continued facing a harsh occupational landscape. Domestic labor and household employment— which was unregulated and the lowest-paying occupation for women in the US economy—remained one of the few options available to them to make a living. Black women across socioeconomic classes persisted in their resistance to labor exploitation into the early 20th century. For example, the National Association of Colored Women's Clubs (NACWC) was established in 1896 to advocate for Black women's right to vote and establish social services for Black communities that had been denied to them during the Jim Crow era. The NACWC reached far and wide, creating local clubs in several hundred small and large cities in every state of the United States except Alaska. In each locale, NACWC leaders and members who managed the clubs provided vital resources for Black women and their children: daycare services, kindergarten classes, lodging, libraries, literacy and literary courses, and employment assistance, just to name a few (White 1999: 33–36).

One of the primary goals of the NACWC was to improve the working conditions of Black women on a national scale. Members conducted on-the-ground research, prepared reports, and delivered speeches, culling data that did not previously exist to create what we would think of today as a national database of research about the working and living conditions of Black women workers.

NACWC members conducted community research to produce previously nonexistent quantitative and qualitative data about racial, class, and gender inequalities that contributed to the unequal wages of Black and white women workers. Clubwomen used their data to advocate for state and federal labor legislation to eradicate wage disparities, work with white women on labor issues, and create their own labor organizations to address the poor working and living conditions of Black women.[3]

NACWC member Elizabeth Ross Haynes, a sociologist born in Mount Willing, Alabama, is why we have federal data today about the disparate working conditions of women along the lines of race and occupation. Haynes' groundbreaking research about women's wages laid the foundation for explaining what Black economist Michelle Holder refers to today as the double gap, or the unequal wages between white and Black women (Holder 2020). Haynes produced research studies while working at the Women in Industry Service (later renamed the Women's Bureau) of the US Department of Labor in 1919 and in her position as the Domestic Service Employment Secretary at the US Employment Service in Washington, D.C., from 1920 to 1922 to bring attention to the national problem of Black women earning substandard wages.

Haynes traveled across the country gathering statistics and qualitative data from employment agencies and from her own interviews with domestic workers, household employers, and employment agencies. She disaggregated the primary source data and labor census statistics of the US Department of Labor to create a comprehensive record of the working conditions and earnings of domestic workers according to race and gender. Haynes' intersectional analysis and research provided solid documentation revealing that Black women on average made far less than their Black male and white female counterparts in household employment (Haynes

1923: 418). Haynes also concluded that employment agencies rendered Black women vulnerable to labor exploitation at a higher rate than native-born and immigrant white domestic workers. The scholar-activist put her intersectional research into action to advocate for government oversight of employment agencies to intervene in the disproportionate exploitation of Black women in domestic service. As she concluded in her proposal: "The service rendered by them [employment agencies] is on the whole poor. The harm inflicted upon society by many of them is irreparable. Public control of employment agencies has great possibilities for social betterment" (Haynes 1923: 442).

Prior to publishing her research and recommendations as a master's thesis at Columbia University in 1923, Haynes mobilized a cross-class group of NACWC members, including first NACWC president Mary Church Terrell, who were educators, writers, and factory workers, to advocate for a cross-racial women's labor union at the 1919 International Congress of Working Women (ICWW) in Washington, D.C. The ICWW was the first and largest gathering of women labor organizers from around the world.

Haynes and her NACWC colleagues saw the historic conference as a prime opportunity to create global and national alliances with women labor activists across race and ethnicity to improve the working conditions of Black women in domestic service. Although the majority of conference attendees were white women, Haynes and her colleagues believed that their shared labor experiences as women was a foundation from which they could together organize against both racial and gender inequalities in the economy.

Haynes and her co-organizers authored a petition to form a coalitional union for domestic workers that Maud Schwartz, leader of New York's Women's Trade Union League, read aloud to the majority white women audience at the conference. The petition included a detailed statistical and qualitative analysis of the labor exploitation of women workers in the US economy, primarily highlighting the working conditions of Black domestic workers. It stated, moreover, "We, a group of Negro women, representing those two millions of Negro woman wage-earners, respectfully ask for your active cooperation in organizing the Negro women workers of the United States into unions that they may have a share in bringing about industrial democracy and social order in the world" (Burroughs et al. 1919). They appealed to the league to incorporate Black women's labor issues into their agenda because Black women had "very limited means of making their wishes known and of having their interests advanced through their own [male] representatives" (Burroughs et al. 1919).

The ICWW did not join the NACWC members' efforts to unionize with Black women (Vapnek 2014: 166). They claimed that they would discuss it later and never did—probably out of refusal to address both race and gender discrimination in the labor market. Nevertheless, Haynes' research and organizing shaped what would in 1920 become the Women's Labor Bureau, which is still in operation today. For the past century, the bureau has documented racial and gender disparities in the labor sector that disproportionately impact women of color, and the data collected have been instrumental to several studies and key pieces of legislation introduced by government officials and labor organizers to raise the federal minimum wage, better the working conditions of women of color, and end the double gap (Frye 2020; Wilson and Kessa 2020).

Nannie Helen Burroughs, Haynes' NACWC colleague and co-author of the ICWW petition, never gave up on their 1919 vision of establishing a labor union for domestic workers. In 1921, the native of Orange, Virginia, and founder of the National Training School for Women and Girls in Washington, D.C., used data from Haynes' research and the petition to launch the National Association of Wage Earners (NAWE). The NAWE was the first national Black women's labor organization of the early 20th century dedicated to improving the working conditions of domestic workers.

While the core objective of the NAWE was to unionize domestic workers, organizational members included women and men across social class and from a wide array of occupations including educators, domestic workers, professors, pastors, beauticians, insurance agents, and farmers, just to name a few (NAWE Membership Cards, no date). Together, Burroughs and members of the NAWE declared that domestic workers could become "towers of strength in the labor world" through labor organizing ("Colored Women to Organize" 1924: 22).

Burroughs and her NAWE comrades used several strategies to recruit such a diverse membership. Guided by an intersectional frame, they had a keen understanding of how racial, class, and gender inequalities in the US economy impacted a wide range of laborers. Burroughs believed that domestic workers experienced the most glaring forms of labor exploitation and remedying their struggles would reverberate to all other workers who were subjected to discrimination. Welcoming everyone into the NAWE, Burroughs declared in a promotional pamphlet: "This is an organization for every worker—skilled or unskilled. This is an organization for every woman—high or low, servant or secretary, college president or field hand. Working together we can advance to a place of influence and respect in the Labor World" (Burroughs/NAWE Files, no date).

Similar to the focus of the Washing Society of Atlanta, Burroughs and NAWE officers relied on women's vast social, religious, and occupational networks for recruitment. The national officers, district chapter president Sadie Henson, and local D.C. organizers collectively drew an NAWE membership of 5,000 people across 37 states and Washington, D.C., within two years of the organization's existence. The majority of NAWE officers were members of the NACWC who recruited members outside of Washington, D.C., and molded its national reputation through their leadership in national and state women's and civil rights organizations. The officers were Mary McLeod Bethune, vice president (Florida); Minnie L. Bradley, executive secretary (Connecticut); Elizabeth C. Carter, chair of the investment board (Massachusetts); Lizzie Foust, registrar (Kentucky); Maggie L.

Walker, treasurer (Virginia); Georgine Kelly Smith, chair of the advisory council (New York); and Maude A. Morrisey, recording secretary (Pennsylvania) ("The First Annual Meeting" 1924). D.C. organizers complemented the efforts of national officers by recruiting a local cross-class coalition of women and men laborers into the NAWE. Sadie Henson met professionals ranging from teachers to lawyers to domestic workers while working as a truant officer in the public schools and through her leadership positions in the Women Wage Earners Association, a local church, and local chapters of the NACWC and the Freemasons Order of the Eastern Star ("Women Form Organization" 1917; "Women Wage Earners Organize" 1917).

Within one year of organizing, Henson convinced 50 people from her networks to join the NAWE (Murphy 2018: 26). The NAWE's expansive vision of achieving economic freedom for all women and Black people inspired Lucy E. Holland to join the organization and recruit others. As an organizer, she mobilized the NAWE's comprehensive agenda by recruiting people who labored in or were closely connected to the service industry, such as maids, charwomen, laundresses, housewives, and security guards (Murphy 2018: 27).

Similar to Elizabeth Ross Haynes' work, local NAWE organizers gathered their own data to routinely document the experiences of members and took that research to push for labor legislation to standardize the wages of household employment. They also employed their research to identify the needs of domestic workers and create vital resources that they were not getting through their jobs. With the assistance of Burroughs' NACWC colleague Maggie Lena Walker, the NAWE provided a death benefits fund for its members. Walker was the first woman in the United States to establish and serve as president of a bank. Her support helped alleviate stress for domestic workers of the organization, who often had to pool resources to bury their loved ones because domestic service employers did not offer benefits to workers.[4] Burroughs believed in sharing with the surrounding D.C. community the NAWE's research as well as other studies about the exploitation of Black domestic workers.

She organized public forums at the NAWE's headquarters and local churches to educate people in D.C. about the exploitation of domestic workers and draw their support for labor legislation to regulate household employment ("The First Annual Meeting" 1924).

While presiding over the NAWE, Burroughs co-founded the National League of Republican Colored Women (NLRCW) in 1924 to combat voter suppression, which she believed was necessary for achieving labor rights and eradicating racial, class, and gender discrimination. As she announced in her prophetic 1915 article in *The Crisis*, "The world is going to get a correct estimate of the Negro woman" when they are granted the right to vote. She predicted that Black women would have an indescribable impact on the country that "poets have never sung, orators have never spoken, and scholars have never written" (Burroughs 1915). While president of the NLRCW, Burroughs collected national data to report intimidation of Black women voters at the polls and inspire Black women to vote. As she explained, "Since Negro women have the ballot, they must not undervalue it. They must study municipal problems—men and measures, parties and principles … They must organize to fight discrimination and class legislation" ("Colored Women in Politics" c. 1924).

After the 1924 presidential election, Burroughs created an extensive questionnaire of 29 questions to measure Black women's participation in state, local, and national policies and to document voter intimidation. Urging Black women to complete the survey, she noted in its introduction that they were essential for "fighting discrimination and class legislation" and becoming "a factor in the body politic" ("Colored Women in Politics" c. 1924).

The NLRCW was successful at using data to inspire Black women across the country to vote and convince politicians why they needed to take Black women voters seriously. Burroughs also used the information from the survey to propose federal legislation to address the suppression of Black women voters, especially in relation to their occupation. As she argued, domestic workers were the most susceptible to harassment because they worked in the homes of white families who would threaten to fire them if they voted.

The NAWE and NLCRW were relatively short-lived, but Burroughs achieved tremendous results with each organization. The NAWE declined in 1926 as a result of financial issues, yet Burroughs' labor union provided the model for future labor organizations that conduct intersectional labor research and tap into women's social and occupational networks to mobilize voters. One of these organizations is the National Domestic Workers Alliance, an organization that registered hundreds of voters who participated in the historic Georgia Senate election. Burroughs never gave up on her mission after the NAWE and NLCRW disbanded. Similar to the Atlanta washerwomen and Elizabeth Ross Haynes, Burroughs believed in the power of directly challenging government to push for an equitable labor system along the lines of race, class, and gender.

In 1937, Burroughs wrote a scathing analysis of the federal government for excluding domestic workers in the 1935 Social Security Act. In an article published by the *Atlanta Daily World* and reprinted by the *Norfolk Journal and Guide*, Burroughs wrote: "Society has always seemed to delight in penalizing those who wear caps, aprons, and work with their hands. … Now along comes the Federal Government … by a sweeping legislative act of exclusion makes domestic workers the mudsill of the new social order" (Burroughs 1937: 2). Although deeply angered and disappointed by the federal government's refusal to address Black women's labor issues, Burroughs continued fighting for comprehensive voting and labor rights through her school, community work, and leadership in the civil rights movement until her death in 1961.

Early Black women labor organizations and leaders such as the Washing Society, Elizabeth Ross Haynes, and Nannie Helen Burroughs, along with Black women who did similar work, should be frequently referenced in public discussions about labor movements and integrated into the curricula of labor studies programs across the nation. Their "behind the scenes" work of extracting data about workplace conditions from racially indeterminate data, mapping out the racial, class, and gender demographics of counties and districts, assembling cross-class coalitions, writing protest literature, and developing incisive questions for community surveys to expose overlapping inequalities that impact a wide range of workers led to some of the most progressive and comprehensive labor and civil rights initiatives in US history. Black women organizers are continuing these intellectual and organizing traditions that are poised to transform labor politics in the foreseeable future.

CONCLUSION

The United States is facing similar labor dilemmas to what Black women analyzed and fought against in the late 19th and early 20th centuries. There is no federal legislation to protect domestic workers from labor exploitation, and there are no specific laws that address the particular racial, class, and gendered experiences of women workers across employment sectors. Looking at the history of Black women's intellectual work, however, moves us closer to developing more data and policies that will truly address systemic inequalities with such deep historical roots.

Black women's intellectual traditions are also instructive course correctives to "race and gender neutral" approaches to labor analyses and organizing. Their intersectional analyses complicate discussions of workers as an undifferentiated mass of people, which in turn reinforces the privileging of white male workers. White working-class men have had the benefit of being seen as a group of workers with diverse and critical needs since the rise of labor unions in the 19th century. Politicians and lawmakers always angst over the racial and economic grievances, working conditions, and mental health of the white male working-class every election season. Their focus leads to questions of how the government can better their lives through policy changes. When it comes to women, there is always a focus on suburban (read: white) women and their concerns. These questions are rarely asked about Black people, and they are certainly not asked about Black women in particular, although Black women have been among the most consistent block of organizers and voters in the United States for over two centuries.

Now is the opportune time to change the course of history and move closer to comprehensive labor justice. This can only become a reality when we center the rich genealogy of southern Black women's and other women of color's intersectional approaches in labor studies and our labor movements.

ENDNOTES

1. The American Federation of Labor's website features a story about the strike ("Atlanta's Washerwomen's Strike," https://bit.ly/34PYjjL). New America, a collective of policy experts and

public intellectuals, highlighted the strike on their website and touts them as a guide for resistance today ("The Atlanta Washerwomen Strike of 1881: A Lesson in Unity and Persistence," https://bit.ly/3KhhCCJ). Classroom instruction blogs also include teaching materials about the strike (https://bit.ly/3I8D2Af and https://bit.ly/3GzEGud).

2. For histories of how Black women asserted political power through churches during the late 19th and early 20th centuries, see Barkley Brown (1994) and Higginbotham (1993).

3. For example, Mary Church Terrell, Memphis-born activist, educator, and the first president of the NACWC, launched the Woman's Wage Earners' Association in Washington, D.C., in 1917 to research the labor struggles of Black women workers and encourage them to unionize (Parker 2020: 202).

4. The NAWE could offer burial assistance and safe housing for its members because of the support of Elizabeth Carter and Maggie Lena Walker. Carter was president of the NACWC from 1908 through 1912 and supervised the Young Women's Christian Association's building in Washington, D.C., where she provided lodging arrangements for NAWE members (https://bit.ly/3FFMgT6). Walker, whose mother was a washerwoman, was a leader in the Independent Order of Saint Luke in Richmond and the first Black woman president of a bank in the United States. She contributed significantly to the NAWE's death benefits fund (Garrett-Scott 2019: 62–72).

REFERENCES

11Alive Staff. 2021. "Women of Color in Georgia Showed Up in Record Numbers to Make Their Voices Heard for 2020 Election." January 6. https://bit.ly/3GBxs9d

Aiello, Thomas. 2016. *The Battle for the Souls of Black Folks*. Santa Barbara: ABC-CLIO.

Anderson, Carol. 2016. *White Rage: The Untold Truth of Our Racial Divide*. Camden: Bloomsbury.

Bailey, Chelsea. 2020. "Stacey Abrams: The Woman Behind Biden's Biggest Surprise." *BBC News*. November 10. https://bbc.in/33IpPiC

Barkley Brown, Elsa. 1994. "Negotiating and Transforming the Public Sphere: African American Political Life in the Transition from Slavery to Freedom." *Public Culture* 7 (1): 107–146.

BlackPast. No date. "Structured Academic Debate: Booker T. Washington and W.E.B. Du Bois." https://bit.ly/3nytiY4

Blight, David W. 2001. *Race and Reunion: The Civil War in American Memory*. Cambridge: Harvard University Press.

Burroughs, Nannie Helen/NAWE Files. No date. "We Must Paddle Our Own Canoe." NAWE Files, New York University's Tamiment Library and Wagner Labor Archives.

Burroughs, Nannie Helen. 1915. "Black Women and Reform." *The Crisis*. August 1.

Burroughs, Nannie Helen. 1937. "Domestic Workers Excluded." *Atlanta Daily World*, January 21; reprinted as "The Social Security Act Looks Down On Us Who Toil With Our Hands." *The Pittsburgh Courier*. January 23.

Burroughs, Nannie Helen, Elizabeth C. Carter, Mamie R. Ross, Leilia Pendleton, Dr. A.G. Green, Eva A. Wright, Mary Church Terrell, Carrie Roscoe, Caroline Clifford, and Elfizabeth Ross Haynes. 1919. "First Convention of International Conference of Working Women." International Federation of Working Women Records, Schlesinger Library, Harvard University, Folder 3.

"Colored Women in Politics." c. 1924. Questionnaire. NHB papers, Manuscript Division, c:308, Library of Congress.

"Colored Women to Organize Domestic Workers: Miss Nannie Helen Burroughs of Washington and Mrs. Mary McLeod Bethune of Florida Behind Movement." 1924. *The Pittsburgh Courier*. March 22.

Crenshaw, Kimberlé. 1989. "Demarginalizing the Intersection of Race and Sex: A Black Feminist Critique of Antidiscrimination Doctrine, Feminist Theory, and Antiracist Politics." *The University of Chicago Legal Forum* 1 (8): 139–167.

Crenshaw, Kimberlé. 2016. "The Urgency of Intersectionality." TED Talk. December 7. https://bit.ly/3rpvGBM

Frontline. 1998. "The Debate Between W.E.B. Du Bois and Booker T. Washington." PBS. February 10. https://to.pbs.org/3nAUPrX

Frye, Jocelyn. 2020. "On the Frontlines at Work and at Home: The Disproportionate Economic Effects of the Coronavirus Pandemic on Women of Color." *American Progress*. April 23. https://ampr.gs/3GEzHse

Garrett-Scott, Shennette. 2019. *Banking on Freedom: Black Women in US Finance Before the New Deal*. New York: Columbia University Press.

Glenn, Evelyn Nakano. 2001. *Unequal Freedom: How Race and Gender Shaped American Citizenship and Labor*. Cambridge: Harvard University Press.

Haynes, Elizabeth Ross. 1923. "Negroes in Domestic Service in the United States." *Journal of Negro History* 8 (4): 384–442.

Higginbotham, Evelyn Brooks. 1993. *Righteous Discontent: The Women's Movement in the Black Baptist Church, 1880–1920*. Cambridge: Harvard University Press.

Holder, Michelle. 2020. "The 'Double Gap' and the Bottom Line: African American Women's Wage Gap and Corporate Profits." Roosevelt Institute. March 31. https://bit.ly/3Fwxw8J

Hunter, Tera. 1997. *To 'Joy My Freedom: Southern Black Women's Lives and Labors After the Civil War*. Cambridge: Harvard University Press.

Kelly, Mary Louise 2021, "Black Voters Matter Co-Founder: Black Voters in Georgia Fuel 'New Southern Strategy.'" National Public Radio. January 6. https://n.pr/3A9iMeQ

Murphy, Mary-Elizabeth B. 2018. *Jim Crow Capital: Women and Black Freedom Struggles in Washington D.C., 1920–1945*. Chapel Hill: University of North Carolina Press.

National Domestic Workers Alliance. No date. "We Dream in Black. An NDWA Project." https://bit.ly/3KnroDI

NAWE Membership Cards. No date. Nannie Helen Burroughs papers, Box 71, Manuscript Division, Library of Congress.

Parker, Alison M. 2020. *Unceasing Militant: The Life of Mary Church Terrell*. Chapel Hill: University of North Carolina Press.

Schott-Bresler, Kayla. 2014. "Wheat Street Baptist Church, Atlanta, Georgia (1869–)." BlackPast. March 14. https://bit.ly/3nBmV6y

"Stacey Abrams Showed the Power of Up-Close and Personal Politics." 2021. *South Florida Sun Sentinel*. January 12. https://bit.ly/3A8PNId

"The First Annual Meeting of The National Association of Wage Earners" Program. November 11–12, 1924, Box 3, Folder 42, Mark Solomon and Robert Kaufman Research Files on African Americans and Communism, Tamiment Library and Robert F. Wagner Archives, New York University.

"The Washerwomen's Strike" 1881. *Atlanta Constitution*. July 20.

Vapnek, Lara. 2014. "The 1919 International Congress of Working Women: Transnational Debates on the Woman Worker." *Journal of Women's History* 26 (1): 160–184.

"Women Form Organization." 1917. *Washington Bee.* April 15.

"Women Wage Earners Organize." 1917. *Washington Bee.* April 20.

White, Deborah Gray. 1999. *Too Heavy a Load: Black Women in Defense of Themselves, 1894–1994.* New York: W.W. Norton.

Wilson, Valerie, and Melat Kessa. 2020. "Black Women Workers Are Essential During the Crisis and for the Recovery but Still Are Greatly Underpaid." Working Economics Blog, Economic Policy Institute. August 2020. https://bit.ly/3IjkvS1

CHAPTER 5

"Disorganize the State":
The Black Workers Congress's Visions of
Abolition-Democracy in the 1970s

AUSTIN MCCOY

West Virginia University
Department of History

Abstract

Since the George Floyd uprisings of 2020, more activists and scholars have adopted "defund the police" as a central demand in confronting police killings of Black people. Such calls have galvanized workers and labor unions to link struggles for improved working conditions and power with those seeking to confront police violence. These solidarity actions among labor unions highlight a gap in scholarship around the history of post-1960s working-class organizing and violent policing. "Disorganize the State" brings these histories together by illustrating how the Black Workers Congress (BWC) devised and articulated an abolitionist–democratic politics amid a moment of "rank-and-file rebellion," growing antifascist consciousness, and a burgeoning counterrevolution of capital. The BWC's vision of abolition-democracy emphasized the dismantling of the carceral and warfare state, as well as capitalism. The organization also called for extending democracy to workers in factories and demanded the expansion of a social wage.

INTRODUCTION

During Labor Day weekend in 1971, around 300 Black and "Third World" workers and activists gathered in Gary, Indiana, for the first national conference organized by the Black Workers Congress (BWC). Black workers and activists in Detroit founded the BWC to bring together the various Black- and brown-led revolutionary union movements that arose throughout the United States in the wake of the Dodge Revolutionary Union Movement's (DRUM) emergence in Detroit in May 1968. While 300 workers and activists hardly represented a mass movement, the group saw the gathering as not just one to demonstrate a "unified struggle against

US imperialism and its lackeys" but the beginnings of a national radical working-class movement led by Black laborers and other workers of color ("Organize the Revolution" 1971: 1).

In the BWC's first issue of *Siege*, the group titled their front-page story reporting on the conference "Organize the Revolution; Disorganize the State!" While the organization's attempt to bring together "delegates" from other worker organizations led by people of color illustrated their desires to "organize the revolution" behind a vanguard of Black workers around principles of industrial and economic democracy, the second demand ("disorganize the state!") underscored the BWC's critiques of the various aspects of the racial capitalist state, such as the criminal legal system, the military, and capitalism. Advocating for an abolitionist–democratic vision—demands to abolish the military, police, prisons, and courts, and capitalism—arose out of these critiques ("Organize the Revolution" 1971: 1).

Contemporary abolitionist activists such as Angela Davis and Ruth Wilson Gilmore often point to W.E.B. Du Bois's conception of "abolition-democracy" articulated in *Black Reconstruction in America* (Davis 2003, 2005; Du Bois 1992; Gilmore 2017: 231). Du Bois's description of abolition-democracy during the Reconstruction period emphasized not only the destruction of racial slavery by what he argued was a massive general strike and war but also the attempts to radically transform Black life in the South by restructuring property relations and building institutions that would ensure Black political and economic freedom (Du Bois 1992: 182–236). Davis and Gilmore emphasize this point in their work to demonstrate both the necessity to dismantle institutions that perpetuate harm, especially for the most marginalized, and the transformative and constructive aspects of abolitionism (Davis 2005; Gilmore 2017).

However, while Davis, Gilmore, and other activist–intellectuals such as Patrisse Khan-Cullors, Mariame Kaba, and Geo Maher often emphasize the incompatibility of capitalism with abolitionism, there is only sporadic discussion about the possible role that organized labor—and the working-class—can play in this process (Heatherton 2016: 40; Kaba 2021; Maher 2021: 224–227). And while some of these discussions of the relationship among organized labor, capitalism, and abolition have appeared in academic and political publications, the best illustrations of these politics arose out of actions such as the International Longshore and Warehouse Union's solidarity strike in June 2020 when workers shut down 29 ports along the West Coast in solidarity with the George Floyd uprisings and in commemoration of Juneteenth (Cole 2020; Piser 2020). Another contemporary example of labor organizing against state violence as part of a fight for racial justice and labor rights is the Graduate Employees Union's (GEO) "abolitionist strike" at the University of Michigan in September 2020 (Stark, Ehrhardt, and Fleischmann 2020).

This chapter suggests that, despite the organization's very short life, labor unions and workers in our contemporary moment could point to the BWC's vision of abolition-democracy in the early 1970s for historical inspiration. In addition to organizing their first, and only, national conference, the BWC produced various texts, including manifestos, lists of demands, articles, and ephemera, articulating and transmitting calls to dismantle the police and warfare state and to transform society into one organized around various expressions of democracy, whether in unions, in factories, or in the larger society. In effect, the organization desired abolition in every sense of the word.

The BWC is an understudied organization in labor and Black radical historiographies. The group often appears passively in analyses of labor histories after the 1960s, if they appear at all (Dawson 2013; Elbaum 2002; Georgakas and Surkin 1998; Geschwender 1977; Taylor 2010).[1] And when scholars and activists consider the BWC, much attention is paid to its leaders' personalities and the group's split, particularly James Forman's central role in conceiving the organization and its dissolution. Dan Georgakas and Marvin Surkin's important study, *Detroit, I Do Mind Dying*, is an exception: They contextualize the BWC in the history of Black radical organizing in the city during the early 1970s. The BWC's fleeting presence in the history of post-1960s Black radicalism and labor unions overshadows its abolitionist platform.

It is true the BWC arrived late on the scene, in the 1970s, and the group faltered as its members struggled to develop a sustainable organization. However, for historians of labor movements, especially those led by Black workers, the BWC's visions are overlooked expressions of abolition-democracy in the black radical tradition (BRT) (Kelley 2002: 2–3; Robinson 2020). And while this chapter asserts that their speeches and manifestos should be considered key and influential components of the BRT, it is important to note that the BWC also contributed to intellectual traditions of industrial and economic democracy. Like many of their predecessors, such as the International Workers of the World and the Congress of Industrial Organizations and communist activists such as Detroit's Charles Denby, the BWC advocated for democratizing unions and demanding greater "workers' control at the point of production" at a time when the postwar collective bargaining regime constrained the ability of workers to challenge poor working conditions and enable them exert more control over production (Watson 1967). With a desire to institute an industrial democracy, the BWC called for dismantling police, prisons, and the military, and they advocated for expanding social democratic rights such as free education, healthcare, and daycare, as well as access to better housing. The BWC reminds labor scholars and activists that racial justice, abolition, and internationalism should be at the center of visions for worker rights and economic democracy, whether inside the factory or in broader society.

What follows is, first, an analysis of the emergence of the BWC amid a burgeoning counterrevolution in Detroit and the United States. The BWC arose out of a rebellion by grassroots workers; however, these protests coalesced during an expanding counterrevolution. As philosopher Herbert Marcuse, the counterrevolution was "preventative," in that state and capitalist institutions sought to disorganize and stamp out liberation movements before they gained too much traction (Marcuse 1972: 1–2). Consequently, it entailed a "frontlash" in policing and repression—a scaling up and intensification of surveillance and violence directed at all radicals, especially those working in Black-led organization (Weaver 2007). The counterrevolution also featured a reorganization of capitalism, which, as historian Scott Kurashige and other scholars and theorists of neoliberalism have demonstrated, capitalists' assault on labor, which featured capital disinvestment and deindustrialization, automating production, and forcing labor unions into a pattern of concessionary bargaining, as well as organizing opposition to economic reforms (Kurashige 2017: 30–51). But, as historians such as Judith Stein have demonstrated, policy makers and elected officials on both sides of the aisle also helped facilitate the transformation of the US economy from one based in manufacturing to one organized around finance and service (Stein 2010).

Next, I illustrate how the BWC articulated the organization's abolitionist–democratic vision in its manifesto. I also contextualize the organization's manifesto within burgeoning campaigns against state violence and what many considered a creeping fascism. Lastly, I conclude the chapter by considering the organization's weaknesses, the ongoing reorganization of capitalism and the state's repressive institutions, and the meanings of the BWC's vision of abolition-democracy for contemporary labor activists and scholars.

CONTEXT: THE EMERGENCE OF THE BLACK WORKERS CONGRESS AMID A CAPITALIST COUNTERREVOLUTION

The origins of the BWC lay in rank-and-file rebellion in Detroit. On May 2, 1968, more than 4,000 workers participated in a wildcat strike that paralyzed the Dodge Main plant in Hamtramck (Allen 1979: 71). Dodge disproportionately held Black workers responsible, firing and suspending dozens (Taylor 2010: 318). Immediately after the strike, General Baker Jr., along with Mike Hamlin, John Watson, Kenneth Cockrel, and others formed the Dodge Revolutionary Movement (DRUM) to defend the fired Black workers. Like the other rank-and-file uprisings of the period, DRUM founders saw leading trade unions like the United Auto Workers (UAW) and AFL-CIO as too bureaucratic and obstructive when it came to workers seeking to acquire more control of the conditions of work. Thus, DRUM aimed to organize Black workers to challenge the discrimination and deplorable work conditions in Dodge plants, as well as racism in the UAW.

DRUM arose at a time of revolt and counterrevolution at the end of the 1960s and in the 1970s. Between 1968 and 1975, especially, it appeared as if a new, grassroots, working-class insurgency was on the rise across the United States. These labor insurgencies included hotel workers organizing in Atlantic City, the efforts of Edward Sadlowski and mine workers to democratize the United Mine Workers of America, and the attempts of public sector workers to enact a "Wagner

Act for public employees" (Cowie 2010: 23–74; McCartin 2008). DRUM, however, saw themselves as the vanguard of the next working-class revolution in the United States. As DRUM activist Mike Hamlin told Jim Jacobs and David Wellman for *Leviathan*, "We had certain radical ideas and a certain revolutionary line: that black workers would be the vanguard of the liberation struggle in this country" (Jacobs 1970: 11). The group inspired Black workers in other plants, in and outside of Detroit, to create their own revolutionary union organizations.[2] The proliferation of other Black worker organizations throughout Detroit led DRUM organizers to form the League of Revolutionary Black Workers. Viewing themselves as the vanguard, DRUM members, and eventually League members, distinguished themselves from the other rank-and-file insurgencies by linking issues related to union and workplace democracy with other facets of the counterrevolution, especially that of police violence.

DRUM also entered the local scene amid turmoil in Detroit at the end of the 1960s and early 1970s. Nearly a year before DRUM's founding, Detroiters responded to years of police abuse and harassment by confronting police officers who raided a "blind pig" (an establishment that sold alcohol during Prohibition). The uprising that began on the night of July 23 expanded beyond the blind pig on Twelfth Street to include hundreds of participants, resulting in four days of attacks on property and police (Kurashige 2017: 14). The Detroit uprising, as historian Scott Kurashige suggests, represented a crucial node in the global struggle against racism, imperialism, and capitalism taking place in the United States (with Detroit following uprisings in Watts and Newark) and throughout the world (Kurashige 2017: 14–15).

The Black revolutionary worker rebellion also arose at a time of transformation of the city's capitalist economy. As historian Thomas Sugrue documents, uneven postwar metropolitan development—deindustrialization, suburbanization, white violence, and white flight—created conditions ripe for rebellion in the streets and the factories (Sugrue 2005). And while the rebellion did not cause white and job flight from Detroit, those forces accelerated following the 1967 civil disturbance. Businesses continued their flight out of the city—the Budd Company and K-Mart moved out, while Ford Motor Company and Chrysler Corporation started building facilities in nearby suburbs (Conot 1974: 786-787; Lichtenstein 1997: 413). Job and population loss strained city budgets as the city faced budget deficits of $21 million and $39.5 million in the 1969–70 and 1970–71 fiscal years ("Report to Mayor Roman S. Gribbs" 1970). Amid its crisis during the 1970s, Detroit continued to hemorrhage residents, losing one-fifth of its population, and "nearly a quarter-million jobs evaporated from the city" (Kurashige 2017: 43).

DRUM members, however, were responding to dangerous work conditions and recent firings of Black workers when they decided to strike in May 1968. Many activists cited speedups, mandatory overtime, and other conditions, in a factory where 60% of its workforce was Black, as the source of frustration and alienation

(Jones 2013: 276). Yet, while racism in hiring and racial segregation of work tasks, as well as speedups and mandatory overtime were not exceptional to Detroit's plants, the city's factories were among the first to deploy automated production during the 1950s and 1960s (Sugrue 2005: 130). And Black workers in the city's plants, like autoworkers and intellectual-activists Charles Denby and James Boggs, reported increased layoffs amid a steady uptick in manufacturing productivity after World War II (Boggs 2009; Denby 1960). As Dan Georgakas and Marvin Surkin reported in *Detroit, I Do Mind Dying*, "In 1946, some 550,000 auto workers had produced little more than three million vehicles, but in 1970 some 750,000 auto workers had produced more than eight million vehicles" (1998: 85).

Yet, according to Georgakas and Surkin, "Niggeration, not automation" was "clearly the watchword" for Detroit's Black workers (1998: 85). DRUM members advanced "niggermation" as a racialized theory of auto manufacturing to explain increased productivity and alienation. DRUM organizer John Watson explained the concept in a 1969 interview with the radical publication, the *Fifth Estate*, "Niggermation is simply when you hire one black man to do the job which is previously done by two or three or four white men" (Watson 1967: 2). Following the left's critique of automation stemming from Marx, members of DRUM maintained that automation represented a weapon aimed at disciplining and dominating workers, particularly Black laborers.

In the years following the 1967 uprising, the frontlash in policing, surveilling, and brutalizing activists continued apace. In 1968, Detroit police officers attacked anti-racist demonstrators during multiple protests. Detroit Police Department (DPD) officers raided the New Bethel Church after a shootout between them and the Black nationalist Republic of New Africa (RNA), shooting four members and arresting 142 of them in the process (McCoy 2021: 6). Mayor Jerome Cavanagh and his successor Roman S. Gribbs, along with prominent figures in the private sector, led the frontlash in Detroit. They advocated for "tough on crime" policies during this period as well. Mayor Cavanagh supported efforts to institute stop-and-frisk measures as he and business leaders linked rising crime with a decline in consumption. "People are unwilling to come into the city after dark," Cavanagh told the Common Council (i.e., city council) (McCoy 2021: 7). In an exchange with other business leaders, Thomas L. Disk wrote that it was necessary for the city to address its "criminal element" if the city hoped to attract capital investment (McCoy 2021: 9). Detroit's counterrevolution during the early 1970s culminated as the DPD killed at least 108 residents between 1971 and 1973. Twenty-two of these deaths came after the DPD's creation of its new undercover unit, "Stop the Robberies, Enjoy Safe Streets" (STRESS), to curb what Gribbs and DPD officials believed was a rise in street crime. This unprecedented brutality and death inspired much of the city's left, including members of the BWC, to take action ("STRESS and Radical Response" 2021).

FORMING THE BLACK WORKERS CONGRESS

In early 1969, Mike Hamlin invited James Forman to visit Detroit so, as Forman wrote, "I could observe the league in action" (Forman 1990: 543; Hamlin and Gibbs 2013: 28). Boasting a national profile after serving as the Student Nonviolent Coordinating Committee's (SNCC) executive director and his brief collaboration with the Black Panther Party, Lucius Walker from the Interreligious Foundation for Community Organization also invited Forman to address the Black Economic Development Conference (BEDC) planned for April 1969, which he agreed to do despite his belief that "there could be no solution to the economic problems of black people within the framework of capitalism" (Forman 1990: 544).

At the conference, Forman delivered his "Black manifesto" speech, where he demanded $500 million in reparations from white Christian churches. Forman explained, "Since the conference was being staged by 'Christians,' we felt it was the right occasion to demand reparations from the Christian churches for the centuries of exploitation and oppression which they had inflicted on black people around the world" (Forman 1990: 545). The BEDC envisioned using the funds to construct a southern land bank, publishing houses, job training centers, among other ventures (Georgakas and Surkin 1998: 78–83). Cockrel, Watson, and fellow League member Mike Hamlin served on the organization's committee.

The political interests of Forman and these Detroit activists converged around building a national Marxist–Leninist–Maoist-inspired anticapitalist federation of workers of color. The League leaders' work with Forman exacerbated tensions within the League, which led Cockrel, Watson, and Hamlin to split from it on June 12, 1971. Other important strategic disagreements also fractured the organization. Cockrel, Watson, Hamlin, and others saw labor–community organizing and establishing links with other like-minded revolutionary union movements outside of Detroit, and outside the industrial sector, as necessary to building Black working-class power—while those critical of such an approach desired that the organization continue to focus more on in-plant organizing (Taylor 2010: 330–331).

Shortly after their split, Hamlin, Cockrel, Watson, and others established the BWC. Rather than just focusing on organizing workers at the point of production in Detroit's factories, the BWC sought to build a broad coalition of workers of color. Thus, the group appealed for support from all workers, especially from "Third World" groups such as Asian, Arab, Indigenous, Hispanic, and Latinx peoples. To build its organization quickly, James Forman, serving as the "titular national leader," utilized his connections while leading SNCC to organize activists and like-minded groups of workers across the country (Georgakas and Surkin 1998: 137–143).

Even though the BWC established itself as a national organization, Detroit served as the group's headquarters. Although Forman spent much of his time traveling throughout the United States establishing connections, Hamlin, Cockrel, and Watson remained key figures. Hamlin occupied the position of chairman, while Cockrel served as a prominent spokesperson, and Watson as its leading intellectual. Other local activists, including Michelle Russell, Helen Jones, and Gregory Hicks, served in important organizing roles during its brief existence ("Agenda Suggestions" 1972).

The BWC also established a short-lived newspaper, Siege, and planned its first national conference for September 1971. The organization, however, was more centralized than the League with Forman at the head. Forman was the driving force behind the BWC's aspirations to establish political education institutions (the Frantz Fanon Institutes), as well as the group's publishing company, Black Star Publishing, which aimed to "publiciz[e] ideas that would help the formation of a political party capable of leading the American revolution" (Georgakas and Surkin 1998: 138).

In addition to forming a national organization linking revolutionary union movements and radical workers in a fight against capitalism, imperialism, and racism, such a formation might also allow them to present a popular front against police violence and prevent the state's attempts to repress radical workers of color (Georgakas and Surkin 1998: 132). Founders of the organization identified repression in an internal planning document titled, "Statement of the Problem and Some Suggestions for a Solution" (no date) in which they identified organizing a "mass organization of black workers" to use "their productive power as a weapon against the racist capitalists." The Black Panthers, nationwide as well as members of its Detroit chapter, offered a cautionary tale for Black liberation activists as the FBI and police forces across the United States waged war against the organization. This entailed jailing its leaders and members and keeping them tied up in courts and prison, pitting the Panthers against other Black- and brown-led political organizations and gangs, and even assassinating and killing members such as Bobby Hutton. And, most infamously, the Chicago Police Department collaborated with the FBI to assassinate Illinois Panther Chapter leader Fred Hampton. The League and the BWC expressed solidarity with the incarcerated Angela Davis, who faced the death penalty after being accused of providing weapons to Jonathan Jackson, who then sought to free his brother, prisoner activist, George Jackson.[3] Governor Nelson Rockefeller's decision to send in the National Guard to put down a prisoner rebellion at the prison in Attica, New York, also galvanized members of the League and the BWC. In addition, George Jackson was murdered at San Quentin State Prison (Bloom and Martin 2013; Thompson 2016a).

The BWC also operated within a growing, more explicit, antifascist movement developing in the United States. Intellectuals such as Herbert Marcuse, Angela Davis, and George Jackson, as well as organizations such as the Black Panther Party, all warned of a creeping fascism in American and Western life (Jackson 1972; Toscano 2020). During the late 1960s and early 1970s, radicals from various backgrounds organized and participated in conferences where they strategized how to organize in a repressive atmosphere. In January 1970, Kenneth Cockrel and other activists participated in the Liberation Conference Against Repression held at St. Joseph's Church in Detroit. The program featured several speakers of national importance, including leader of the Students for a Democractic Society Weather Underground, Bernadine Dohrn; Chicago Eight defendant and activist Rennie Davis; formerly exiled civil rights leader Robert F. Williams; and Black Panther David Hilliard (*Fifth Estate* 1970).

Representing the League of Revolutionary Black Workers, Cockrel outlined some of the League's efforts to defend targets of repression in Detroit. However, he also spoke "on the revolutionary need to avoid arrest." While expressing sympathy and solidarity with organizations such as the Black Panthers, who were confronting the full weight of counterrevolutionary repression, Cockrel also reminded the audience, "But we feel that the principal responsibility of persons who are concerned about doing political work is that they first of all have an obligation to conduct themselves in such a way as to avoid incarceration, because the primary responsibility of revolutionaries is to be about the business of doing revolutionary work" (Cockrel 1971: 82). This perspective does not seem to account for the mission of law enforcement, especially federal law enforcement, to confront Black radicals and neutralize revolutionary groups by any means necessary, including violence.

On the surface, Cockrel's criticisms appeared individualist and behavioral. However, the following sentence in Cockrel's critique reveals a strategic argument: "And that means that your first responsibility is to do everything in your power to avoid becoming a defense organization" (Cockrel 1971: 82). Essentially, law enforcement's ability to incarcerate radicals not only robbed organizations of members and prominent leadership, but it also robbed those groups of financial resources and energy that they could have used elsewhere. While the Panthers maintained their community survival programs into the 1970s, Huey P. Newton de-emphasized "picking up the gun" because the state drained the Panthers of people and money. Law enforcement's ability to hem in the Panthers eventually forced Newton to reorganize the Panthers and use Oakland as its "base of operation" (Bloom and Martin 2013: 385 Self 2005: 299).

Also, rather than focus solely on police repression, Cockrel presented an expanded analysis that incorporated racist violence of individuals as well as the participation of schools, employers, and unions in repressing Black workers and DRUM leaders such as Ron March, who sought elective office in the UAW. For Cockrel, and eventually the other founding members of the BWC, the only way to adequately confront a repressive society was to mobilize on behalf of an expansive view of the working class. He declared, "We say that all people who don't own, rule, and benefit from decisions which are made by those who own and rule are workers." To beat back repression, Cockrel ultimately suggested it was necessary to take control over the means of production, but "in order to do this, we've got to develop a political machine." While Cockrel did not call directly for participating in electoral politics as a reference to building a political machine suggests, his comment eventually caused some tension among him and members of the League and, eventually, the BWC (Cockrel 1971: 87-88).

Over the next two years, the Black Panther Party hosted, or were featured prominently in, two antifascist gatherings—the Revolutionary Conference for a United Front Against Fascism in Oakland and the Revolutionary People's Constitutional Convention. At the former, the Panthers hoped to build "a broad people's revolutionary alliance" that included students, workers, and those in the "lumpenproletariat," as well as Black Americans, Chicanos, Puerto Ricans, Asian Americans, and radical white Americans (Bloom and Martin 2013: 299–300; Toscano 2020). Out of the conference arose demands to undermine the carceral and warfare state by advocating for community control of police, banishing military presence on college and university campuses, and releasing political prisoners (Bloom and Martin 2013: 298).

The Revolutionary People's Constitutional Convention in September 1970, attended by more than 10,000 people, represented a high point in the Panthers' attempts to build a multiracial and multinational popular front against fascism (Katsiaficas 1987: 203). Drawing language from the US revolutionary tradition, Newton declared that "in order to insure our international constitution, we, the people of Babylon, declare an international bill of rights: that all people are guaranteed the right to life, liberty, and the pursuit of happiness, that all people of the world be free from dehumanization and intervention in their internal affairs by a foreign power" (Katsiaficas 1987: 265).

Participants in workshops at the conference also produced a comprehensive list of demands in various aspects of social, economic, political, and cultural life. They called for self-determination for "street people," the "liberation" of land for public use, and free food, housing, clothing, and medical care. The workshop on the self-determination of women advanced critiques of family life, called for full reproductive freedom "including abortion, available on demand," the end of gender discrimination in the workplace, a guaranteed income, and access to self-defense training. Members of the convention also advanced demands for the free expression of lesbian, gay, and queer identities (Katsiaficas 1987: 269–271).

Convention participants also sought a democratic transformation of the system of justice. This entailed greater public participation in policing—community control—and the administration of justice with ordinary citizens participating in periodic reviews of judges and police. Ultimately, if legal systems continued to oppress people, they proclaimed "the right to … alter or abolish all existing legal structures, and to reorganize the society for the benefit of all people" (Katsiaficas 1987: 274).

The comprehensive series of transformative demands emerging from the various workshops at the Revolutionary People's Constitutional Convention anticipated the BWC abolitionist–democratic manifesto that it produced a year later. Convention attendees, too, would articulate an expansive vision of society advocating for the eradication of the carceral, police, and warfare state. The BWC would also advocate for industrial and social democracy at a time of counterrevolution and revolt.

ABOLITIONIST MANIFESTO OF THE BLACK WORKERS CONGRESS

The BWC's manifesto is the group's clearest expression of abolitionist–democratic politics. The 32-point document is comprehensive, incorporating a variety of demands calling for the elimination of racism, sexism, imperialism, and various forms of state violence while also advocating for various aspects of industrial and economic democracy. The BWC advanced proposals in their manifesto such as "workers' control," free health- and childcare, the abolition of police and other law enforcement agencies such as the FBI, and dismantling of the US military. The BWC also expressed a Third World internationalism in the document, calling for "the ending of the exploitation of workers in Africa, Asia, Latin America, and the Caribbean" and "the right of the Palestinian people to their homeland in the Middle East" ("International Black Workers Congress: Draft Proposal," no date).

Aligning themselves with other antifascist Black radicals such as George Jackson, Angela Davis, and the leadership of the Black Panther Party, the BWC in their sixth objective called for the end of "the growing repression and increasing fascism of the United States, the militarization of the police, the arming of right wing forces" and "the repeal of all repressive legislation" ("International Black Workers Congress: Draft Proposal," no date). Again, this demand sprung from the expanding counterintelligence apparatus that extended its reach into many Black radical organizations. However, and this was the case in Detroit, members of the BWC most likely paid attention to how many white Americans and law enforcement institutions reacted to urban rebellions during the mid to late 1960s. According to historian Sidney Fine, rumors of racial violence swirled through the city as "Blacks heard rumors that whites would try to murder blacks, that the police were training suburban whites to shoot, and that the police were anxious for a riot 'to get even' with blacks" (Fine 1989: 385). And while this scenario never came to pass, arms sales in Detroit skyrocketed to the point where Cavanagh believed there was "an arms race inside the city" (Fine 1989: 385).

Also, as scholars and experts such as historians Elizabeth Hinton and Max Felker-Kantor and journalist Radley Balko have noted, the rebellions accelerated the militarization of police forces in cities such as Los Angeles and Detroit (Balko 2013: Felker-Kantor 2018; Hinton 2016). And as police developed more tactical units to confront what they believed was rising criminalized activity in cities, the US Congress also included an "anti-riot" provision in the 1968 Civil Rights Act, forbidding interstate travel for the purposes of participating in a civil disturbance ("President Signs Civil Rights Bill" 1968). For activist organizations such as the BWC and the Black Panther Party and activists George Jackson, Angela Davis, and James Boggs, this constellation of individual, policy, and institutional responses illustrated the pernicious ways that fascism subtly manifested itself as an anti-Black force. Antifascism as anti-Blackness represented the most formidable external threat to organizing a Black working-class vanguard (Boggs 2009; Jackson 1972; Toscano 2020).

While the BWC alerted prospective members and readers of its manifesto to a burgeoning fascism in the United States, the group presented their carceral and warfare state abolitionist demands in objectives 19 through 23. The organization called for the "abolition of the brutal penal system of the United States," the "elimination and smashing of the Federal Bureau of Investigation, the Central Intelligence Agency, the Counter-Insurgency forces," and "a destruction of all of the armed, vicious, brutal, militaristic police forces in the United States that kill people at random, terrorize the population" ("International Black Workers Congress: Draft Proposal," no date).

Like the Black Panthers and those who attended the Revolutionary People's Constitutional Convention in Philadelphia in September 1970, the BWC called for the complete dismantling of the US warfare state, if not the US empire. They called for the "elimination and smashing" of the CIA and "a withdrawal of all United States troops from overseas countries and a total dismantling of the military force of the United States" ("International Black Workers Congress: Draft Proposal," no date; Katsiaficas 1987: 265). The BWC supported their demands by expressing solidarity with the Vietnamese and other groups from the Global South in their publications.

The BWC also planned a Third World Summit Conference in Gary, Indiana, in early June 1972 in response to the US's war in Vietnam. According to the organization, more than 300 people and "representatives from more than fifty organizations and united front coalitions that represent a broad, mass base of Chicanos, Red people, Asians, Blacks and Puerto Ricans attended." At the conference, the attendees agreed to create a "national clearing house" to forge connections between like-minded groups, to sign a Unity Treaty of Oppressed Minorities "expressing solidarity and pledges of good-will and cooperation," and a solidarity committee to support the Vietnamese and others fighting against the US military in Southeast Asia ("Third World People Unite" 1972). Out of the Third World Summit Conference, the BWC declared a "Vietnam summer offensive," which directed workers to continue organizing in the plants but to also plan to attend a Solidarity Day protest planned for August 19, 1972 ("BWC Calls for a Summer Offensive" 1972). Also, James Forman, along with other members, traveled to China and Vietnam to forge links with officials (Georgakas and Surkin 1998: 140).

Outside of the BWC's anti-imperialism and foreign affairs, the organization fused democracy—worker control and other aspects of transformative and economic justice—to abolition. For example, they followed their call for the abolition "of the brutal penal system" with a demand for the "establishment of people's reorientation centers for those who misunderstand the workers' society and commit crimes against the people." While the BWC did not advance any explicit demands for community control of police like Huey Newton did, the group expressed a desire to build institutions aimed at rehabilitation, if not re-education, as suggested in the assumption that criminal activity arose from a "misunderstanding" of "the workers' society" ("International Black Workers Congress: Draft Proposal," no date). Continuing in the tradition of labor radicals, the BWC made workers' control the first objective in their list of demands. "Workers' control of their places of work—the factories, mines, fields, offices, transportation service, communication facilities—so that the exploitation of labor will cease and no person or corporation will get rich off the labor of another person, but all people will work for the collective benefit of humanity," stated the manifesto ("International Black Workers Congress: Draft Proposal," no date). BWC's manifesto also expressed more detailed objectives related to work, such as the reduction of work time limited to 20 hours per week.

Echoing the Black workers serving in the revolution union movements, the group also demanded the "elimination of speed-up, compulsory overtime, unsafe working conditions, inadequate medical facilities on the job, [and] brutality and terror in the mines, factories and industrial plants of the United States and Puerto Rico" ("International Black Workers Congress: Draft Proposal," no date). While it is possible that determining the use of automated machinery is implied in the demand for control by workers, an analysis of automation and its role in alienating and displacing workers, especially Black workers, remained conspicuously absent considering DRUM's and John Watson's focus on "niggermation" as an expression of racism in the Dodge factories ("To the Point of Production" 1962: 2).

The BWC, in effect, called for the total transformation of society, into one that at least was more socialist. Work, according to the manifesto, should be for the social good—not for the benefit of "parasitic capitalistic vultures," who needed to "be eliminated." The BWC expressed a rather comprehensive vision of a new society. The organization advanced social demands such as free education, healthcare, and 24-hour daycare centers "so that mothers and fathers will be able to engage in other work and activities and the care of children will be socialized" ("International Black Workers Congress: Draft Proposal," no date). The organization also called for "safe, clean, uncrowded housing where there are no rats and roaches," which reflected the demands of many Black women dwellers in cities across the United States (Keeanga-Yamhatta 2019: 168–209). BWC's abolition-democracy also extended to caring for the Earth, and it incorporated an environmental justice demand to end "the pollution of the atmosphere, forests, … rivers, and living quarters of all the people by the giant corporations" ("International Black Workers Congress: Draft Proposal," no date).

But industrial and economic democracy could not be achieved without justice for the oppressed throughout the world. Rather than focus on white churches like Forman when he read the Black manifesto in 1969, the BWC also called for reparations to be paid by the United States and "all white racist institutions" to people in the Global South.

Worker control, in the context of the manifesto, implied an anticapitalist possibility. The organization fused abolition and democracy in their call for the "destruction of all the armed, vicious, brutal, and militaristic police forces in the United States" when they suggested that police and intelligence agencies would not be necessary "with workers control of the means of production, transport services, and communication facilities " ("International Black Workers Congress: Draft Proposal," no date).

RESPONSE OF THE BLACK WORKERS CONGRESS TO POLICE KILLINGS IN DETROIT

The BWC's response to the STRESS unit of the DPD's killings and its limited participation in the campaign to stop police violence demonstrated the organization's abolitionist politics in action. Because the BWC focused much of its attention on institution building, the DPD's STRESS unit continued a pattern of unlawful violence against its Black residents. Charged with stopping street crime, STRESS officers engaged in "decoy" tactics that entailed them posing as likely victims such as drunks (McCoy 2021: 8). In practice, however, the officers engaged in harassment and entrapment as a form of deterrence to catch perceived suspects. While similar units also emerged in Los Angeles, Atlantic City, and Boston, STRESS's deadly results distinguished it from the other units as officers shot and killed ten residents in the first nine months in operation (Fischer 2019; Lipsitz 2016; McCoy 2021: 9; Simon 2004).

The killings of teenagers Ricardo Buck and Craig Mitchell on September 19, 1971, inspired the creation of a broad-based political coalition to reform, then eventually abolish, the STRESS unit. This coalition included liberal organizations such as the city's NAACP chapter and the Southern Christian Leadership Conference, progressive groups such as the National Lawyers Guild, and radical groups such as the RNA, the Motor City Labor League, and another organization Kenneth Cockrel worked for in his capacity as a lawyer—the Labor Defense Coalition (LDC), a group devoted to providing legal defense to Black activists and workers. Still, understanding the existential threat police repression and state violence posed to the city's Black working-class, some BWC members, such as Cockrel, involved themselves in the formation of the State of Emergency Committee (SEC), a coalition of radical and liberal activists and politicians devoted to confronting police violence (McCoy 2021: 10–12).

The SEC organized a demonstration under the slogan "Close the Schools" and "Shut Down" [the city's factories] to protest the killings of Mitchell and Buck for the week after the BWC Gary Convention. On September 23, around 4,000 people marched in protest and in solidarity with Angela Davis and in memory of the prisoners slain at Attica. Following this demonstration, a coalition of liberal and radical political groups in Detroit including the NAACP and the LDC, waged a three-year struggle to end STRESS. In doing so, the anti-STRESS coalition raised questions about police violence, and it laid the groundwork for Coleman Young to win the mayoralty after campaigning on a promise to discontinue the unit (Hamlin and Gibbs 2012: 31, McCoy 2021: 23–27).

The BWC participated marginally in the campaign outside of Cockrel's legal work. However, the group sounded off on the DPD's criminality, deplorable conditions in the Wayne County Jail, and a prisoner rebellion at New Orleans Parish Prison, as well as what the organization viewed as political repression of workers and activists ("Brother Rainey" 1971; Brown 1971; Rutledge 1971). Reporting on the events leading up to the protest in the BWC's newspaper, *Siege*, Carolyn Ramsey claimed the BWC "declared a state of emergency" and "that an on-going State of Emergency Committee would be formed in Detroit to address itself actively to any and all aspects of official war against Black people" (Ramsey 1971). The organization also published an update in their second issue of *Siege*, "STRESS: Guilty as Charged," focusing on the successful defense by Cockrel and his LDC colleagues of Nathaniel Johnson, who was acquitted on a felonious assault charge against a STRESS officer. Joining in the chorus of voices calling for the end of the STRESS unit, the story concluded with the words "the abolition of STRESS is absolutely necessary" ("STRESS: Guilty as Charged" 1971).

In the spring of 1972, Cockrel emerged as a leading figure in the campaign, serving among the lawyers who filed a lawsuit against Mayor Gribbs, Police Commissioner Nichols, and Wayne County Prosecutor William Cahalan, on behalf of 30 political organizations, the victims, and their families. The goal for Cockrel and the legal team was to put "STRESS on trial" and use the proceedings to further educate Detroiters about the undercover unit's abuses. However, this effort failed when the Michigan State Court of Appeals struck down the case before it began (McCoy 2021: 16).

The anti-STRESS movement outlasted the BWC because the latter experienced many schisms, splits, and departures. The group collapsed under the weight of a few strategic debates around organizing strategy. Forman's tendency toward autocracy and personality politics irritated Cockrel to the point where he accused him of "incompetence and egotism" (Georgakas and Surkin 1998: 144). The anti-STRESS campaign served as another point of severing within BWC as Cockrel, whose profile rose amid the campaign, decided to focus more attention on abolishing STRESS. Cockrel's decision put him on a path toward focusing more on building an organization flexible enough to participate in various forms of politics, including the electoral arena (Plotke 1980). John Watson, according to Hamlin, "simply walked away" out of fear and stress caused by police surveillance. Commenting on some of the BWC turmoil, Hamlin said, "We lost that argument in the context of the Black Workers Congress but won it in the streets when we formed the Labor Defense Coalition" (Hamlin and Gibbs 2013: 30).

CONCLUSION: END OF THE BLACK WORKERS CONGRESS AND LABOR-INSPIRED ABOLITIONIST POLITICS TODAY

By 1975, Mike Hamlin was the remaining working-class leader engaging in BWC work. However, as he acknowledged later, "I left organizational work in the middle of the 1970s as a matter of personal survival" (Hamlin and Gibbs 2013: 49). By then, the BWC was a shell of its former self, with much of its principal leadership departed. Most importantly, and this was the case with DRUM and the League as well, much of the working-class base eroded, too, between job losses and recession and further absorption of Black workers into existing unions (Taylor 2010: 326). As DRUM activist Ernie Allen remarked, "Without the mass upsurge which had initially brought the League into being, it was a matter of time before the BWC itself would experience a number of purges, resignations, and ultimate collapse" (Allen 1979: 102). Much of the revolutionary workers' movement had transformed by then as well. While occasional wildcats continued in Detroit, other Black workers took the lead (Berry et al. 1974; Thompson 2016b). And the remaining members of the League, like General Baker, moved into working with "new communist" organizations such as the Communist League. Baker, like Cockrel, even tried his hand at electoral politics, unsuccessfully running for state representative (Allen 1979: 103).

Rather than disorganizing the state, various political and economic developments by 1975 had demobilized and disorganized the Black working-class revolutionary movement that emerged in 1968. Detroit's unemployment rate increased from 12.5% to 17.4%, while the country's rate rose from 5.6% to 8.5% during the 1974–75 recession (Anton 1983: 6–7). Fiscal crisis provoked Mayor Coleman Young to enact austere measures, while the near failure of the Chrysler Corporation used its own crisis as an excuse to force the UAW to accept wage concessions during the late1970s and early 1980s (Hill 1983: 109–110; McCoy 2016: 35). Wider trends also disorganized labor unions and disrupted worker solidarity, generally, since the end of the 1960s. Workers and labor unions encountered political headwinds as policy makers and elected officials from both major political parties focused on developing and implementing policies buttressing finance capital, further protecting the private property rights of businesses and corporations and tightening the private sector's grip on its control over production and capital investment. These policies, along with the privatization of public goods and services, helped redistribute wealth upward and impoverish workers further (McCartin 2010: 219).

The other aspect of the counterrevolution—state repression in the form of police violence, surveillance, and incarceration—also drained radical social movements. Law enforcement continued to surveil and neutralize the remaining radical groups and activists by jailing them (Bloom and Martin 2013; Marcuse 1972). Deindustrialization, automation, and job loss eroded local tax bases and economies, and criminalized drug markets took their place. Politicians and policy makers continued advocating for growing police departments and more draconian law-and-order policies, which led to the explosion of mass incarceration (Hinton 2016). And it is important to note that these forces did not stamp out Black radicalism or Black working-class politics completely during the 1970s and 1980s. Black workers continued mounting campaigns for labor rights and defenses against factory closures (Williams 2021; "BWC Calls for a Summer Offensive" 1972). However, as in the case with the BWC, the base of workers shrunk considerably.

In his book, *Stayin' Alive: The 1970s and the Last Days of the Working Class*, historian Jefferson Cowie argued that the various rank-and-file rebellions of the early 1970s "achieved little lasting institutional presence in the labor movement, left almost no legacy in American politics, and, most significantly, failed to become an enduring part of the class awareness of the nation's workers" (Cowie 2010: 70). It is true that counterrevolutionary elements put labor on the defensive toward the end of the 1970s and beyond. However, it appears that the Great Recession, the emergence of Black Lives Matter, calls to "defund the police," and unionization drives and a tightening labor market resulting from the coronavirus pandemic have opened a new political opportunity for working-class organizing and unionization. This also means that our contemporary moment is ripe for reappraising old models of Black working-class radical politics, including the BWC's model of abolition-democracy.

What Cowie's claim misses, however, is the resilience of the Black radical imagination and how ideas can, as Mary Frances Berry argues, reverberate long after an organization's or movement's decline (Berry 2018: 4). While pundits hailed the election of the first Black US president and declared the end of "Black politics" and the arrival of post-racialism, few anticipated the emergence of the Black Lives Matter movement, let alone its architects presenting Ella Baker's organizing philosophy as a guide (Cobb 2016; Ransby 2003, 2020).

There is no reason, amid a growing consciousness around abolitionist thinking and organizing, that contemporary labor activists, scholars, and organizations could not return to the labor politics of the past to find useful models for organizing. Labor studies scholars are in a great position to uncover lesser-known examples from the past to help activists forge a comprehensive radical democratic vision derived from critiques of state violence and capitalism. It may be time for labor organizers to (re)examine BWC's manifesto as they consider how to adopt abolitionist demands. Most important, all organizers should understand how the BWC, as advocates of abolition-democracy, envisioned a new society in spite of the leaders' and members' differences and a repressive environment.

ENDNOTES

1. The best treatment of the Black Workers Congress remains Dan Georgakas and Marvin Surkin's, *Detroit, I Do Mind Dying: A Study in Urban Revolution*.
2. See Georgakas and Surkin (1998), Allen (1979), and Taylor (2010) for critical histories of the organization.

3. Angela Davis was accused in playing a role in Jonathan Jackson's attempts to take hostages to free his incarcerated brother, George, in August 1970. Jackson, who served as one of Davis's bodyguards, entered a courtroom with three other prisoners and took Judge Harold Haley, district attorney, and members of the jury hostage. Jackson sought to exchange hostages for George's freedom. However, San Quentin guards fired on the van where Jackson held the hostages and killed him, Haley, and two of the prisoners (James 1998: 10–11).

REFERENCES

"Agenda Suggestions for Detroit Organizing Commission." January 23, 1972. Dan Georgakas Papers, Box 1, Folder 23, Walter Reuther Library, Wayne State University, Detroit.

Allen, Ernie. 1979. "Dying from the Inside: The Decline of the League of Revolutionary Black Workers." In *They Should Have Served That Cup of Coffee*. Dick Cluster, ed. Boston: South End Press.

Anton, Thomas J. 1983. *Federal Aid to Detroit*. Washington, DC: The Brookings Institution.

Balko, Radley. 2013. *Rise of the Warrior Cop: The Militarization of America's Police Forces*. New York: PublicAffairs.

Berry, Mary Frances. 2018. *History Teaches Us to Resist: How Progressive Movements Have Succeeded in Challenging Times*. Boston: Beacon Press.

Berry, Millard, Ralph Franklin, Alan Franklin, Cathy Kauflin, Marilyn Werbe, Peter Werbe, and Richard Wieske. 1974. *Wildcat: Dodge Truck, June 1974*. Detroit: Black & Red.

Bloom, Joshua, and Waldo E. Martin Jr. 2013. *Black Against Empire: The History and Politics of the Black Panther Party*. Berkeley: University of California Press.

Boggs, James. 2009. *The American Revolution: Pages from a Negro Worker's Notebook*. New York: Monthly Review Press.

"Brother Rainey Fights Draft Charges." 1971. *Siege* 1 (1): 5.

Brown, Francine. 1971. "Parish Prison Rebellion." *Siege* 1 (1): 5.

"BWC Calls for a Summer Offensive." 1972. *Point of Production* July: 5, 18.

Cobb, Jelani. 2016. "The Matter of Black Lives." *The New Yorker*. March 6. https://bit.ly/3HM8RyY

Cockrel, Kenneth. 1971. "From Repression to Revolution." *Radical America* 5 (2): 81–89.

Cole, Peter. 2020. "The Most Radical Union in the U.S. Is Shutting Down the Ports on Juneteenth." *In These Times*. June 16. https://bit.ly/3uLCjBv

Conot, Robert. 1974. *American Odyssey*. New York: Morrow.

Cowie, Jefferson. 2010. *Stayin' Alive: The 1970s and the Last Days of the Working Class*. New York: The New Press.

Davis, Angela. 2003. *Are Prisons Obsolete?* New York: Seven Stories Press.

Davis, Angela. 2005. *Abolition Democracy: Beyond Empire, Prisons and Torture*. New York: Seven Stories Press.

Dawson, Michael. 2013. *Blacks In and Out of the Left*. Cambridge: Harvard University Press.

Denby, Charles. 1960. "Workers Battle Automation." *News & Letters* 5 (7): 1–8.

Du Bois, W.E.B. 1992. *Black Reconstruction in America*. New York: Free Press.

Elbaum, Max. 2002. *Revolution In the Air: Sixties Radicals Turn to Lenin, Mao, and Che*. New York: Verso.

Felker-Kantor, Max. 2018. *Policing Los Angeles: Race, Resistance and the Rise of the LAPD*. Chapel Hill: University of North Carolina Press.

Fifth Estate. 1970. January 22.

Fine, Sidney. 1989. *Violence in the Model City: The Cavanagh Administration, Race Relations, and the Detroit Riot of 1967.* Ann Arbor: University of Michigan Press.

Fischer, Anne Gray. 2019. " 'This Place Is Gone!': Policing Black Women to Redevelop Downtown Boston." *Journal of Social History* 53 (1): 7–26.

Forman, James. 1990. *The Making of Black Revolutionaries.* Seattle: Open Hand.

Georgakas, Dan, and Marvin Surkin. 1998. *Detroit, I Do Mind Dying: A Study in Urban Revolution.* Cambridge: South End Press.

Geschwender, James A. 1977. *Class, Race, & Worker Insurgency: The League of Revolutionary Black Workers.* Cambridge: Cambridge University Press.

Gilmore, Ruth Wilson. 2017. "Abolition Geography and the Problem of Innocence." In *Futures of Black Radicalism.* Gaye Theresa Johnson and Alex Lubin, eds. New York: Verso.

Hamlin, Mike, and Michelle Gibbs. 2013. *A Black Revolutionary's Life in Labor: Black Workers Power in Detroit.* Detroit: Against the Tide Books.

Heatherton, Christina. 2016. "#BlackLivesMater and Global Visions of Abolition: An Interview with Patrisse Cullors." In *Policing the Planet: Why the Policing Crisis Led to Black Lives Matter.* Christina Heatherton and Jordan T. Camp, eds. New York: Verso.

Hill, Richard Child. 1983. "Crisis in the Motor City: The Politics of Economic Development in Detroit." In *Restructuring the City: The Political Economy of Urban Development,* revised edition. Susan S. Fainstein, Norman I. Fainstein, Richard Child Hill, Dennis R. Judd, and Michael Peter Smith, eds. 80–125. New York: Longman.

Hinton, Elizabeth. 2016. *From the War on Poverty to the War on Crime: The Making of Mass Incarceration in America.* Cambridge: Harvard University Press.

"International Black Workers Congress: Draft Proposal." No date. Madison James Foster Bentley Papers, Box 1, Folder: Black Workers Congress, Bentley Historical Library, University of Michigan, Ann Arbor.

Jackson, George. 1972. *Blood in My Eye.* New York: Random House.

Jacobs, Jim. 1970. "Our Thing Is DRUM!" *Leviathan* 2 (2).

Jones, Jacqueline. 2013. *A Dreadful Deceit: The Myth of Race from the Colonial Era to Obama's America.* New York: Basic Books.

James, Joy, ed. 1998. *The Angela Y. Davis Reader.* Boston: Blackwell Publishing.

Kaba, Mariame. 2021. *We Do This 'Til We Free Us: Abolitionist Organizing and Transforming Justice.* Chicago: Haymarket Books.

Katsiaficas, George. 1987. *The Imagination of the New Left: A Global Analysis of 1968.* Cambridge: South End Press.

Keeanga-Yamhatta, Taylor. 2019. *Race for Profit: How Banks and the Real Estate Industry Undermined Black Homeownership.* Chapel Hill: University of North Carolina Press.

Kelley, Robin. 2002. *Black Freedom Dreams: The Black Radical Imagination.* Boston: Beacon Press.

Kurashige, Scott. 2017. *The Fifty-Year Rebellion: How the U.S. Political Crisis Began in Detroit.* Oakland: University of California Press.

Lichtenstein, Nelson. 1997. *Walter Reuther: The Most Dangerous Man in Detroit.* Urbana: University of Illinois Press.

Lipsitz, George. 2016. "Policing Place and Taxing Time on Skid Row." In *Policing the Planet: Why the Policing Crisis Led to Black Lives Matter.* Jordan T. Camp and Christina Heatherton, eds. 123–140. London: Verso.

Maher, Geo. 2021. *A World Without Police: How Strong Communities Make Cops Obsolete.* New York: Verso.

Marcuse, Herbert. 1972. *Counterrevolution and Revolt.* Boston: Beacon Press.

McCartin, Joseph. 2008. "'A Wagner Act for Public Employees': Labor's Deferred Dream and the Rise of Conservatism, 1970-1976. *Journal of American History* 95 (1): 123–148.

McCartin, Joseph. 2010. "Solvents of Solidarity: Political Economy, Collective Action, and the Crisis of Organized Labor, 1968–2005." In *Rethinking U.S. Labor History: Essays on the Working-Class Experience, 1756–2009.* Donna T. Haverty-Stacke and Daniel J. Walkowitz, eds. 217–239. New York: Continuum.

McCoy, Austin. 2004. *Jonathan Simon, Boardwalk of Dreams: Atlantic City and the Fate of Urban America.* New York: Oxford University Press.

McCoy, Austin. 2016. "No Radical Hangover: Black Power, New Left, and Progressive Politics in the Midwest, 1967–1989." PhD diss., University of Chicago.

McCoy, Austin. 2021. "'Detroit Under STRESS': The Campaign to Stop Police Killings and the Criminal State in Detroit." *Journal of Civil and Human Rights* 7 (1): 1–34.

"Organize the Revolution. Disorganize the State!" 1971. *Siege* 1 (1): 1.

Piser, Karina. 2020. "Unions Are Taking a Stand for Black Lives." *The Nation.* June 24. https://bit.ly/3gF6LVV

Plotke, David. 1980. "Politics in Detroit: An Interview with Ken Cockrel." *Socialist Review* 49 10 (1): 77.

"President Signs Civil Rights Bill; Pleads for Calm." 1968. *New York Times.* April 12.

Ramsey, Carolyn. 1971. "State of Emergency." *Siege* 1 (1): 3.

Ransby, Barbara. 2003. *Ella Baker and the Black Freedom Movement: A Radical Democratic Vision.* Chapel Hill: University of North Carolina Press.

Ransby, Barbara. 2020. "Ella Baker's Legacy Runs Deep. Know Her Name." *New York Times.* January 20. https://nyti.ms/3JmPBbN

"Report to Mayor Roman S. Gribbs from Alfred M. Pelham, Deputy Controller, Re: Current Fiscal Status of the City of Detroit." January 9, 1970, 1a-5a. Roman S. Gribbs Papers, Box 70, Folder 1. Burton Historical Collection, Detroit Public Library.

Robinson, Cedric. 2020. *Black Marxism: The Making of the Black Radical Tradition.* Chapel Hill: University of North Carolina Press.

Rutledge, Charles. 1971. "Wayne County Inmates File Suit." *Siege* 1 (1): 5.

Self, Robert O. 2005. *American Babylon: Race and the Struggle for Postwar Oakland.* Princeton: Princeton University Press.

Simon, Jonathan. 2004. *Boardwalk of Dreams: Atlantic City and the Fate of Urban America.* New York: Oxford University Press.

Stark, Alejo, Jasmine Ehrhardt, and Amir Fleischmann. 2020. "University of Michigan Graduate Workers Are on Strike." *Jacobin.* September 11. https://bit.ly/3HMsK9j

"Statement of the Problem and Some Suggestions for a Solution." No date. Madison James Foster Papers, Box 1, Folder: Black Workers Congress, Bentley Historical Library, Ann Arbor.

Stein, Judith. 2010. *Pivotal Decade: How the United States Traded Factories for Finance.* New Haven: Yale University Press.

"STRESS and Radical Response, 1971–1973." 2021. *Detroit Under Fire: Police Violence, Crime Politics, and the Struggle for Racial Justice in the Civil Rights Era.* University of Michigan Carceral State Project. https://bit.ly/34xGjLt

"STRESS: Guilty as Charged." 1972: *Siege* 1 (2): 3.

Sugrue, Thomas. 2005. *The Origins of the Urban Crisis: Race and Inequality in Postwar Detroit.* Princeton: Princeton University Press.

Taylor, Kieran. 2010. "American Petrograd: Detroit and the League of Revolutionary Black Workers." In *Rebel Rank and File: Labor Militancy and Revolt from Below During the Long 1970s.* Aaron Brenner, Robert Brenner, and Cal Winslow, eds. New York: Verso.

"Third World People Unite: Resolutions of the Third World Summit Conference." 1972. *Point of Production.* July: 7.

Thompson, Heather. 2016a. *Blood in the Water: The Attica Prison Uprising of 1971 and Its Legacy.* New York: Knopf Doubleday.

Thompson, Heather. 2016b. *Whose Detroit? Politics, Labor, and Race in a Modern American City.* New York: Pantheon.

"To the Point of Production: An Interview with John Watson of the League of Revolutionary Black Workers." 1969. Boston: New England Free Press.

Toscano, Alberto. 2020. "The Long Shadow of Racial Fascism." *Boston Review.* October 28. https://bit.ly/3BgS4BR

Watson, John. 1967. "TO THE POINT ... OF PRODUCTION." *To the Point of Production,* NA-10. Ann Arbor: Radical Education Project.

Weaver, Vesla M. 2007. "Frontlash: Race and the Development of Punitive Crime Policy." *Studies in American Political Development* 21 (2): 230–265.

Williams, Naomi R. 2021. "Sustaining Labor Politics in Hard Times: Race, Labor, and Coalition Building in Racine, Wisconsin." *LABOR: Studies in Working-Class History* 18 (2): 41–63.

CHAPTER 6

Racial Capitalism at Work:
Evidence from a COVID-Era Survey

SANJAY PINTO
Rutgers School of Management and Labor Relations
Worker Institute at Cornell ILR

Abstract

The past two years have laid bare long-running dynamics of structural racism in multiple arenas, from the labor market to healthcare institutions to the criminal legal system. Amid the different crises and ideological cross currents of the moment, the conceptual framework of "racial capitalism" offers an important prism for understanding our contemporary predicament. Recognizing racial differentiation as a cornerstone of capitalist development, it provides a means of tracing how racial hierarchies are formed and maintained across a broad range of economic and social processes. It also sheds light on the political fractures that help entrench the racial, class, and gender hierarchies underpinning contemporary capitalist economies and offers insight into the patterning of movements seeking progressive change. In this chapter, I aim to draw out the relevance of racial capitalism for the field of labor and employment relations. The chapter begins by briefly outlining key elements of the framework and addressing common lines of criticism concerning its limitations and blind spots. Then, drawing on original data from a national survey, I discuss how core mechanisms of racial capitalism—exploitation, expropriation, marginalization, and domination—have been at work in the United States during the pandemic and consider how the convergence of these mechanisms connects to prospects for collective action. Finally, in the concluding section, I draw out the implications of this discussion for thinking about the future of labor and employment relations within the broader span of multiple struggles for social equality.

INTRODUCTION

The past two years laid bare long-running dynamics of racial inequality in the United States. In the early stages of the pandemic, Black and Latinx communities experienced a disproportionate toll of illness and death due to COVID-19 (Chen and Krieger 2021), and racially inflected social determinants of health have continued to produce racial disparities in rates of mortality for those contracting the virus (Dalsania et al. 2022). Communities of color have experienced more severe employment impacts from pandemic conditions than other groups and have faced greater challenges maintaining basic economic security (Mabud, Paye, Pinto, and Pinto 2021). And the movement for Black lives has called attention to the structural racism deeply embedded in the criminal legal system and all other social arenas (Jean 2020). These developments have triggered an important set of reckonings with the force and impact of structural racism. All too predictably, though, a backlash has ensued—naming racism as a problem has been posited by many as the reason for outrage, rather than racism itself (Kaplan and Owings 2021).

Amid the multiple crises and ideological cross currents of the moment, the conceptual framework of "racial capitalism" offers a prism for understanding how all of these developments connect. Recognizing racial differentiation as a cornerstone of capitalist development (Robinson 2021[1983]), it offers a way of tracing how racial hierarchies are formed and maintained across a broad range of economic and social processes. It also sheds light on political fractures that help entrench the racial, class, and gender hierarchies underpinning contemporary capitalist economies and offers insight into the patterning of movements seeking progressive change.

This chapter aims to draw out the relevance of racial capitalism for the field of labor and employment relations. It begins by briefly outlining key elements of the framework and addressing common lines of criticism concerning its limitations and blind spots. Then, drawing on original data from a national survey, it discusses how core mechanisms of racial capitalism—exploitation, expropriation, marginalization, and domination—have been at work in the United States during the pandemic period and considers how the convergence of these mechanisms connects to prospects for collective action. Finally, the concluding section draws out the implications of this theoretical and empirical discussion for thinking about the future of labor and employment relations within the broader span of multiple struggles for social equality.

HOW RACIAL CAPITALISM WORKS

The term "racial capitalism" has been used in a variety of ways to capture the connections among race, power, and profit. One usage has addressed how subordinated racial identities are commodified for economic and social gain by white people and white-dominated institutions in the United States (Leong 2012). The conception mobilized here draws on Robinson's (2021 [1983]) seminal formulation to consider how racial differentiation intersects with larger processes of capitalist development (see also Leroy and Jenkins 2021). The relationship cuts both ways. We cannot understand the overall shape of contemporary capitalist systems without considering how racialized distinctions have been exploited to generate economic segmentation and political division. Nor can we grasp the character of racism and racial classification without accounting for how racialized difference has been reified and mobilized in the service of capital accumulation.[1]

Racial capitalism operates at multiple scales. In local, regional, and national contexts, we can see racial capitalism at work in the ways racism shapes the evolution of class and occupational hierarchies: who performs what roles, how these roles are valued, and who gets consigned to positions on the economic and social margins. The workings of racial capitalism are also evident in the shape and evolution of the global division of labor. Racialized distinctions played a central role in justifying transatlantic slavery and European colonization while reconciling these forms of domination with the values of Enlightenment liberalism (see, for example, Dawson 2016; Mehta 2018). In turn, these systems shaped the historical emergence of capitalism and the development of the capitalist world system. As Johnson (2018) put it, "There was no such thing as capitalism without slavery: the history of Manchester never happened without the history of Mississippi."

The global scale of racial capitalism is critical for understanding the analytical reach of the framework. Walzer (2020) questions the scope of racial capitalism by citing national cases where, in his estimation, the framework does not seem to apply—a line of critique blinkered by the sort of rigid methodological nationalism that Robinson (2021 [1983]), Du Bois (2017 [1935]), and others rightly sought to resist. In *Black Reconstruction*, long before "racial capitalism" became a term of art, Du Bois drew attention to how Black and brown workers in the global North and South—"the dark sea of human labor"—remained concentrated in the bottom rungs of a global division of labor, working under the most coercive conditions.[2] For Du Bois, racism played an undeniable role in rationalizing and reinforcing these patterns on a global scale. Accordingly, understanding and confronting this racialized subordination demanded a global perspective (see also Go 2021 and Singh 2021).

Recognizing the global dimensions of racial capitalism is not the same as saying it functions in identical ways across space and time. Some have raised concerns that a racial capitalism framework could lose sight of important differences among racial, ethnic, and national distinctions and the particular valences they assume across various settings (Go 2021; Walzer 2020). Robinson (2021 [1983]), however, left room for recognizing this variation, even while stressing the common threads in how these categories often came to be essentialized and *racialized* across different contexts. "The tendency of European civilization through capitalism was … not to homogenize but to differentiate—to exaggerate regional, subcultural, and dialectical differences into racial ones," Robinson asserted in a notable passage in *Black Marxism*. Following Marx and others, he highlighted the demonization of Irish workers to bolster English nationalism as an early instance of racialized distinctions being mobilized to stifle challenges to capitalist domination.[3]

The racialized othering of "the Irish" emerged within the American context as well, as Ignatiev (2012) has shown. Over time, however, this dynamic receded, a shift that corresponded with the integration of Irish people into American economy and society, even as what Du Bois (2015 [1903]) called the "problem of the color line" continued to shape the life chances of Black people and other racially subordinated groups. The position of Latinx people in the United States reflects the complexities of what Omi and Winant (2014) have referred to as "racial formation" and the ways it connects with capitalist development. The Latina/o/x category is a complex amalgam (Suarez-Orozco and Páez 2002)—broadly coded as "ethnic" within US government data but carrying racial inflections that vary across its subcategories. Darker-skinned people from Mexico and other parts of Latin America—often with Indigenous roots—have frequently faced demonization connected to the low-paying economic roles for which they are recruited (leading to charges of "stealing jobs" from ordinary Americans), even as richer and whiter immigrants from Latin American assimilate far more easily.[4]

A racial capitalism framework centers race and racialized distinctions in the analysis of capitalist dynamics, including the formation and maintenance of class boundaries. However, it does not suggest that race supersedes other categories of analysis such as gender.[5] Indeed, building on feminist accounts addressing the devaluation of paid and unpaid reproductive labor (England, Budig, and Folbre 2002; Federici 2013; Mies 2014), some of the most generative work on racial capitalism has shown how racism and sexism converge in shaping the devaluation of lives and labor that are ultimately essential for social reproduction and the functioning of capitalist economies (see, especially, Bhattacharyya 2018). The discussion below seeks to address these important lines of connection.

MAPPING MECHANISMS OF RACIAL CAPITALISM

The literature on racial capitalism draws attention to several mechanisms through which racialized subordination is perpetuated. The current discussion focuses on four—exploitation, expropriation, marginalization, and domination—that have been discussed at varying levels of depth and precision in the existing literature.[6] Given their underlying interconnectedness, sharp definitions pose somewhat of a challenge, and the characterizations offered below no doubt require further refinement. With that said, this mapping exercise seeks to do two things. First, given that discussion of these mechanisms often proceeds at a fairly high level of abstraction, the aim is to offer some more concrete delineations. Second, with much of the existing literature on racial capitalism shedding new light on the past, the goal here is to mobilize an understanding of these mechanisms to help illuminate contemporary conditions. The discussion addresses in broad strokes how legacies of slavery, colonialism, and conquest continue to reverberate in the present. It also considers how racial capitalism is actively being made and remade in the here and now, shaping patterns of inequality, and, as discussed in the next section of the chapter, conditions for collective action.

To trace the contemporary workings of racial capitalism, the discussion draws on data from the Just Recovery Survey (JRS), an instrument developed by a host of partners [7] in late 2020 to better understand how race, gender, and class were shaping worker experiences during the COVID-19 pandemic (Mabud, Paye, Pinto, and Pinto 2021). The survey relied on an existing nationally representative online panel created by the survey research firm SSRS, reaching 3,100 people across the country. Black and Latinx respondents were oversampled to provide greater statistical power for addressing racial inequalities (the survey team was unfortunately unable to oversample Asian and Indigenous respondents). Individuals in the survey indicated that they were not retired or permanently out of the labor market—that is to say, they were broadly in the labor force or might potentially rejoin it at some point in the future. All differences reported here are statistically significant at a 95% confidence level (for more detail on the survey and quantitative analysis, see the appendix). The aim is not to measure in a totally precise or highly technical way the different mechanisms being discussed but rather to offer a set of data points that are broadly indicative: a preliminary portrait. Richer quantitative and qualitative data are needed to capture more fully the mechanisms under discussion.

Exploitation

Exploitation was a central analytical category for Marx, capturing capital's extraction of "surplus value" from labor, which he saw as a foundational source of inequality in capitalist society (Marx 2007 [1867]).[8] The sense of the term "exploitation" used here draws from Marxist theory but is broader than this classic formulation, encompassing a variety ways in which workers and their labor come to be unfairly devalued economically and culturally by employers and other actors (Cohen 1989).[9]

Cedric Robinson and others have shown how racialized distinctions structure the basic terms of exploitation. The enslavement of Black people in the United States and other parts of the Atlantic world is the paradigmatic example of this phenomenon. Over time, racially differentiated exploitation has occurred both through legalized subordination and more subtle forms of devaluation. Drawing on a wide body of work diverse in its theoretical commitments, we can think of contemporary racialized exploitation as consisting of at least two dimensions: the ways in which racism contributes to the sorting of people into less-valued occupational positions (Weeden, Newhart, and Gelbgiser 2018) and its role in how certain jobs are accorded lesser value in the first place (Catanzarite 2003).[10]

The treatment of direct care workers providing childcare, long-term care, and other services provides an all too vivid illustration of how racialized and gendered exploitation continue to intersect. Women's unpaid reproductive labor has generally been rendered invisible and undervalued culturally (Hartmann 1979), which bleeds over into how it is valued when performed for pay (England, Budig, and Folbre 2002). And, in the United States and many other places, women of color and immigrant women have been concentrated in the most devalued paid care jobs, forming the basis for other women and men to pursue much greater gains in the labor market. Glenn (1992) has noted how many Black women were constrained to domestic service jobs following emancipation, marking continuities with their roles under slavery.

The concentration and undervaluation of Black women and other women of color in paid direct care jobs has been perpetuated not only by private actors but by the state. During the Depression and New Deal era, women of color seeking employment were systematically tracked into domestic service jobs by local government administrators (Glenn 1992), while Southern Democrats intent on maintaining the subjection of Black workers blocked the inclusion of domestic workers and farmworkers in landmark labor and employment protections (Perea 2011). In the publicly funded systems for childcare and long-term care services, policy makers have long set reimbursement rates at low levels based in part on the assumption that women of color can supply these services at low cost (Boris and Klein 2015).

Beneath the rhetoric lionizing "essential" workers, racialized differentiation has been on display within care-related fields during the COVID-19 pandemic. In healthcare, for example, there have been stark differences in the experience of front-line direct care workers and those in more highly professionalized positions.[11] Census data show that Black and Latinx people are far more highly concentrated in "healthcare support" occupations (e.g., home health aides and certified nursing assistants) than in "healthcare practitioner and technical occupations" (e.g., doctors and nurses).[12] A comparison of the two groups using the JRS shows that the former were far more likely than the latter to experience increased difficulty paying bills (including rent, utility, credit card, student loan, medical, and other bills) during the COVID-19 pandemic (50% versus 26%) and less likely to express confidence that they could afford to cover the cost of their own healthcare if seriously ill (38% versus 69%) (Pinto, Campos-Medina, Mabud, and Wagner 2021). These differences in experience reflect a variety of factors, including the ways in which different functions and educational credentials are rewarded in the healthcare field. But there is a substantial body of work showing how race has factored into the invisibility, undervaluation, and lack of mobility for an underclass within this sector (see, for example, Berry and Bell 2018; Boris and Klein 2015; Dodson and Zincavage 2007; Jones 2019).

The JRS question on paying household bills during the pandemic can be taken as a highly imperfect proxy for challenges meeting basic needs,[13] which is an important reflection of exploitation (Snyder 2008): a predicament in which those who sell their labor power within capitalist markets nonetheless struggle to provide for themselves and their families. Not surprisingly, those in the bottom earnings or household income quartiles were more likely than those at the top to experience increased difficulties paying bills during the pandemic (49% versus 24% for the bottom versus the top earnings quartile). Latinx and Black respondents were also more likely to experience increased challenges paying bills during the pandemic than their white counterparts (59%, 50%, and 35% respectively reported increased difficulties paying bills)—differences that held up even after controlling for earnings or household income, along with employment status.

Significantly, there were also racial differences *within* the bottom of the distribution. In the bottom earnings quartile, 72% of Latinx respondents and 58% of Black respondents experienced increased difficulties paying bills, as opposed to 39% of white respondents. What we know from other sources suggests that these differences are due not only to the concentration of Black and Latinx people at the bottom of each earnings and income bracket but to racial wealth gaps—which connect to the next mechanism of racial capitalism discussed here: expropriation.

Expropriation

Expropriation—the separation of people from individual or communal property—has laid the ground for capitalist development in ways that are well established. Capitalist production first took root on a terrain where people were separated from communal lands through which they had met their basic consumption needs, with the enclosure movement forcing them to sell their labor power in order to survive. In Brenner's (1977) classic account, expropriation enabled the particular form of exploitation that defines capitalism.

Alongside racialized exploitation, a substantial literature shows how racialized distinctions have structured the terms of expropriation. In the early history of the United States, Indigenous people were dispossessed of their lands and enslaved Black people were dispossessed of ownership over themselves and their labor power, even as white workers gradually moved toward "free" labor and a mostly white capitalist class accumulated ownership over the means of production (Roediger 1999). Drawing out these historical facts, Harris (1993) has noted how whiteness itself has functioned as a form of property in the American context. And, to further unpack Johnson's (2013, 2018) assertion, this racial ordering of property relations carried global implications: enslaved Black people harvesting cotton on lands appropriated from Indigenous nations supplied the raw material for England's industrialization, feeding its drive to the summit of the world system.[14]

Expropriation continues in the present. Land grabs—both by corporations and governments—continue to separate people from the basic means of subsistence, particularly in the global South (Federici 2018; Harvey 2003; Levien 2018). And expropriation broadly conceived includes not only the *taking* of ownership over land, personhood, and other forms of property, but also their ongoing *denial*. In *Black*

Reconstruction, Du Bois (2017 [1935]) traced how racial subjugation was maintained following emancipation. Rather than 40 acres and a mule, many of the formerly enslaved were forced into sharecropping arrangements that denied them property ownership and left them severely indebted (see also Dawson and Francis 2016). Over time, "redlining" and other forms of racist treatment by corporations and the federal government have continued to create barriers to home ownership and ownership of other assets (Rheingold, Fitzpatrick, and Hofeld 2000), which has contributed, alongside earnings disparities, to the racial wealth gaps clearly documented both for Black and Latinx communities (Sullivan, Meschede, Dietrich, and Shapiro 2015). Even when these communities have been "included" in the American dream of home ownership, it has frequently been on predatory terms that only deepen their financial and housing insecurity (Taylor 2019).

During the pandemic, particularly in its early stages, housing security took on added significance given the importance of "home" as a refuge from the dangers of COVID-19. Although policy makers took some measures to address the issue (e.g., eviction moratoriums), these were time bounded and unevenly applied. In this context, the JRS shows racial disparities in experiences and concerns related to housing security. The share of Black respondents (10%) who experienced or received notice of eviction or foreclosure was substantially higher than that of white respondents (2%). And Black respondents (42%) and Latinx respondents (38%) were far more likely than white respondents to indicate that they were very or moderately concerned about facing eviction or foreclosure within the coming year—differences that held up even after controlling for household income. These patterns broadly reflect a persisting logic of racialized expropriation in the housing arena: the ways in which home ownership is denied and housing rendered more tenuous based on racial distinctions. Other work has shown how these dynamics, including eviction specifically, bear on a host of other inequities including racial disparities in health (Himmelstein and Desmond 2021).

Racialized expropriation conceived as the denial of personhood has also been tragically on display during the pandemic.[15] bell hooks (1981) noted how the violation of Black women and the exploitation of their reproductive capacities under slavery left a lasting mark on perceptions of Black womanhood. Hartman (2016) has argued that categories of "labor" and "labor exploitation" consequently fail to capture fully the harms that were inflicted during slavery and that continue to resonate in its "afterlife." In the public health field, a growing body of work has shown how the failure of clinical providers to recognize the full personhood of Black women continues to shape their treatment and bodily autonomy in very specific ways, contributing to a variety of disparate outcomes including higher rates of maternal morbidity and mortality (Taylor 2020).

During the pandemic, these dynamics were evident in numerous cases where the pain and symptoms of Black women with COVID-19 were ignored or not taken seriously (Givens 2021). The JRS offers a small reflection of such experiences.

Fifty-five percent of Black women reported worrying that racism could affect their care if seriously ill, which was significantly more than other groups. Black men (38%), Latinx men (29%), and Latinx women (28%) were also much more likely to report these fears than white women (4%) or white men (4%) (for a more detailed discussion of these patterns, see McGregor and Pinto, in progress.

Marginalization

The logic of racial capitalism is apparent not just in how value is extracted via exploitation and expropriation but how populations are treated as expendable when there is little or no evident value to appropriate (Bhattacharyya 2018; Kundnani 2021). Bhattacharyya's account of racial capitalism (2018: 26–27) describes the creation of racialized "edge populations" that are positioned on the periphery of mainstream economies and struggle to reproduce their means of subsistence. Drawing on a Marxist lexicon, her discussion also calls to mind a conception of marginalization developed by Young (2011) in *Justice and the Politics of Difference.* "Marginals are people the system of labor cannot or will not use," Young observed, posing marginalization as a process whereby "a whole category of people is expelled from useful participation in social life and thus potentially subjected to severe material deprivation and even extermination" (Young 2011: 53).

For many Indigenous nations in the United States, racialized marginalization has been closely intertwined with expropriation. Even as some Indigenous people were compelled into extractive forms of employment (Jacobson 1984), those surviving the genocides perpetrated under settler colonialism were often pushed to the edges of the American polity and society. This occurred through removal by brute force, and, as Park (2018) shows, by making their lives so intolerable they were compelled to move.

Kundnani (2021: 1) suggests that the market-driven economic logic of the neoliberal era often intensifies the creation of racialized "surplus populations" with "no market value," pushing them farther to the margins of economic and social life. The present discussion aims to tease out this dynamic. However, it conceives marginalization not as a process of complete exclusion but one occurring along more of a continuum, particularly in higher-income countries where informal labor markets and other zones situated "outside the system" have a smaller relative presence than in the global South (Wood and Gough 2006).[16] As Marx recognized, those situated on the margins of labor markets are often subject to particularly intense forms of exploitation.[17]

In the United States, deindustrialization, public sector retrenchment, and other forms of economic restructuring have disproportionately impacted Black, Latinx, and Indigenous communities (Dawson and Francis 2016; Wilson, Roscigno, and Huffman 2013). Racialized marginalization often occurs, though, not through the complete denial of access to economic opportunities. Rather, communities of color experience disproportionate underemployment, nonstandard employment, and more frequent spells of unemployment—and a greater likelihood that these conditions will seriously compromise their economic security.

The JRS provides some rough indications of such patterns amid the COVID-19 pandemic. Government data show that workers of color are overrepresented among the ranks of temporary workers, those who involuntarily work part-time, and those who are misclassified as independent contractors across a number of key sectors (see Golden and Kim 2020; National Employment Law Project 2018; Ruckelshaus et al. 2020). The JRS shows broadly that workers in these categories were substantially more likely to lose income (51%) during the pandemic than those in standard employment arrangements (23%)—a pattern with racially disparate impacts owing to the demographics noted above. Black and Latinx respondents were also more likely than their white counterparts to lose income from paid work, whether or not they managed to retain their jobs. And their employment outlook was considerably bleaker. Fifty percent of Latinx respondents and 48% of Black respondents expressed moderate or serious concern about being able to maintain steady work for the remainder of the year, as opposed to 26% of white respondents. Within the bottom earnings quartile, the difference was even more dramatic: 63% of Black respondents and 59% of Latinx respondents expressed these concerns, versus 32% of their white counterparts.

These disparities should be understood in relation to another set of patterns that emerged in the JRS data. Black (34%) and Latinx (26%) respondents who applied for various forms of unemployment insurance were much more likely than their white counterparts applying for unemployment insurance (14%) to report that their claims were denied.[18] Black and Latinx respondents—particularly Latinx women (28%) and Black women (27%)—were also more likely than white women (12%) and men (9%) to report that they had to take time off from work during the pandemic due to caregiving responsibilities (the figures for Latinx and Black men were 20% and 15%, respectively). Although the JRS does not specifically address the issue of access to care-related benefits, we know from previous work that women of color often face disproportionate barriers to accessing public childcare benefits—barriers that are frequently maintained at the state level by government actors seeking to limit benefits disbursement to those deemed "unworthy" (see, for example, Hardisty 2013). A variety of factors blocking access to key benefits reinforce structural marginalization and economic insecurity.

Domination

Domination is the broadest of the mechanisms discussed here and perhaps the least sharply theorized in the literature around racial capitalism, despite being commonly invoked. Gourevitch (2011), drawing on 19th-century labor republicanism, articulates a two-pronged conception of capitalist domination that provides a useful starting point. First, domination occurs through the ways in which specific employers wield power over specific sets of workers in setting the terms and conditions of work. Second, what Gourevitch terms "structural domination" has to do with the fact that most people must work for *some* employer in order to secure their subsistence—even more so in societies such as the United States with a relatively weak social safety net (Esping-Andersen 1990). Of course, the bargaining power of workers varies substantially across the class and occupational structure.[19] And a racial capitalism framework invites closer consideration of how racism and capitalist domination intersect—for example, how employers wield their individual and structural power in ways that both rely on and reinforce patterns of racial inequality (and how these patterns shift over time in relation to the collective power of different workers and evolving configurations of state power).

The JRS captures some general indications of racially inflected domination in the world of work. The problem of wage theft has been well documented in the low-pay economy (Bobo 2014), and Black workers (14%) were more likely than white workers (6%) to report stolen pay in the form of not being paid at the correct rate, not being paid for all hours worked, not receiving tips, or being made to pay for personal protective equipment. Notably, this difference remained significant even after controlling for occupation and earnings. Employer retaliation for workers responding to unsafe conditions is another problem that reflects unequal relations of power, and one that became particularly concerning during the COVID-19 pandemic. In the JRS, Black workers (21%) were more likely than white workers (11%) to fear retaliation for reporting unsafe conditions and for refusing to work under unsafe conditions (30% and 18%, respectively)[20]—differences that again remained significant even after accounting for variation in occupation and earnings. Together, these data points broadly indicate the ways in which race can inflect a specific kind of employer domination: the ability to flout or signal the power to flout established institutional rules of the game.

More broadly, strategies of racial domination often help to reinforce capitalist domination.[21] In *Black Reconstruction*, Du Bois (2017 [1935]) identified a "public or psychological wage" of whiteness that prevented many white workers from seeing the interests they shared with workers of color in challenging the unfairness flowing from capitalist domination. Roediger (1999) builds on Du Bois's formulation to trace how the "wages the whiteness" evolved historically in the American context, as white workers observing Black enslavement came to associate their position as "free" laborers with their racial superiority. Even once emancipation was declared in 1865, this sense of superiority stuck, ginned up by political and economic elites looking to reinforce white supremacy and capitalist domination.[22] Over time, it hampered the creation of more robust and encompassing labor and social protections of the sort seen in other advanced democracies (Alesina and Glaeser 2004), divided and weakened the labor movement (Roediger 1999), and helped to provide backing for varying forms of ongoing racial oppression.

Against this historical backdrop, the pandemic period has seen an upsurge in organizing around structural racism and the specific devaluation of Black lives in the criminal legal system and other arenas (Bell, Berry, Leopold, and Nkomo 2021; Jee-Lyn García and Sharif 2015; Rickford 2016). In the summer of 2020, the police killings of George Floyd, Breonna Taylor, and numerous other Black Americans sparked a new round of uprisings demanding accountability for the people and institutions responsible for this violence, along with recognition of the intrinsic value of Black lives. Often intersecting with organizing in the world of work (Williams and Davis-Faulkner 2021), these protests came at a moment when the highly disproportionate economic impacts of the pandemic on communities of color were becoming apparent, and COVID-19 was striking those same communities the hardest even as they faced higher barriers to receiving the healthcare they needed. While the strategy and tactics of racial justice organizing have been debated across the political spectrum, responses to the assertion that "Black lives matter" served as a kind of litmus test for views on racism in society— the contention that structural racism has effectively made Black lives matter less and that something should be done to change this.

The JRS indicated cross-racial differences in favorability toward #BLM. However, it also showed majority support across different groups: 80% of Black respondents, 70% of Latinx respondents, and 53% of white respondents reported favorable views. Moreover, when accounting for ideology (conservative, moderate, liberal), the JRS showed that white conservatives were the real outliers (17% support), with all others at majority or very-near majority support. Although public opinion has continued to ebb and flow since the time the survey was conducted in late 2020 (Horowitz 2021), the appearance of this pattern following an uptick in #BLM organizing is significant in light of the historical dynamic captured by Du Bois.[23]

CONVERGING STRUGGLES AND COLLECTIVE ACTION

Data from the JRS roughly indicate some ways in which key mechanisms of racial capitalism have been at work amid the COVID-19 pandemic. We can also use these data to observe whether and how these mechanisms converge. Broadly, for example, we might expect a convergence of marginalization in the labor market with expropriation in the housing market, and we see this in the fact that those concerned about maintaining steady work were far more likely to be worried about eviction or foreclosure (55%) than those who did not indicate such concerns (14%). And race moderated this relationship: Black respondents and Latinx respondents who were concerned about maintaining steady work were more likely than white respondents with similar concerns to indicate worries about eviction or foreclosure (64% and 63% versus 47%, respectively). These patterns speak to the compounding ways in which racial capitalism shapes people's experiences both as workers and consumers.

In light of historical experience, we might also imagine that conditions of marginalization and expropriation would connect to greater exploitation and domination in the world of work. The JRS data show that those with concerns about maintaining steady work were more likely than those without such concerns to report wage theft (18% versus 5%) and fears of retaliation that would prevent them from raising health and safety concerns (24% versus 9%) or refusing to work under unsafe conditions (34% versus 14%). Race did not moderate these relationships. However, with racial distinctions shaping both sets of patterns in the ways discussed above, we can see how the convergence of uncertain unemployment prospects with different forms of employer domination would be a more likely scenario for workers of color—one that might compel them to exit their jobs entirely.

Despite this sobering picture, the JRS data also speak to significant and largely untapped collective active potential (albeit with a limited lens focused on the world of work). The early stages of the pandemic saw a surge in workplace actions demanding hazard pay and workplace health and safety protections, and the JRS showed substantial support for a specific form of action: the strike. Most respondents (56%) agreed that "labor strikes can boost workers' wages, benefits, and working conditions"—a majority that held across racial lines. The JRS also captured significant interest in workplace representation. Among currently employed working people without union representation, nearly half (45%) said they would like to join a union if they could. Nonunion Black workers (62%) were more likely than nonunion white workers (42%) or nonunion Latinx workers (44%) to express interest in joining a union—differences that remained significant even after controlling for occupation. These patterns accord with other recent public opinion polling, and they also call to mind long-running historical patterns (Taylor 2016). For example, during the heyday of Congress of Industrial Organizations (CIO) organizing between the New Deal era and the early postwar period, Black workers were often the most enthusiastic early supporters of unionization, perceiving most clearly what they stood to benefit (Nelson 1996).

The JRS also points to some specific ways in which mechanisms of racial capitalism may shape conditions for collective action. Among nonunion, currently employed respondents, those who said fear of retaliation might prevent them from raising workplace health and safety concerns were more likely to say that they would be interested in joining a union (60%) than those who did not report such fears (38%). And, among Black respondents who were nonunion and currently employed, fully 90% of those who feared retaliation for reporting health and safety issues said they would join a union if they could. In other words, both in spite of and because of the disproportionate challenges they confront in the world of work, Black workers are poised to be at the leading edge of helping to realize the collective action potential of the current moment. Granted, historical experience also provides reason for pause—even as Black workers played a key role in CIO organizing during the mid-20th century, for example, they were often constrained to less-valued occupational roles and marginalized within union decision-making processes (Hill 1996; Nelson 1996).

Finally, it's worth touching on how movements for racial justice in society at large might help to gradually shift conditions in the world of work. Amid the crescendo in #BLM organizing in the summer of 2020, many employers made statements supporting #BLM, with some announcing measures to address racial equity and inclusion. In the JRS, 38% of respondents indicated that their employer had made "statements in support of the Black Lives Matter movement or addressing racial equity in American society," and 29% said their employer "had taken specific action aimed at addressing racial inequity." And, among respondents reporting that their employers made statements supporting #BLM, took action to address racial equity, or did both, racial disparities in fears of retaliation for responding to workplace health and safety concerns virtually disappeared, falling to well within the survey margin of error. In no way can we draw any causal connections here. But these patterns broadly indicate how a willingness among employers to take certain kinds of stands may correlate with less unequal workplace conditions.

RACIAL CAPITALISM, LABOR RELATIONS, AND PATHWAYS TO EQUALITY

A racial capitalism framework offers a set of lenses for understanding how racism structures labor and employment relations as part of broader processes of capitalist development. It furnishes a set of historical resources for understanding more fully how racialized distinctions structure evolving class and occupational hierarchies. It provides a framework for linking compounding, racially inflected challenges in the world work and other domains—for example, how concerns about maintaining steady work coincide with concerns about maintaining a roof over one's head. And it lends insight into dynamics of collective action and coalition formation that carry implications for challenging structural racism and reversing rising economic inequality.

Applying and elaborating a racial capitalism framework can help to deepen our understanding of how racialized distinctions structure labor and employment relations within a broader field of social relationships. Multiple interlocking mechanisms of racial capitalism shape people's experiences as workers and consumers, among other social roles. Amid the COVID-19 pandemic, the JRS showed important differences in a variety of outcomes for Black, Latinx, and white respondents in the United States, and including Indigenous people and those of Asian descent would further complicate the picture (even before accounting for all the variation and subcategories with these broad racial/ethnic groupings). Pulling on existing contributions, teasing out how the mechanisms of racial capitalism shape the spectrum of experience for different groups across the labor market and other domains could move us toward a more holistic understanding of patterns of racial stratification (Hao 2007; Krivo and Kaufman 2004), fault lines that engender social conflict (Bonacich 1973; Cho 1993), and shared struggles that foster parallel or common lines of resistance (Ortiz 2018).

In contrast to perspectives that regard race as a distraction from class or conceive racial equity and inclusion in ways largely bereft of a class analysis,[24] a racial capitalism framework can also help to probe more fully the relationships between race/ethnicity, on the one hand, and class/occupation on the other. Though not measuring class in any precise sense, the JRS pointed to challenges maintaining basic security that affected substantial numbers of Black, Latinx, and white respondents in lower earnings and income brackets. At the same time, many of the racial disparities in the JRS flow from the concentration of Black and Latinx people in more disadvantaged economic positions, reflecting long histories of racial capitalism at work. And, notably, Black and Latinx respondents at the bottom end of the economic distribution also tended to indicate a more complex array of challenges maintaining well-being (e.g., paying bills, maintaining steady housing) than white respondents in broadly similar positions. Applying a racial capitalism framework can lend further insight into how racialized distinctions factor into a variety of mechanisms that bear on class formation, occupational closure, the differential valuation of lives and labor, and conditions for maintaining basic well-being.

Through continuing integration with feminist scholarship, a racial capitalism framework can help to work out how race and gender converge in shaping a variety of economic and social processes, including the paid and unpaid labor of social reproduction on which all other activity depends.[25] Long considered residual, there has been some progress in recognizing the essential character of paid care labor in particular, owing in part to its growing centrality in the economy (Schulze-Cleven 2021)—e.g., demand for home care has skyrocketed amid longer lifespans, the aging of the baby boomer generation, and growing preferences for aging in place (Osterman 2017).[26] Using the JRS to tease out mechanisms of racial capitalism offers some general insight into the challenges confronting front-line healthcare workers who are disproportionately women of color and shows that, despite their outsized role in these and other essential care occupations, Black and Latinx women confront particular barriers securing different forms of care they need for themselves and their families. As Hartman (2016) emphasizes, a narrow workerism fails to grasp the scope of these challenges. A more expansive framework also opens up space for connecting the dots across multiple areas where women of color have driven change in care systems, from being on the front lines of unionizing direct care jobs and strengthening protections for domestic workers to advancing welfare rights and reproductive justice (Boris and Klein 2006; Nadasen 2004, 2015; Roberts 2015).

In addition to strengthening our grasp of how racism and sexism interlink with occupational stratification and class inequality, a racial capitalism framework offers purchase for better understanding the positioning of key sets of actors in the labor and employment relations arena, including employers/capital, policy makers/the state, and workers/labor. The JRS provides some broad indications of how racial distinctions shape employer treatment of workers, and the results on fears of mistreatment in the healthcare system touch on racism in the treatment of customers—an issue that has received growing attention across different sectors, including retail (see, for example, Pittman 2020). In the context of #BLM organizing, the JRS broadly suggests that the willingness of employers to directly address racism may help to mitigate certain forms of racial inequity. Recent labor shortages may also compel more employers to rethink a set of practices that have long exploited a disproportionately Black and brown low-wage workforce. However, a racial capitalism framework calls attention to the racially inflected individual and structural power that employers continue to wield, which has only been consolidated in the neoliberal era through decades of deregulation and union decline (Dawson and Francis 2016). In this context, voluntary efforts may effect some meaningful improvements but will likely have limited impact in addressing broad patterns of racial stratification and employer domination.

In the United States, the historical record shows how law and policy have shaped dynamics of racial capitalism, including in the post–civil rights era. In the 1970s, enforcement of antidiscrimination protections enacted as part of the Civil Rights Act helped put a dent into race-based occupational segregation within firms, but this progress plateaued under the Reagan administration in the 1980s, as enforcement was curtailed (Stainback, Robinson, and Tomaskovic-Devey 2005). For policy makers interested in advancing workplace fairness and social equality, the JRS data show the importance of breaking down silos, addressing multiple forms of racialized exploitation, expropriation, marginalization, and domination. It also speaks to the ongoing importance of policy enforcement and implementation, providing some indications of racial disparities in access to key benefits.[27] In light of past experience, uneven enforcement and implementation across states and localities will be a problem to watch should progressive "infrastructure" legislation that sits in Congress at the time of this writing ever make its way into law.

As these political battles unfold in the American context, it is worth briefly revisiting the issue of how racial capitalism takes shape across different national settings. Among today's richest nations, the strongest and most encompassing forms of social democracy have taken root in small, open economies noted for their relative racial and ethnic homogeneity.[28] In the United Kingdom, a close cousin to the United States among national varieties of capitalism (Hall and Soskice 2001), the relative distance of racialized others positioned "out there" in the colonies meant that, well into the 20th century, working-class identity was not fissured by race in the same was it was in the United States (Bonnett 1998). Today, however, amid immigration flows shaped by old colonial circuits and the intra-European core-periphery dynamics traced by Cedric Robinson (2021 [1983]), there are growing parallels in the kinds of labor market segmentation we see across Europe and North America—and in the racism and xenophobia coursing through Far Right political formations. In many cases, these parties have made inroads among segments of the working class that have been core constituencies within Left political coalitions (see, for example, Adorf 2018). At a time when capital is challenging long-standing labor and social settlements even in the heartlands of coordinated capitalism (Streeck 2009), these fractures could be hugely consequential. Building on existing work (see, for example, Roemer et al. 2007), we need a comparative political economy of labor relations and social policy that grapples more searchingly with the realities and impacts of racial capitalism.[29]

In the United States, the fragmentation of the labor movement has paradoxically left greater room for experimenting with strategies to organize and build power in low-paid services where Black, brown, and immigrant workers are overrepresented (Turner 2014). And, while many unions in these and other parts of the economy have been decimated recently by lockdown conditions and slowdowns in economic activity, the JRS underscores the collective action potential of the current moment. Given patterns of precarity and marginalization emerging in the data, further developing structures that extend power and representation beyond any single employer or industry will be important in realizing this potential. So, too, will supporting the leadership of Black workers who have already been at the forefront of many recent union organizing victories and reckoning with the labor movement's complicated history of entanglements with racial capitalism (for more on this history, see Pinto, forthcoming). The wages of whiteness clearly remain a potent force in American life. But the JRS points towards a broad multiracial coalition that acknowledges the force of structural racism. Perhaps with expansive, strategic organizing, the grip of racial domination might weaken in the coming period, opening new horizons for labor and social relations.

APPENDIX

This methodological overview is excerpted from Mabud, Paye, Pinto, and Pinto (2021). The instrument for the JRS was developed with input from the Alianza de Campesinas, Arise Chicago, Gig Workers Rising, Koreatown Immigrant Workers Alliance, Make the Road New York, National Black Worker Center Project, National Domestic Workers Alliance, ONE DC, Restaurant Opportunities Center, and Workers Defense Project. These ten organizations represent workers—primarily Black, Latinx, and Asian, and many of them women—in a wide range of occupations, industries, and work arrangements across the United States.

The survey was designed to examine multiple indicators within three broad and overlapping determinants of worker well-being and power in the COVID-19 economy and beyond: economic security (including access to paid work and steady income, access to unemployment supports and paid leave, ability to pay bills and maintain steady housing, and unpaid care and paid work trade-offs), health and safety (including impact of COVID-19 on personal networks, access to healthcare, and workplace safety), and agency and voice (including workplace collective action, civic engagement, and political participation).

The JRS was administered by the survey research firm SSRS in September and October 2020 using its online SSRS Opinion Panel, in coordination with the Cornell Survey Research Institute. The survey included respondents from 50 US states and the District of Columbia who indicated that they were not retired or permanently out of the labor market. Black and Latinx respondents were oversampled to allow analysis of variables by race (n = 3,100 total; n = 1,783 white/ other respondents; n = 722 Hispanic respondents; and n = 595 Black respondents). The survey was conducted both in English (n = 3,020) and Spanish (n = 80). Survey weights were developed and applied to provide estimates representative of the US adult population 18 years of age and older in the labor market and with Internet access. The mean survey completion time was 13.6 minutes.

SSRS Opinion Panel participants are recruited randomly based on nationally representative address-based sampling combined with targeted recruiting for hard-to-reach demographic groups in the Omnibus survey platform, a nationally representative bilingual random digit dialing telephone survey. In all, 5,382 panelists were invited to participate in the survey, which was administered online. Participants received modest incentives in the form of an electronic gift card. A base weight was first developed to account for the probability of selection into the survey panel and then further weighted to match population targets, including sex by age, sex by education, race and Hispanic ethnicity, Census region, civic engagement, and population density. The design effect for this survey was 1.95 overall, and the survey margin of error is 2.5. Subgroups reported in the analysis are coded in the following way:

Race and Ethnicity: We coded respondents as white, Black, Latinx, Asian, or other based on SSRS's panel-reported ethnoracial survey item. The white category included only those respondents who identified as non-Hispanic. The Black category included respondents who identified as both Hispanic and non-Hispanic. The Latinx category included respondents who identified as Hispanic (excluding those who said they were both Black and Hispanic, who were included in the Black category). The Asian category included respondents who identified as non-Hispanic; due to sample size, data on Asian respondents are not reported for all items. We coded as "people of color" those respondents who identified as Black, Latinx, Asian, Native Hawaiian and other Pacific Islander, Native American/American Indian/Alaska Native, or a combination.

Gender: We coded respondents as women and men based on survey responses to a preexisting question in the SSRS panel (the sample size for gender-nonconforming individuals was not large enough to report results).

Income: We used SSRS's panel-reported household income item, which has the following categories: <$15k, $15k–<$25k, $25k–<$30k, $30k–<$40k, $40k–<$50k, $50k–<$75k, $75k–<$100k, $100k–<$150k, $150k–<$200k, $200k–<$250k, and $250k or more. We divided this variable into quartiles, which corresponded to the following categories: Less than $40k, $40k–<$75k, $75k–<$100k, and $100k or more.

Earnings: We used an item that asked workers who performed paid work since January 2020 to estimate their weekly earnings in wages or salary, before taxes, from their most current or most recent main job. We then dropped observations that reported above the 95th percentile, which is $5,300 per week. We divided this variable into quartiles, which corresponded to the following categories: $500 or less, $504–$902, $924–$1,500, and $1,501 or more.

ENDNOTES

1. Some have questioned whether racial capitalism posits a necessary relationship between racialized distinctions and capitalist development (see, for example, Walzer 2020). As Táíwò and Bright (2020) have suggested, this line of argumentation is a *non sequitur*. The point is to consider how racism has actually intersected with capitalist development historically and continues to do so.

2. Walzer (2020) suggests that the "key issue is exploitation, not racism," going on to explain that "even in a democratically or social democratically regulated global system, the majority of workers and the majority of managers—the underclass and the overclass—will be non-white." A racial capitalism framework highlights how exploitation and racism are intertwined, often leading to the "super-exploitation" of Black and brown workers. And it is not logically inconsistent to recognize that exploitation clearly does occur on a large scale within racial groups while appreciating the role racism has played historically in explaining why Black and brown workers are highly overrepresented, relative to their population shares, in the most exploited positions globally.

3. Robinson notes that English and Irish workers did act in concert in the late 18th century, including as part of the Chartist movement. However, by the mid-19th century, English nationalism had largely overwhelmed this nascent class solidarity, and "the English people were at one with respect to the Irish Question" (2021: 39–41). Go (2021) observes that Marx did address these kinds of dynamics in his journalistic writings but that racialized differentiation did not assume a central role in his general theory of capital, which became the crux of Robinson's critique of orthodox Marxism.

4. García (1981) traces the history of the racially charged and militarized targeting of Mexican guestworkers during "Operation Wetback" in the 1950s. Of course, discourses that demonize "illegal aliens" from Mexico also elide long histories through which colonial powers and their imperial conflicts displaced Indigenous nations from their lands.

5. See Ralph and Singhal (2019) for a line of critique suggesting, among other things, that a racial capitalism framework tends not to sufficiently account for "intersectionality."

6. Exploitation and expropriation have been addressed most extensively in the literature to date. For useful discussion and debate on the historical unfolding of these mechanisms, see Dawson (2016), Fraser (2016), and Camp, Heatherton, and Karuka (2019).

7. The partners were Color of Change, National Employment Law Project, TIME'S UP Foundation, and the Worker Institute at Cornell ILR.

8. Marx (2007 [1867]) conceptualized this surplus as the value extracted beyond what was given to workers to cover their means of subsistence.

9. Cohen suggested that "a person is *exploited* when unfair advantage is taken of him" (1989: 908).

10. Granted, there is debate on the role of racial composition in occupational valuation. For another empirical exploration, see Jacobs and Blair-Loy (1996).

11. As Dodson and Zincavage (2007) suggest in their discussion of the nursing home context, the very discourses praising the "familial" sacrifice and commitment and women of color concentrated in front-line positions often obscure the challenges they confront and serve to enable racialized exploitation.

12. Women are also somewhat more highly concentrated in healthcare support versus healthcare technical and professional occupations.

13. For those with higher income and earnings, not being able to cover bills is far less likely to correlate with not being able to cover basic needs like food and housing (even if some adjustment in standard of living is required). As such, differences in ability to pay bills no doubt underestimate earnings- and income-related disparities in ability to meet basic needs.

14. There is long-running disagreement over whether the development of external trade relationships or shifts in internal class relations drove different national trajectories of development (Brenner 1977; Denemark and Thomas 1988; Wallerstein 1974; Williams 1994 [1944]). Johnson (2013, 2018) makes a convincing case that the former was crucial in the pace and magnitude of England's industrial development (even if it was internal shifts in class relations that permitted this development to assume a specifically capitalist form).

15. Dawson's (2016) discussion is helpful for conceptualizing expropriation in this more expansive sense.

16. Under conditions of what Sassen (2014) terms "expulsion" that are occurring via land grabs largely though not exclusively in the Global South, strategies for challenging marginalization can also look quite different than in the global North. A rich array of movements in the South are looking to reclaim a territorial basis for subsistence beyond the domain of the market, rather than seeking to participate in the market on more equal terms. For an example from the Indian context, see Vaidya (2014). For a more theoretical discussion, see Federici (2018). Although such movements and impulses can be seen in the global North, they are undoubtedly smaller in relative scope and influence.

17. Marx (2007 [1867]) noted relative surplus populations that were left unexploited or underexploited by capital, stuck in conditions of unemployment of underemployment. But this "reserve army" helped to discipline the working class and was susceptible to superexploitation because of its precarity.

18. The Governmental Accountability Office (GAO) has noted similar patterns (Costa 2021). A news story on the GAO release noted some of factors that might help account for these patterns, including overrepresentation of BIPOC workers in nonstandard work arrangements, concentration in states that set more stringent limits on unemployment benefits (reflecting a racial logic dating back to the Reconstruction era), and racial disparities in the resources needed to navigate online systems for receiving benefits (Carino 2021). Of course, in light of historical experience, straight-up racism on the part of benefits administrators could also be a factor.

19. As Wright (1998) notes, more professionalized workers and those with higher credentials may be caught in "contradictory class locations," potentially perceiving their interests to reside more firmly with capital than labor.

20. The figures reported here differ from those reported in Mabud, Paye, Pinto, and Pinto (2020) because they reflect only "yes" responses to questions on fears of retaliation (the figures in the report reflect both "yes" and "maybe" responses).

21. It is worth here noting recent discussions that have identified racial domination as a barrier to achieving racial justice, albeit without fully teasing out what this means in the context of capitalism specifically. Allen and Somanathan (2020) propose, among other things, scrutiny of patterns of nonproportional racial representation in different institutional settings for evidence of racial domination. Desmond and Emirbayer (2009) put forward a somewhat thicker conception of racial domination that includes various forms of institutional racism (from the apportioning of rights and opportunities to control over norms and culture) and interpersonal racism (including everyday manifestations that are often subtle and unconscious).

22. Defending interests in white supremacy and capitalist domination do not always coincide, of course. And the convergence of these interests often occurs via complex coalitional dynamics—for example, the alliance between northern Republicans more concerned with maintaining capitalist domination and southern Democrats more concerned with maintaining racial domination during the New Deal era.

23. That said, there are numerous factors standing in the way of multiracial coalitions being positioned to support change through the electoral system in particular, from structures of representation in the US Congress to efforts to curb voting access that are both racially motivated and carry racially disparate effects. The JRS, fielded just before the 2020 election, showed that Black respondents (68%) and Latinx respondents (62%) were more likely than their white counterparts (53%) to express concern that problems at the polls or with mail-in ballots would prevent their vote from counting.

24. Left-liberal accounts lamenting the eclipse of class by a focus on "identity" proliferated during the 1990s in particular (see, for example, Gitlin 1995). For more on neoliberal ideologies and practices of racial inclusion/progress that sidestep a serious confrontation with the entwinement of race and class, see Dawson and Francis (2016).

25. For an account defining different kinds of reproductive labor, see Duffy (2005).

26. Granted, as Winant (2021) observed in a discussion focusing on the healthcare sector, front-line direct care workers are "indispensable" in a collective sense but rendered "disposable" as individuals.

27. Although the JRS data itself do not permit detailed analysis of the reasons for racial and gender disparities, we know from previous work that these kinds of inequities often stem form bias among policy administrators as well as inadequate outreach within communities most in need of support.

28. That said, recent accounts complicate this assumption and the precise role "homogeneity" has played in the development trajectories of the Nordic countries (see, for example, Keskinen, Skaptadóttir, and Toivanen 2019; Moene and Wallerstein 2020).

29. Following Du Bois, we also need a more fleshed out *global* political economy of contemporary racial capitalism, which would include probing in greater depth how racialized distinctions shape patterns of devaluation within global value chains. For a relevant historical discussion, see Manjapra (2018). For a theoretical discussion that touches on the convergence of gender, race, and class in dynamics of devaluation within contemporary global value chains, see Dallas, Ponte, and Sturgeon (2019).

REFERENCES

Adorf, Philipp. 2018. "A New Blue-Collar Force: The Alternative for Germany and the Working Class." *German Politics and Society* 36 (4): 29–49.

Alesina, A., and E.L. Glaeser. 2004. *Fighting Poverty in the US and Europe: A World of Difference.* Oxford: Oxford University Press.

Allen, Danielle, and Rohini Somanathan. 2020. *Difference Without Domination: Pursuing Justice in Diverse Democracies.* Chicago: University of Chicago Press.

Bell, Myrtle P., Daphne Berry, Joy Leopold, and Stella Nkomo. 2021. "Making Black Lives Matter in Academia: A Black Feminist Call for Collective Action Against Anti-Blackness in the Academy." *Gender, Work & Organization* 28: 39–57.

Berry, Daphne, and Myrtle P. Bell. 2018. "Worker Cooperatives: Alternative Governance for Caring and Precarious Work." *Equality, Diversity and Inclusion* 37 (4): 376–391.

Bhattacharyya, Gargi. 2018. *Rethinking Racial Capitalism: Questions of Reproduction and Survival.* Lanham: Rowman & Littlefield.

Bobo, Kim. 2014. *Wage Theft in America: Why Millions of Americans Are Not Getting Paid— And What We Can Do About It.* New York: The New Press.

Bonacich, Edna. 1973. "A Theory of Middleman Minorities." *American Sociological Review* 38 (5): 583–594.

Bonnett, Alastair. 1998. "How the British Working Class Became White: The Symbolic (Re) Formation of Racialized Capitalism." *Journal of Historical Sociology* 11 (3): 316–340.

Boris, Eileen, and Jennifer Klein. 2006. "Organizing Home Care: Low-Waged Workers in the Welfare State." *Politics & Society* 34 (1): 81–108.

Boris, Eileen, and Jennifer Klein. 2015. *Caring for America: Home Health Workers in the Shadow of the Welfare State.* Oxford: Oxford University Press.

Brenner, Robert. 1977. "The Origins of Capitalist Development: A Critique of Neo-Smithian Marxism." *New Left Review* 104 (1): 25–92.

Camp, Jordan T., Christina Heatherton, and Manu Karuka. 2019. "A Response to Nancy Fraser." *Politics/Letters* 15. https://bit.ly/3GVxg3K

Carino, Meghan McCarty. 2021. "Analysis Finds Racial Disparity in Pandemic Unemployment Benefits." Marketplace. https://bit.ly/3I0ZDPx

Catanzarite, Lisa. 2003. "Race–Gender Composition and Occupational Pay Degradation." *Social Problems* 50 (1): 14–37.

Chen, Jarvis T., and Nancy Krieger. 2021. "Revealing the Unequal Burden of COVID-19 by Income, Race/Ethnicity, and Household Crowding: US County Versus Zip Code Analyses." *Journal of Public Health Management and Practice* 27 (1): S43–S56.

Cho, Sumi. 1993. "Korean Americans vs. African Americans: Conflict and Construction." *Reading Rodney King/Reading Urban Uprising.* Robert Gooding-Williams, ed. New York: Routledge.

Cohen, Gerald A. 1989. "On the Currency of Egalitarian Justice." *Ethics* 99 (4): 906–944.

Costa, Thomas. 2021. "Management Report: Preliminary Information on Potential Racial and Ethnic Disparities in the Receipt of Unemployment Insurance Benefits during the COVID-19 Pandemic." Washington, DC: US Government Accountability Office.

Dallas, Mark P., Stefano Ponte, and Timothy J. Sturgeon. 2019. "Power in Global Value Chains." *Review of International Political Economy* 26 (4): 666–694.

Dalsania, Ankur K., Matthew J. Fastiggi, Aaron Kahlam, Rajvi Shah, Krishan Patel, Stephanie Shiau, Slawa Rockicki, and Michelle DallaPiazza. 2022. "The Relationship Between Social Determinants of Health and Racial Disparities in COVID-19 Mortality." *Journal of Racial and Ethnic Health Disparities* 9: 288–295.

Dawson, Michael C. 2016. "Hidden in Plain Sight: A Note on Legitimation Crises and the Racial Order." *Critical Historical Studies* 3 (1): 143–161.

Dawson, Michael C., and Megan Ming Francis. 2016. "Black Politics and the Neoliberal Racial Order." *Public Culture* 28 (1): 23–62.

Denmark, Robert A., and Kenneth P. Thomas. 1988. "The Brenner–Wallerstein Debate." *International Studies Quarterly* 32 (1): 47–65.

Desmond, Matthew, and Mustafa Emirbayer. 2009. "What Is Racial Domination?" *Du Bois Review: Social Science Research on Race* 6 (2): 335–355.

Dodson, Lisa, and Rebekah M. Zincavage. 2007. "'It's Like a Family': Caring Labor, Exploitation, and Race in Nursing Homes." *Gender & Society* 21 (6): 905–928.

Du Bois, W.E.B. 2017 [1935]. *Black Reconstruction in America: Toward a History of the Part Which Black Folk Played in the Attempt to Reconstruct Democracy in America, 1860–1880.* New York: Routledge.

Du Bois, William Edward Burghardt. 2015 [1903]. *The Souls of Black Folk.* New Haven: Yale University Press.

Duffy, Mignon. 2005. "Reproducing Labor Inequalities: Challenges for Feminists Conceptualizing Care at the Intersections of Gender, Race, and Class." *Gender & Society* 19 (1): 66–82.

England, Paula, Michelle Budig, and Nancy Folbre. 2002. "Wages of Virtue: The Relative Pay of Care Work." *Social Problems* 49 (4): 455–473.

Esping-Andersen, Gosta. 1990. *The Three Worlds of Welfare Capitalism.* Princeton: Princeton University Press.

Federici, Silvia. 2013. "The Reproduction of Labour Power in the Global Economy and the Unfinished Feminist Revolution." In *Workers and Labour in a Globalised Capitalism: Contemporary Themes and Theoretical Issues.* Maurizio Atzeni, ed. 85–107. Basingstoke: Palgrave Macmillan.

Federici, Silvia. 2018. *Re-Enchanting the World: Feminism and the Politics of the Commons.* Oakland: PM Press.

Fraser, Nancy. 2016. "Expropriation and Exploitation in Racialized Capitalism: A Reply to Michael Dawson." *Critical Historical Studies* 3 (1): 163–178.

García, Mario T. 1981. *Operation Wetback: The Mass Deportation of Mexican Undocumented Workers in 1954.* Westport: Greenwood.

Gitlin, Todd. 1995. *The Twilight of Common Dreams: Why America Is Wracked by Culture Wars.* New York: Henry Holt.

Givens, Raymond. 2021. "One of Us." *New England Journal of Medicine* 384 (6): e18.

Glenn, Evelyn Nakano. 1992. "From Servitude to Service Work: Historical Continuities in the Racial Division of Paid Reproductive Labor." *Signs* 18 (1): 1–43.

Go, Julian. 2021. "Three Tensions in the Theory of Racial Capitalism." *Sociological Theory* 39 (1): 3–47.

Golden, Lonnie, and Jaesung Kim. 2020. "The Involuntary Part-Time Work and Underemployment Problem in the U.S." Center for Law and Social Policy. https://bit.ly/3LBVqUF

Gourevitch, Alex. 2011. "Labor and Republican Liberty." *Constellations* 18 (3): 431–454.

Hall, Peter A., and David Soskice. 2001. "An Introduction to Varieties of Capitalism." In *Varieties of Capitalism: The Institutional Foundations of Comparative Advantage.* Peter Hall and David Soskice, eds. 1–68. Oxford: Oxford University Press.

Hao, Lingxin. 2007. *Color Lines, Country Lines: Race, Immigration, and Wealth Stratification in America.* New York: Russell Sage Foundation.

Hardisty, Jean. 2013. "Between a Rock and Place: Race and Childcare in Mississippi." Wellesley Centers for Women, Wellesley College.

Harris, Cheryl I. 1993. "Whiteness as Property." *Harvard Law Review* 106 (8): 1707–1791.

Hartman, Saidiya. 2016. "The Belly of the World: A Note on Black Women's Labors." *Souls* 18 (1): 166–173.

Hartmann, Heidi I. 1979. "The Unhappy Marriage of Marxism and Feminism: Towards a More Progressive Union." *Capital & Class* 3 (2): 1–33.

Harvey, David. 2003. "Accumulation by Dispossession." In *The New Imperialism.* David Harvey, ed. Oxford: Oxford University Press.

Hill, Herbert. 1996. "The Problem of Race in American Labor History." *Reviews in American History* 24 (2): 189–208.

Himmelstein, Gracie, and Matthew Desmond. 2021. "Eviction and Health: A Vicious Cycle Exacerbated by a Pandemic." Health Affairs. https://bit.ly/3GWfayT

hooks, bell. 1981. *Ain't I a Woman: Black Women and Feminism.* New York: Routledge.

Horowitz, Juliana. 2021. "Support for Black Lives Matter Declined After George Floyd Protests, But Has Remained Unchanged Since." Pew Research Center. https://pewrsr.ch/3GSN4Er

Ignatiev, Noel. 2012. *How the Irish Became White.* New York: Routledge.

Jacobs, Jerry A., and Mary Blair-Loy. 1996. "Gender, Race, Local Labor Markets and Occupational Devaluation." *Sociological Focus* 29 (3): 209–230.

Jacobson, Cardell K. 1984. "Internal Colonialism and Native Americans: Indian Labor in the United States from 1871 to World War II." *Social Science Quarterly* 65 (1): 158–171.

Jean, Tyra. 2020. "Black Lives Matter: Police Brutality in the Era of COVID-19." Issue Brief #31, Lerner Center for Public Health Promotion, Maxwell School of Citizenship & Public Affairs, Syracuse University. https://bit.ly/33pIujq

Jee-Lyn García, Jennifer, and Mienah Zulfacar Sharif. 2015. "Black Lives Matter: A Commentary on Racism and Public Health." *American Journal of Public Health* 105 (8): e27–e30.

Johnson, Walter. 2013. *River of Dark Dreams.* Cambridge: Harvard University Press.

Johnson, Walter. 2018. "To Remake the World: Slavery, Racial Capitalism, and Justice." Forum. Boston Review. https://bit.ly/3I377Sk

Jones, Alethia. 2019. "Agents of Change: How Allied Healthcare Workers Transform Inequalities in the Healthcare Industry." In *Structural Competency in Mental Health and Medicine.* Helena Hansen and Jonathan M. Metzel, eds. 191–209. London: Springer Nature.

Kaplan, Leslie S., and William A. Owings. 2021. "Countering the Furor Around Critical Race Theory." *NASSP Bulletin* 105 (3): 200–218.

Keskinen, Suvi, Unnur Dís Skaptadóttir, and Mari Toivanen. 2019. *Undoing Homogeneity in the Nordic Region: Migration, Difference and the Politics of Solidarity.* London: Taylor & Francis.

Krivo, Lauren J., and Robert L. Kaufman. 2004. "Housing and Wealth Inequality: Racial–Ethnic Differences in Home Equity in the United States." *Demography* 41 (3): 585–605.

Kundnani, Arun. 2021. "The Racial Constitution of Neoliberalism." *Race & Class* 63 (1): 51–69.

Leong, Nancy. 2012. "Racial Capitalism." 126 *Harvard Law Review* 2151.

Leroy, Justin, and Destin Jenkins. 2021. *Histories of Racial Capitalism*. New York: Columbia University Press.

Levien, Michael. 2018. *Dispossession Without Development: Land Grabs in Neoliberal India*. Oxford: Oxford University Press.

Mabud, Rakeen, Amity Paye, Maya Pinto, and Sanjay Pinto. 2021. "Foundations for a Just and Inclusive Recovery: Economic Security, Health and Safety, and Agency and Voice in the Covid-19 Era." National Employment Law Project, Worker Institute at Cornell, TIMES UP Foundation, and Color of Change.

Manjapra, Kris. 2018. "Plantation Dispossessions: The Global Travel of Agricultural Racial Capitalism." In *American Capitalism*. Sven Beckert and Christine Desan, eds. 361–388. New York: Columbia University Press.

Marx, Karl. 2007 [1867]. *Capital: A Critique of Political Economy*. Durham: Duke University Press.

McGregor, Alecia, and Sanjay Pinto. In progress. "Race, Gender, and Concerns About Healthcare Access During COVID-19."

Mehta, Uday Singh. 2018. *Liberalism and Empire: A Study in Nineteenth-Century British Liberal Thought*. Chicago: University of Chicago Press.

Mies, Maria. 2014. *Patriarchy and Accumulation on a World Scale: Women in the International Division of Labour*. New York: Bloomsbury.

Moene, Karl Ove, and Michael Wallerstein. 2020. *Social Democracy as a Development Strategy*. Princeton: Princeton University Press.

Nadasen, Premilla. 2004. *Welfare Warriors: The Welfare Rights Movement in the United States*. New York: Routledge.

Nadasen, Premilla. 2015. *Household Workers Unite: The Untold Story of African American Women Who Built a Movement*. Boston: Beacon Press.

National Employment Law Project. 2018, "America's Nonstandard Workforce Faces Wage, Benefit Penalties, According to U.S. Data." https://bit.ly/3uTn0H9

Nelson, Bruce. 1996. "Class, Race and Democracy in the CIO: The 'New' Labor History Meets the 'Wages of Whiteness.'" *International Review of Social History* 41 (3): 351–374.

Omi, Michael, and Howard Winant. 2014. *Racial Formation in the United States*. New York: Routledge.

Ortiz, Paul. 2018. *An African American and Latinx History of the United States*. Boston: Beacon Press.

Osterman, Paul. 2017. *Who Will Care for Us? Long-Term Care and the Long-Term Workforce*. New York: Russell Sage Foundation.

Park, K-Sue. 2018. "Self-Deportation Nation." 132 *Harvard Law Review* 1880.

Perea, Juan F. 2011. "The Echoes of Slavery: Recognizing the Racist Origins of the Agricultural and Domestic Worker Exclusion from the National Labor Relations Act." *Ohio State Law Journal* 72: 95.

Pinto, Sanjay. Forthcoming. "Economic Democracy Against Racial Capitalism: Seeding Freedom." In *Democratizing the Corporation*. Isabelle Ferreras, Tom Malleson, and Joel Rogers, eds. Brooklyn: Verso.

Pinto, Sanjay, Patricia Campos-Medina, Rakeen Mabud, and K.C. Wagner. 2021. "The Gender Policy Report: Seizing the Moment to Make Our Care Systems More Equitable." Cornell University ILR School. https://bit.ly/3sK6OW1

Pittman, Cassi. 2020. "'Shopping While Black': Black Consumers' Management of Racial Stigma and Racial Profiling in Retail Settings." *Journal of Consumer Culture* 20 (1): 3–22.

Ralph, Michael, and Maya Singhal. 2019. "Racial Capitalism." *Theory and Society* 48 (6): 851–881.

Rheingold, Ira, Michael Fitzpatrick, and Al Hofeld Jr. 2000. "From Redlining to Reverse Redlining: A History of Obstacles for Minority Homeownership in America." *Clearinghouse Review* 34: 642.

Rickford, Russell. 2016. "Black Lives Matter: Toward a Modern Practice of Mass Struggle." *New Labor Forum* 25 (1): 34–42.

Roberts, Dorothy. 2015. "Reproductive Justice, Not Just Rights." *Dissent* 62 (4): 79–82.

Robinson, Cedric J. 2021 [1983]. *Black Marxism: The Making of the Black Radical Tradition.* London: Penguin UK.

Roediger, David R. 1999. *The Wages of Whiteness: Race and the Making of the American Working Class.* Brooklyn: Verso.

Roemer, John E., S. Elizabeth, Woojin Lee, U-jin Yi, and Karine van der Straeten. 2007. *Racism, Xenophobia, and Distribution: Multi-Issue Politics in Advanced Democracies.* Cambridge: Harvard University Press.

Ruckelshaus, Catherine, Judy Conti, Rebecca Smith, Brian Chen, and Maya Pinto. 2020. "Comments on RIN 1235-AA34: Independent Contractor Status Under the Fair Labor Standards Act." National Employment Law Project. https://bit.ly/3LE12hb

Sassen, Saskia. 2014. *Expulsions.* Cambridge: Harvard University Press.

Schulze-Cleven, Tobias. 2021. "Beyond Market Fundamentalism: A Labor Studies Perspective on the Future of Work." Working Paper Series, The Center for Women and Work, School of Management and Labor Relations, Rutgers University. https://bit.ly/34MfenC

Singh, Nikhil Pal. 2021. *Black is a Country.* Cambridge: Harvard University Press.

Snyder, Jeremy C. 2008. "Needs Exploitation." *Ethical Theory and Moral Practice* 11 (4): 389–405.

Stainback, Kevin, Corre L. Robinson, and Donald Tomaskovic-Devey. 2005. "Race and Workplace Integration: A Politically Mediated Process?" *American Behavioral Scientist* 48 (9): 1200–1228.

Streeck, Wolfgang. 2009. *Re-Forming Capitalism: Institutional Change in the German Political Economy.* Oxford: Oxford Univesity Press.

Suarez-Orozco, Marcelo, and Mariela Páez. 2002. *Latinos: Remaking America.* Berkeley: University of California Press.

Sullivan, Laura, Tatjana Meschede, Lars Dietrich, and Thomas Shapiro. 2015. "The Racial Wealth Gap: Why Policy Matters." Dēmos, Institute for Assests and Social Policy, Brandeis University. https://bit.ly/3GYhnKf

Taylor, Jamila K. 2020. "Structural Racism and Maternal Health Among Black Women." *Journal of Law, Medicine & Ethics* 48 (3): 506–517.

Taylor, Keeanga-Yamahtta. 2016. *From #BlackLivesMatter to Black Liberation.* Chicago: Haymarket Books.

Taylor, Keeanga-Yamahtta. 2019. *Race for Profit: How Banks and the Real Estate Industry Undermined Black Homeownership.* Chapel Hill: University of North Carolina Press.

Turner, Lowell. 2014. "Organizing Immigrant Workers." In *Mobilizing Against Inequality: Unions, Immigrant Workers, and the Crisis of Capitalism*. Lee Adler, Maite Tapia, and Lowell Turner, eds. 3–13. Ithaca: Cornell University Press.

Táíwò, Olúfẹmi O., and Liam Kofi Bright. 2020. "A Response to Michael Walzer." *Dissent*. August 7. https://bit.ly/33w5E7Y

Vaidya, Anand Prabhakar. 2014. "The Origin of the Forest, Private Property, and the State: The Political Life of India's Forest Rights Act." PhD diss., Harvard University.

Wallerstein, Immanuel. 1974. "The Rise and Future Demise of the World Capitalist System: Concepts for Comparative Analysis." *Comparative Studies in Society and History* 16 (4): 387–415.

Walzer, Michael. 2020. "A Note on Racial Capitalism." *Dissent*. August 7. https://bit.ly/38wbfwY

Weeden, Kim A., Mary Newhart, and Dafna Gelbgiser. 2018. "Occupational Segregation." In *State of the Union: The Poverty and Inequality Report*. Stanford: Stanford Center on Poverty and Inequality.

Williams, Eric. 1994 [1944]. *Capitalism and Slavery*. Chapel Hill: University of North Carolina Press.

Williams, Naomi R, and Sheri Davis-Faulkner. 2021. "Worker Mobilization and Political Engagement: A Historical Perspective." In *Revaluing Work(ers): Toward a Democratic and Sustainable Future*. Tobias Schulze-Cleven and Todd E. Vachon, eds. 121–140. Champaign: Labor and Employment Relations Association.

Wilson, George, Vincent J. Roscigno, and Matt L. Huffman. 2013. "Public Sector Transformation, Racial Inequality and Downward Occupational Mobility." *Social Forces* 91 (3): 975–1006.

Winant, Gabriel. 2021. "Deindustrialization, Working-Class Decline, and the Growth of Health Care." *New Labor Forum* 30 (2): 54–61.

Wood, Geof, and Ian Gough. 2006. "A Comparative Welfare Regime Approach to Global Social Policy." *World Development* 34 (10): 1696–1712.

Wright, Erik Olin. 1998. *The Debate on Classes*. Brooklyn: Verso.

Young, Iris Marion. 2011. *Justice and the Politics of Difference*. Princeton: Princeton University Press.

CHAPTER 7

Reconceptualizing Labor Contestation by Marginalized Workers Through Critical Race Theory

SALIL R. SAPRE

MAITE TAPIA

Michigan State University

School of Human Resources and Labor Relations

Abstract

Over the past four decades, labor scholars have lamented the sharp decline in the incidence of labor militancy in the United States. While traditional perspectives of contentious action encompass strikes and work stoppages, these conceptualizations have mostly underscored class-based struggles over terms and conditions of employment anchored in the workplace. This emphasis has largely occurred at the expense of attention to contestation rooted in the social identity of workers—race, gender, and other markers of oppression—outside of class and the workplace. In this chapter, we focus on recent mobilizations in the context of the Black Lives Matter movement and COVID-19 crisis using critical race theory (CRT). Specifically, we use a counternarrative approach of CRT to understand labor contestation. This approach allows us to push for a reconceptualization of labor militancy by grounding contentious action more deeply in the contexts, embodied experiences, and strategies of the struggles of marginalized workers. We articulate three attributes of resistance, deployed especially by marginalized workers, that have been relatively overlooked by labor scholars and practitioners. These aspects of worker resistance bring valuable lessons not just to our scholarship but to a dwindling labor movement as well.

INTRODUCTION

The year 2020 will not be easily forgotten. The world was taken hostage by a global pandemic in which, at the time of writing, over 270 million people were infected and more than five million people worldwide died. In the United States, the situation has been extremely dire, with more than 50 million people infected and more than 900,000 deaths so far (Johns Hopkins University, no date). At the same time, COVID-19 has sharply exposed the preexisting inequalities as Black, brown, and Indigenous communities have been disproportionately impacted by this pandemic. In many states across the country, hospitalization, infection, and death rates have been disproportionately higher for communities of color—often situated at the bottom of our capitalist economy working in public transportation, meatpacking industries, and cleaning services (Tai et al. 2021).

The year 2020 has also seen one of the largest strike and protest waves in US history (Buchanan, Bui, and Patel 2020). Many workers have gone on strike to demand proper personal protective equipment, hazard pay, and paid sick leave because they felt unsafe and exposed to the virus. Workers across the country protested and struck against a range of employers, private and public, that tried to put capital and money-making before health, dignity, and human well-being. For example, McDonald's workers in Oakland, California, went on strike after some employees were told to wear dog diapers as masks after they got sick (Associated Press 2020); garbage workers in New Orleans went on strike and were subsequently fired and replaced by prison labor (Elk 2020); and in Boston, over 350 paratransit drivers went on strike after their employer proposed to increase their health insurance costs in the midst of a pandemic (Cote 2020). According to some sources, over 1,100 wildcat strikes have been identified since March 2020 (Elk 2021).

Furthermore, the police killings of Breonna Taylor (March 13, 2020), George Floyd (May 25, 2020), and Rayshard Brooks (June 12, 2020), among many others, ignited Black Lives Matter (BLM) protests across the United States. Between May 26 and June 28, 2020, more than 4,700 demonstrations took place in about 2,500 towns and cities. An estimated 15 to 26 million people participated, making this the largest movement in US history (Buchanan, Bui, and Patel 2020). And while those demonstrations focused on racial inequity and police brutality, the linkages between issues of race and class were not understated by protesters.

Yet, perhaps unsurprisingly, many industrial relations scholars, some labor commentators, or even labor practitioners consider movements such as BLM as something artificially separate from worker strikes or even worker power (for an exception, see Lee and Tapia 2021). However, owing to the unique experiences of oppression, these workers' struggles articulate a much broader worldview rather than a restricted approach embedded in class or based on issues in a particular workplace. For women of color, for example, agendas of organizing or acts of resistance have never been unidimensional, given multiple overlapping inequalities to which they are subjected. Along similar lines, the recent BLM protests demonstrated a resistance to various overlapping oppressions. Specifically, they encompassed reactions to the economic devastation that disproportionately affected communities of color during the pandemic, indicating the intertwined nature of racism and class issues in the context of such mass movements (Pessin 2020).

Following these elements of contemporary protest and strike actions, this chapter uses a counternarrative approach central to critical race theory (CRT) to make explicit the connections between various dimensions (class, race, gender, migration status, etc.) of workers' social identity. It further asserts that their struggles for social justice are as much embedded in class issues as they may be, for example, in antiracist objectives. We show that understanding these contemporary mobilizations of people of color (PoC) through a CRT lens more profoundly accounts for the complexities of social identity in the world of work and allows researchers as well as labor practitioners to expand the scope of empirical cases (Lee and Tapia 2021).

Essentially, we reimagine labor contestation using counternarratives by going beyond a workplace-based, color/gender-blind focus and argue for an integration of additional attributes in how labor contestation is conceptualized. These attributes are grounded in workers' social location at the intersection of various forms of oppression. Specifically, we push for industrial relations scholarship to be more receptive to (1) the possibility of interclass solidarity on issues anchored in the experiences of both employers and marginalized workers but which still entail contentious action by workers, (2) contestation originating from supra-workplace issues (e.g., systemic racism) that adversely affect underrepresented workers, (3) and, finally, nonconventional, radical tactics including resistance aimed at new targets in addition to the immediate employer.

We believe that embracing these important counternarratives will advance not only the somewhat narrow industrial relations scholarship on worker power but also bring important lessons to the trade union movement with regard to different forms or meanings of militancy, justice, and democracy. We therefore engage with labor scholars on reconceptualizing labor contestation based on the attributes mentioned above; we articulate the attributes further in the subsequent sections. We also speak to labor practitioners and highlight possibilities for the reversal of union decline that stronger support from organized labor for the struggles of marginalized workers may catalyze.

ISSUES WITH EXISTING SCHOLARSHIP ON LABOR CONTESTATION

The failing of mainstream [industrial relations] has been its compartmentalization of both conflict and the sources thereof within the employment relation.

—Godard 2011: 299

Over the past four decades, labor scholars and observers have lamented the sharp decline in the incidence of labor militancy in the United States. Industrial relations scholars examining labor contestation have mostly focused on union collective action—more specifically on strikes and to a lesser degree on other actions such as overtime bans, working to rule, or go-slows. While there are not a lot of data available on these other forms of collective action, at the same time, strikes are also considered the most powerful tool at the disposal of unions and reflect the "underlying sources of conflict that derive from the institutional structures of capitalism" (Godard 2011: 297). More specifically, these forms of labor resistance (such as strikes) are primarily examined against the backdrop of structural inequalities in the employment relationship (Rhomberg and Lopez 2021).

In the United States, the Bureau of Labor Statistics (BLS) gathers data on major work stoppages or work stoppages involving 1,000 or more workers lasting one shift or longer. While the data don't distinguish between strikes and lockouts (initiated by management), the latter are quite rare, so work stoppages are often considered a proxy for strikes (Shierholz and Poydock 2020). Data show that the use of strikes has significantly declined since the early 1980s—with the exception of an important upsurge between 2018 and 2020 (Shierholz and Poydock 2020; US Bureau of Labor Statistics 2020a) (Figure 1). The changing structure of the economy with the decline in manufacturing and union density, as well as critical policy decisions, are considered some of the reasons behind this drop (McCartin 2007). Indeed, many scholars point to the 1981 PATCO strike as a key event in weakening the US labor movement and its use of strikes as President Ronald Reagan promptly fired the striking air traffic controllers and legitimized the use of permanent replacement workers (McCartin 2007).

Importantly, scholars have pointed out the challenges with the reported strike data. For example, according to Gall (2013), what is not captured in these data is the deinstitutionalization of collective action—in other words, collective action in the political rather than industrial sphere taken by unions as a result of being a political outsider (Korpi and Shalev 1979). According to Godard (2011), there might be an increase in overt conflict that ultimately gets reflected through broader political unrests. Instead of blaming individual employers, workers attribute the injustice to political elites. This means there is likely an increase in political strikes—targeted toward the government as the legislator, the executive, or for public sector workers the ultimate employer—and demise of the economic or industrial strikes. As a result, strike data are likely to underreport workers' strike activity.

Not all such acts of resistance are union led, however. While actions by unionized workers aren't outside the purview of this chapter, acts of resistance may also be organized by labor-oriented nonunion organizations such as worker centers or by "seemingly" nonlabor community/professional organizations (e.g., those championing antiracist struggles) that may not, at the outset, be perceived to center labor issues.

Furthermore, across different contexts, these declining incidences of collective action (especially strikes but also other actions) show a potentially shifting repertoire of contention (e.g., Kelly 2015). In other words, just as the ultimate conditions that ignite strikes may pertain to the employment relation, there could be new manifestations

Figure 1
Number of Workers Involved in Major Work Stoppages, 1973–2019

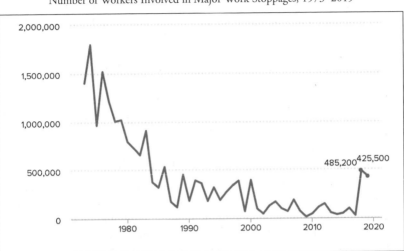

Source: US Bureau of Labor Statistics 2020b.

Note: The Bureau of Labor Statistics does not distinguish between strikes and lockouts in its work stoppage data. However, lockouts (which are initiated by management) are rare relative to strikes, so it is reasonable to think of the major work stoppage data as a proxy for data on major strikes. Data are for work stoppages that began in the data year.

of conflict that might not be directly or overtly linked to the employment relationship. While Godard (2011) points toward a blurring of the boundaries between home and work life—or the societal and employment systems—that might bring more conflict, we focus on the broader systemic structures that have always been in place in which inequities in work, housing, education, healthcare, and other spheres are interlinked and particularly affect marginalized people.

In 2021, scholars at Cornell University launched a new Labor Action tracker to "provide a comprehensive database of strike and labor protest activity across the United States displayed on an interactive map" (ILR School, no date). It includes stoppages by workers with demands that may not be workplace related, as well as labor protests that are not work stoppages but whose central demand is workplace related. While it is an important tool that goes beyond the traditional BLS definition of a strike, social justice protests by nonlabor organizations in which work demands are not perceived to be central will likely not be tracked. Additionally, the tracker quantitively records contentious actions very well but relatively overlooks qualitative attributes of such actions, such as social identity and related vulnerabilities of participants. We argue that many of these contestations, in fact, often come out of struggles rooted in racialized and gendered societal structures and are inextricably linked with labor issues.

In this chapter, we focus on strikes and protests, especially during 2020, demonstrating that labor contestations with nonconventional attributes already exist but have gone largely unnoticed by labor scholars and practitioners. Interestingly, these contentious actions are intersectional in nature and go beyond the workplace, are not always directed at the employer, and are not necessarily seen in traditional labor strongholds. In essence, although labor contestation forms the backbone for expression of labor power, many manifestations of resistance—such as militant action by marginalized people under the auspices of the BLM movement, as well as COVID-19 strikes—remain outside of the purview of mainstream labor contestation scholarship.

CRITICAL RACE THEORY AND COUNTERNARRATIVES

As evident in the previous section, mainstream industrial relations scholarship has largely overlooked contestation outside of the class context and beyond the workplace. This means that labor contention pertaining to race, gender, and other social identity issues originating outside the workplace but inextricably linked and important to workers has received limited scholarly attention. As some researchers have argued (e.g., Lee and Tapia 2021), an adequate understanding of the situatedness of individuals within the web of intersecting social identities and oppressions has been found wanting in the traditional industrial relations literature.

An examination of labor contestation scholarship through a CRT lens underscores the limitations of color-blind and nonintersectional perspectives of labor struggles. Such perspectives result in a deemphasis or "erasure" of contention—of which marginalized workers of color (WoC) are key drivers—that does not fit the framework of traditional labor confrontation. CRT perspectives, however, can bring such contestation into focus. To assist in reversing the neglect around militant action by underrepresented workers, CRT can help highlight "ignored" attributes of labor contestation and also explain the absence of these narratives in the mainstream labor discourse (see Delgado and Stefancic 2001; Lee and Tapia 2021).

Based on racialized experiences of legal jurisprudence, the CRT conceptualization argues that institutions—legal or otherwise—cannot truly serve society unless the erasure of embodied realities of subordinated groups is reversed (Matsuda et al. 1993, in Dixson and Rousseau 2005). This is a critical step toward full emancipation of all individuals. While the CRT framework comprises many important themes (Delgado and Stefancic 2001, Dixson and Rousseau 2005), this chapter borrows from legal and education research in CRT and leverages the counternarratives approach to rearticulate labor contestation. It treats counternarratives as a research method aimed at eradicating oppression by linking CRT theorization with critical reflection for transformative change (see Miller, Liu, and Ball 2020; Milner and Howard 2013).

As an instrument for social justice–oriented research, the counternarrative methodology is predicated on challenging and dismantling the dominant "deficit-informed" renderings of reality that privilege white, middle/upper class, heterosexual, able-bodied, cis males, and on bringing to the fore experiences of those at the margins of society (Solórzano and Yosso 2002). Principally, these dominant stories stem from and perpetuate privilege in ways that reinforce negative assumptions held by privileged groups about those historically oppressed. Indeed, they suppress the experiences of subordinated groups and over time become accepted as normative while alternative lived realities are invalidated or erased from public discourse (Delgado and Stefancic 2001). Therefore, in situations where the accepted reality is singular or unidimensional, counternarratives pave the way forward as a tool to account for alternative versions of lived experiences of the marginalized.

CRT, in fact, asserts that it is by "look[ing] to the bottom" and listening to the "special voice" of underrepresented groups (Matsuda 1995: 63) that counternarratives can amplify their embodied experiences (see also Crenshaw 1989, on intersectionality). As Dixon and Rousseau (2005) have argued, counternarratives go beyond a quantitative approach of analyzing oppression by emphasizing both process and outcomes from a qualitative standpoint through which lived experiences of the oppressed may be amplified. These stories are presented as powerful self-contained pieces of evidence to demonstrate inequality in society and to dispel prevalent notions of liberalism, objectivity, and color blindness in the socioeconomic order. Importantly, counternarratives also encompass praxis in the form of critical reflections and emancipatory solutions as a cyclical process toward societal equity (Miller, Liu, and Ball 2020).

Counternarratives also help affirm commonality of experiences of oppression, raise awareness about injustice and shared trauma, and build social, political, economic, and cultural resistance to the expunging of accounts of the oppressed. Notably, the propagation of counterstories reassures oppressed individuals that their experiences are not singular and that there are systemic forces at play. Counternarratives therefore help call out specific types of oppression—such as discrimination, microaggressions, and systemic racism—so that they can be dismantled (Delgado and Stefancic 2001).

CRT recognizes marginalized people as active producers of counternarratives. Scholars such as Solórzano and Yosso (2002) have, in fact, identified three strategies for presenting counternarratives: personal stories in which authors primarily borrow from their own insights (Milner and Howard 2013), others' stories, which highlight experiences of oppression articulated from a third person's perspective (Dixon and Rousseau 2005), and composite stories involving autobiographical or biographical analyses and creatively building composite characters placed in contentious situations—for example, see the chapter "Space Traders" in Bell (1992) on the disposability of Black people.

Relatedly, some scholars have perceived counternarratives as a research method or an important instrument for data collection (see Miller Liu, and Ball 2020) that guides how counterstories are presented. These researchers have proposed two approaches for doing so: the *whole narrative* approach, which elicits stories from participants and uses the accounts as they are; and the *narrative factor* approach involving the collection of various types of data and constructing counterstories to highlight specific inequities and injustices. Fundamentally, counternarratives are based on data from one or more of these sources: interviews, observations, and similar methods; extant literature; and one's own personal and professional experiences (Solórzano and Yosso 2002).

This chapter follows the narrative factor approach, relying on information obtained from academic and popular literature as well as informal engagements with other scholars and practitioners within the sphere of our professional experiences. The chapter is, essentially, anchored in counternarratives as a methodology that informs a priori our rationales and decision making about what kind of data to collect and how to present our arguments. We articulate our counternarratives in the next sections.

COUNTERNARRATIVES OF LABOR CONTESTATION

Labor contestation, as is commonly understood, involves power struggles between labor and capital. However, some characteristics of resistance bring into question the very nature of labor contestation as it is conventionally perceived. Through CRT, and specifically counternarratives, we examine three important attributes of labor contestation most often deployed by marginalized workers, which tend to be neglected in traditional industrial relations scholarship. While these attributes are treated as analytically distinct, they often overlap in practice and are nonexhaustive. Importantly, however, they demonstrate the inadequacy of existing scholarship in grasping the nature of emerging and often innovative ways in which marginalized people have exercised agency. These accounts also call for a more critical view of who gets to participate in the labor movement and which groups remain outsiders.

Employee–Employer Cooperation

Traditionally, industrial relations scholarship has viewed labor–capital dynamics as a zero-sum game in which workers' gains are perceived as employers' losses and vice versa. Conventionally, notions of labor contestation picture employers and workers engaged in confrontation over power and control of the workplace. However, recent protest waves challenge prevalent imaginations of labor struggles as they highlight how employer and worker interests may also coincide in moments of crises.

The 2020 BLM movement, for example, has witnessed cooperation between small business owners and WoC. For instance, as Elk (2020) has reported, around 250 businesses closed on June 12, 2020, in Seattle and King County after BLM activists issued calls for a general strike to protest against police brutality. Many employers acknowledged the trauma experienced by Black workers and shut shop for a day in solidarity. Similarly, workers shut more than 44 small businesses in Chattanooga, Tennessee, as part of a "revenue strike" in which protesting workers and employers demanded reallocation of the city budget from law enforcement to the support of underrepresented communities (Fortune 2020). Workers and employers may indeed find common ground in shared experiences of oppression—for example, systemic racism—transcending the class divide. Cedric Robinson (1983), as an example, notes in his important thesis on Black Marxism the formation of racial solidarity transcending the class divide. He shows that European conceptualization of class struggle as it was imported into the United States did not sufficiently account for the unique positionality of Black people and other racial minorities in America. As the American working class—a majority of which was white—became infused with racialized notions of white superiority, famously termed by Du Bois as psychological "wages of whiteness," it failed to grasp the intertwined nature of capitalism with slavery in the past and institutionally embedded less overt forms of racism into the present. Slavery and racism pitted poor white workers against Black workers and undermined class solidarity. As a result, many generations of shared struggles of Black people against systemic racism have now given way to "imperatives of broader collectivities" and an overarching Black identity as a response to racial capitalism. Although conflicts between the Black bourgeoisie and proletariat have existed (Burden-Stelly 2020), broader solidarity reflects struggles that emphasize common experiences of racial oppression in a manner that may periodically circumvent class differences.

This was seen in case of Black employers participating in BLM protests shoulder to shoulder with the Black working class. Some of these small business owners also suffered economically when their stores were vandalized following the protests. However, they acknowledged the accumulating frustration of their communities with the arbitrary killing of Black people and empathized with the protesters (Bhattarai 2020). Employers from other racialized communities have also echoed these views. An Asian fast food entrepreneur, for example, emphasized that stores are replaceable, but lives lost due to state violence are a much bigger issue (Wang 2020).

Black business owners under the auspices of US Black Chambers, Inc., have also vehemently criticized corporate America's resistance to increasing the minimum wage to $15 an hour as COVID-19 ravaged the country while the Fight for $15 movement, which constituted an overrepresentation of marginalized workers, continued steadfastly. Their assertions were critical considering the disproportionate impact of the pandemic on communities of color and the positive effect of increasing the minimum wage on reducing pay disparity along racial and gendered lines (Busby 2021).[1]

As such, militant action by workers in these contexts may not always be directed against the employer and therefore is less likely to be characterized as "contentious" from a traditional labor resistance standpoint. Moreover, as some have argued, many employers may support these actions to portray allyship with antiracist struggles and win social approval lest they lose business absent such support (Elk 2020). These arguments indeed need deeper scrutiny and have critical ramifications for the sustainability of worker power.

The mass actions elucidated above have been geared toward achieving systemic transformation and shaping perspectives about injustice while targeting neoliberal policy makers and economic elites. While constituting worker–employer solidarity, they have also accentuated the symbolic power of workers. For instance, through visuals of closed businesses, protesters have demonstrated their capability to halt regional commercial activity *as workers*. They mobilized the support of progressive businesses and pressured others to close. These tactics, activists have argued, can shape a critical mindset, inspire resistance against socioeconomic injustice, and encourage membership gains for organized labor (Elk 2020). Others have further contended that such strategies emphasize the intersections of working class and racialized identities and are potential precursors to general strikes (see Afridi 2017). Such contestation, therefore, needs to be understood from a historical perspective, and more attention needs to be paid to radicalism shaped by common experiences of oppression transcending class. These counternarratives are critical in amplifying distinctive actions by marginalized workers navigating between partnering with employers on various social issues or resisting employer actions.

Expanding the Agenda of Labor Contestation: Supra-Economic Causes of Labor Militancy

A second attribute of the struggles of underrepresented workers pertains to the source of labor contestation. Arguably, labor militancy is centered on conflict related to the employment relationship, while attention paid to supra-workplace issues is relatively scant. Put differently, individuals participating in radical action are perceived to be doing so primarily as workers or part of the working class. Oftentimes, as a result, only the causes for conflict emanating from within the employment relationship are seen relevant for industrial relations research (Budd 2012), while external ones are somewhat overlooked or considered extraneous to industrial relations scholarship.

Labor historians, however, have long acknowledged the intersection of issues for workers, going beyond the workplace per se. For example, Phillips-Cunningham (2020) has written about how Black women in Georgia have a long history of fighting for labor, criminal justice, and voting reform. She has cited events starting from a critical laundry strike in 1881 to campaigns against labor exploitation of Black prisoners in the late 19th century to registering domestic workers to vote in the late 1960s to, most recently, the 2020–21 Georgia Senate runoff campaign. Evidently, Black women have been pioneers "in shaping American democracy," encompassing matters of labor as well as criminal justice and voting reform (Phillips-Cunningham 2020). Along similar lines, working-class historian Williams (2020) has also emphasized a need to center worker agency and acknowledge how race, gender, and ethnicity shape class politics that go beyond the workplace.

Indeed, as stated at the onset, people of color (and women specifically) seldom face unidimensional issues given their oppression along overlapping inequalities.

Workers from marginalized communities have therefore traditionally engaged in contestation as workers *and* people of color, arguing that capitalist exploitation cannot be divorced from systemic racism (Schermerhorn and Sustar 2020). They have, in fact, emphasized that racism is not a by-product of capitalism but that capitalism is built on racial hierarchies.

Some scholars have further articulated the interplay between subordination based on race, class, and other social identities. They cite the subordination of PoC under the capitalist superstructure and have called such a system "racialized capitalism" (Virdee 2019). They argue that systems of "unequal exchange" based on social differences are established such that a periphery of underpaid racialized and gendered workers enriches a core of capitalists and is denied dignity, rights, or access to union membership (Cox 1962, cited in Burden-Stelly 2020; Edwards 2021).

Marable (2015) further demonstrates the overlapping linkages between social identity and oppression in his classic treatise on US capitalism. In that seminal work, he specifically examines how capitalism has "underdeveloped" Black America. The following newly available data provide a glimpse into the interlinkages between class and race, validating his contention. According to the Economic Policy Institute (Gould and Wilson 2020), Black people, as compared with non-Hispanic whites, are more likely to be unemployed (6.1% vs. 3% in 2019), live below the poverty line (20.7% vs. 8.1% in 2018), and have fewer cash reserves to draw on ($8,792 vs. $49,529 in 2016 dollars).

Marable also compellingly asserts that class issues and systematic violence by law enforcement cannot be disentangled from the question of race. For instance, data have shown that a Black person is five times more likely than a white person to be accosted by the police. The likelihood of Black males being questioned by law enforcement is twice that for Black females. Similarly, Black people are five times more likely than white people to be incarcerated (National Association for the Advancement of Colored People 2021). Poverty, police brutality, and incarceration rates, Marable (2015) contends, are interwoven with the Black identity and continue as a covert, if not overt, manifestation of oppression.

Crises such as COVID-19 further exacerbate these inequalities as occupations in which PoC are overrepresented are deemed essential. Observers have noted how individuals doing these jobs have been forced to continue working despite severe health risks, unavailability of protective equipment against pandemic-related hazards, and economic precarity (Edwards 2021).

Contemporary research, however, has also shown the unique contexts in which WoC have engaged in contestation against such forms of oppression (Milkman 2011; Tait 2016; Yu 2014). Owing to their unique experiences of subjugation, these workers' struggles articulate a much broader worldview than the restricted approach embedded in class or a particular workplace. Considering that marginalized workers frequently oscillate between waged work and unemployment, their militant expressions are more likely to encompass broader issues related to affordable housing, environmental degradation in their communities, and the criminal justice system. These broader issues arguably go a longer way in enhancing socioeconomic opportunities for disadvantaged individuals than do economically oriented collective bargaining contracts (Tait 2016). These accounts thus drive home the importance of attending to intersecting identities, as well as call for expansion of the traditional imagination of labor contestation.

Some recent examples further illustrate how intersectional subordination of underrepresented workers is linked to the need for rearticulating contentious action. The Movement for Black Lives (M4BL), for instance, has served as a compelling counternarrative about resistance by marginalized workers facing interlacing oppressions. M4BL as a movement has adopted community-based strategies for the overall welfare of underrepresented workers. It has sought to comprehensively address issues that workers face not only at the workplaces but also in their communities. It has emphasized the intersectional Bargaining for the Common Good approach (see Davis-Faulkner and Sneiderman 2020; Jacobs, Davis-Faulkner, Pumarol, and Sneiderman 2020) and advocated welfare for PoC in the context of institutionalized racism and neoliberalism (Weeks and Sneiderman 2016), thereby effectively highlighting the interlinkages of community and workplace issues pertinent to WoC. Among its diverse goals, M4BL proposes training programs for Black workers, progressive taxation for funding of schools and services in Black communities, and implementation of "ban the box" practices (Weeks and Sneiderman 2016).

Another example demonstrating supra-workplace sources of labor contestation was the militant action of Milwaukee Bucks team members. Their wildcat strike to protest police brutality against Black people was manifested by their stark absence from one of their scheduled NBA matches. Their subsequent interactions with the public were replete with antiracist assertions. Indeed, NBA players' radical measures were not tied to the workplace but spoke to broader issues afflicting the communities in which the players were born and raised. In fact, many players were reluctant to continue the season lest attention be diverted from the racial justice movement unfolding at the time. The players struck, effectively leveraging their celebrity status and symbolic power (Eidlin 2020). They owned their labor *as workers* and chose who watched them play and when (Ahmad 2020; Bryant 2020). Indeed, "the most powerful thing they could do was *not* to work" (Cunningham 2020).

In sum, the counternarratives articulated above push back against a narrow class or workplace-related focus and delineate how the radical action of workers, while rooted in class identity, also intertwines with issues external to the conventional economic perspective of the employment relationship. Indeed, this underscores the effectiveness of counterstories as a tool for legitimizing the experiences and agency of those surviving at the margins of society.

Nonconventional Tactics: Militant Actions and Targets of Labor Contestations

A third attribute of resistance by marginalized workers pertains to nonconventional tactics. In the context of BLM struggles and COVID-19, these strategies comprise active confrontation, including but not limited to labor actions deemed illegal (because of no-strike clauses in particular bargaining agreements) and/or the use of public spaces for making contentious action more conspicuous. At the same time, such tactics may also involve the identification of other targets (in addition to the immediate employer) against whom contestation is directed. These strategies also speak to intersectional identities and highlight the participation of individuals in these actions as workers.

Many of these actions are reflections of the involvement of marginalized workers in direct action as part of their simultaneous participation in social movement activism through radical community organizations and struggles against injustice with deep historical roots.[2] Additionally, the multifaceted and oftentimes systemic vulnerabilities of underrepresented workers also warrant a need to directly engage with policy makers or even to leverage a sense of injustice in the court of public opinion. These aspects shed light on why and how such struggles take particular forms and are also helpful in amplifying unique ways in which these workers express agency even in face of extreme hardship.

In the context of contemporary struggles, the "Scholar Strike" is a compelling example that emphasizes radical action pivoted on intersectional subjugation. Organized in September 2020, participating university faculty across the country, many of them PoC, withheld their labor for two days and engaged in online teach-ins and public outreach to protest the killing of Black people by law enforcement (Madsen 2020). Anthea Butler and Kevin Gannon, lead organizers of the strike, argued that it was important for faculty to bring in their identities as workers because withholding of labor—despite being barred from doing so by faculty bargaining agreements—was an important feature of their resistance. Highlighting these issues was important also because racism has been prevalent on college campuses and has also been a focus of academic research for many protesting faculty (Gannon and Butler 2020). It was also opportune to engage in contentious action around racial issues during the pandemic, given how it ravaged marginalized communities and exacerbated already-existing inequalities.

Minority schoolteachers have also been instrumental in magnifying workplace issues and projecting them on to public forums. For instance, after Breonna Taylor was murdered by a police officer, teachers protesting police brutality and neglect of minority-dominated schools made the cause of racial justice more conspicuous by engaging in visible protests on streets and public junctions. Some organized strikes while others engaged in media outreach, published blogs, and created podcasts. Some teachers also indirectly participated in antiracist contention by assisting protesting students in cases of arrests or tear-gassing (Krauth 2020; Will and Schwartz 2020).

Although schools had been closed because of COVID-19 at the time, teachers engaged in contentious activity as employees of their respective school systems. They recognized that their workplace culture needed to reflect the antiracism they advocated in society. Furthermore, many felt accountable in shaping students' antiracist attitudes and in amplifying marginalized voices in the classroom (Will and Schwartz 2020). Essentially, such examples illustrate not only a confluence of racial and workplace issues but also the innovative acts of resistance in which these individuals participated as working people.

As stated earlier, innovative tactics of contestation also pertain to the target toward which worker opposition is directed. For instance, the intended targets of the Strike for Black Lives movement's activities have been large corporations (or capital in general) involved in profit making at the cost of the well-being of WoC. Although not direct employers, these corporations indirectly employ many underrepresented workers via franchising. Activists' demands in these cases have ranged from pushing corporations to take "unequivocal" measures for ensuring that Black lives matter to advocating for wage increases, unionism without backlash, and childcare support and healthcare benefits (Covert 2020). A push was also generated from within the Strikes for Black Lives movement to pressure and hold politicians accountable for their action against racism. Activists urged movement participants to connect with and demand that local politicians build enabling infrastructure so that all, not just a select few, could thrive (Covert 2020).

Similarly, immigrant WoC have also engaged in direct action. For instance, when government support to their worker centers was withdrawn as a result of a reduction in tax revenue during COVID-19 in June–July 2020, Latinx immigrant workers demonstrated outside New York City Hall. They demanded immediate suspension of these cuts. These worker centers had in fact been instrumental in assisting immigrants in finding dignified jobs requiring OSHA certificates (Frisneda 2020), which helped ensure the socioeconomic well-being of their constituents. Nonetheless, such campaigns were unlike traditional confrontations between workers and employers. Instead, workers (as worker center members) engaged directly with city lawmakers on issues pertaining to decent employment.

Finally, BLM protesters have also targeted traditional labor unions. For example, when the AFL-CIO headquarters building in Washington, D.C., was vandalized during a protest in the night of May 31, 2020, Richard Trumka, former president of the AFL-CIO, responded by "categorically reject[ing] those on the fringes who are engaging in violence and destroying property." He further labeled the "attacks" as "senseless, disgraceful" and accused the protesters of playing "into the hands of those who have oppressed workers of color for generations and detract[ing] from the peaceful, passionate protesters who [were] rightly bringing issues of racism to the forefront" (Gangitano 2020).

However, the counternarrative emphasized by Tamika Mallory, co-founder of Until Freedom, was telling in how it course-corrected the public discourse about the protests and clarified the context of Black people's antiracist struggles:

> What is happening in America is that white nationalism ideology is running wild, and the reason why buildings are burning is because this city, this state, would prefer preserving that white nationalism and that white supremacist mindset over arresting, charging, and helping to convict four officers who killed a Black man. ... Don't talk to us about looting. Y'all are the looters. America has been looting Black people! (Mallory 2020)

Essentially, rather than perceiving these actions as "disgraceful," such counternarratives provide us with a highly nuanced understanding of the historical context of contestation by marginalized communities. For example, the fact that the AFL-CIO had been reluctant to denounce or disaffiliate the International Union of Police Associations was likely a reason the BLM protesters did not feel much empathy for this well-established labor institution. Indeed, as Robinson (1983) argued, mass disruption or massive civil disobedience has long been an important tactic for PoC in delegitimizing the ideologies and institutions that maintain white supremacy in capitalist systems. As underrepresented groups fight for economic, social, and political change, disruptive protests have often been part of their repertoire, given the limited access or ability to affect change through established institutional channels such as unions.

In sum, as some new-age organizers have argued, nonconventional strategies such as those illustrated here are commonly used by PoC. Overlooking these strategies, as has often been the case, does a great disservice to individuals putting themselves on the line for the greater good (Elk 2020). This echoes Robinson's (1983) observations that a holistic critique of contemporary capitalism can be acquired not necessarily from contentious action by industrial workers but from the experiences of the marginalized. A closer focus on the actions of PoC may thus yield deeper insights into new characteristics, contexts, and strategies for labor contestation. A rethinking of labor militancy in industrial relations in conjunction with these aspects is therefore highly imperative going forward.

CONCLUSION

Industrial relations scholars and practitioners tend to emphasize workers' economic struggles at the workplace while the interlinkages between class-based subordination of marginalized workers and other forms of oppression (racial, gendered, etc.) are often overlooked. As a result, traditional industrial relations scholarship has a somewhat blinkered perspective about labor contestation because it sees nontraditional causes and manifestations of contentious actions as unrelated to labor issues. This narrow perspective is also reflected in how statistical information about labor contestation is recorded.

This chapter not only presents a critique of how worker militant action is analyzed and reproduced in research but also problematizes practices of the contemporary labor movement vis-à-vis underrepresented workers. It does so by articulating three attributes of resistance, deployed especially by marginalized workers, that have been relatively overlooked by labor scholars and practitioners.

These attributes of resistance by underrepresented minorities—employee-employer cooperation, supra-economic causes of labor militancy, and nonconventional tactics—undergirded by a counternarrative lens bring to the fore the inadequacies of traditional labor conflict perspectives. Essentially, they shed light on hitherto underacknowledged contexts, embodied experiences, and strategies constituting the struggles of marginalized workers. They also push industrial relations scholars toward integrating these aspects into theorization and empirical analyses of contentious action. Indeed, a renewed focus on underrepresented people's struggles as intentional and serious acts of challenging the status quo, rather than mere blips on the labor resistance radar, can not only provide them with legitimacy but also expand the scope of case studies for labor scholars (Lee and Tapia 2021).

Reimagining a more inclusive conceptualization of labor contestation also has implications for labor practitioners. That the labor movement is likely to lose out on potential sources of leverage and power by ignoring or misclassifying these instances of radical action as unrelated to labor issues seems a perilous but real possibility. However, strategies for a more serious engagement with the marginalized may help mitigate this challenge. Enabling a deeper involvement of activists from underprivileged backgrounds into the labor movement, for instance, may reinvigorate membership and radical consciousness in what has otherwise been perceived as a movement much too close to business interests or as a bastion of the white male. It may also realign the organizing repertoire of unions by introducing innovative tactics into the labor movement and perhaps help in reversing the gradual undermining of labor power.

Marginalized workers also stand to gain from engaging with organized labor; their hitherto atomized actions may be reinforced by the sociopolitical heft of the labor movement. This may also entail greater access to material and organizational resources, which might further translate into political victories.

Labor leaders must therefore act and support these struggles. Reversing the neglect of marginalized groups' radicalism and acknowledging expressions of their agency as well-informed responses to embodied experiences of oppression may indeed be better alternatives for unions to the traditionally bureaucratic—and often gender/color blind—approaches to militant action. This is because these alternatives can undo the erasure of the distinctive lived realities of underrepresented workers and position unions as allies rather than impediments to the self-empowerment of these individuals. This alternative approach can potentially be the tide that lifts all boats and reenergizes organized labor to win the war against injustice to one and all.

ENDNOTES

1. Given the overrepresentation of workers of color in minimum wage jobs, about 31% Black and 26% Latinx workers would benefit from a $15 minimum wage. Similarly, they are likely to make $3,500 per year more through an upward revision in the minimum wage (Economic Policy Institute 2021).

2. See Engeman (2015) for an examination of the embeddedness of WoC in community organizations and Robinson (1983) for a legacy of Black radical struggles rooted in slavery.

REFERENCES

Afridi, L. 2017. "A True General Strike Is Possible in Trump's America." *Al Jazeera.* February 21. https://bit.ly/36fRCIq

Ahmad, A. 2020. "With Their Wildcat Strike, NBA Players Have Pointed the Way Forward." *Jacobin.* August 29. https://bit.ly/3v0Zg3P

Associated Press. 2020. "Oakland McDonald's Workers on Strike After Allegedly Being Told to Wear Dog-Diaper Masks." *Los Angeles Times.* May 26. https://lat.ms/3gZEZDv

Bell, D. 1992. *Faces at the Bottom of the Well: The Permanence of Racism.* New York: Basic Books.

Bhattarai, A. 2020. "For Many Black Business Owners, Importance of Protests Overshadows Cost of Rebuilding." *Washington Post.* June 5. https://wapo.st/3LLzS8k

Bryant, H. 2020. "The Reality of Black Pain Is Breaking American Sports' Status Quo." ESPN. August 27. https://es.pn/3LIQkWJ

Buchanan, L., Q. Bui, and J.K. Patel. 2020. "Black Lives Matter May Be the Largest Movement in U.S. History." *New York Times,* July 3. https://nyti.ms/35a4K18

Budd, J. 2012. *Labor Relations: Striking a Balance.* New York: McGraw-Hill.

Burden-Stelly, C. 2020. "Modern U.S. Racial Capitalism: Some Theoretical Insights." *Monthly Review* July 1. https://bit.ly/3Il0OcZ

Busby, R. 2021. "Op-Ed: Black Businesses Support Raising the Minimum Wage. Why Doesn't the Rest of Corporate America?" CNBC. February 22. https://cnb.cx/3p3LPMC

Gannon, K., and A. Butler. 2020. "Why We Started the #ScholarStrike." CNN. September 8. https://cnn.it/33D2I9C

Cote, J. 2020. "'One Day Stronger': Hundreds of Drivers for MBTA's 'The RIDE' Program Strike Over Health Insurance Cuts." Mass Live. July 13. https://bit.ly/3ByhZ8e

Covert, B. 2020. "Strike for Black Lives: The BLM Movement Comes to Essential Workers." Vox. July 20. https://bit.ly/3H5cjUr

Crenshaw, K. 1989. "Demarginalizing the Intersection of Race and Sex: A Black Feminist Critique of Antidiscrimination Doctrine, Feminist Theory and Antiracist Politics." *University of Chicago Legal Forum* 1989: 139–167.

Cunningham, V. 2020. "The Exhilarating Jolt of the Milwaukee Bucks' Wildcat Strike." *The New Yorker.* August 27. https://bit.ly/3JHipvG

Davis-Faulkner, S., and M. Sneiderman. 2020. "Moneybags for Billionaires, Body Bags for Workers: Organizing in the Time of Pandemics." *New Labor Forum* 29 (3): 82–90.

Delgado, R., and J. Stefancic. 2001. *Critical Race Theory: An Introduction.* New York: New York University Press.

Dixson, A.D., and C.K. Rousseau. 2005. "And We Are Still Not Saved: Critical Race Theory in Education Ten Years Later." *Race Ethnicity and Education* 8 (1): 7–27.

Economic and Policy Institute. 2021. "Why the U.S. Needs a $15 Minimum Wage: How the Raise the Wage Act Would Benefit U.S. Workers and Their Families." Fact Sheet. January 26. https://bit.ly/3I6hWmu

Edwards, Z. 2021. "Racial Capitalism and COVID-19." *Monthly Review.* March 1. https://bit.ly/3sW3zuu

Eidlin, B., 2020. "Last Week's Pro Athletes Strikes Could Become Much Bigger Than Sports." *Jacobin.* August 30. https://bit.ly/3sSQKkT

Elk, M. 2020. "Prison Labor Replaces Striking Garbage Workers in New Orleans." Payday Report. May 9. https://bit.ly/3v2iV3m

Elk, M. 2021. "COVID-19 Strike Wave Interactive Map." Payday Report. https://bit.ly/3o5uQrt

Engeman, C. 2015. "Social Movement Unionism in Practice: Organizational Dimensions of Union Mobilization in the Los Angeles Immigrant Rights Marches." *Work, Employment and Society* 29 (3): 444–461.

Fortune, M. 2020. "Chattanooga Businesses Close to Show Support for Defunding Police." *Chattanooga Times Free Press.* June 16. https://bit.ly/3v4L9L2

Frisneda, R. 2020. "Pro-Immigrant Groups Join BLM Protests at City Hall." City Limits. July 3. https://bit.ly/3I7oRM6

Gall, G. 2013. "Quiescence Continued? Recent Strike Activity in Nine Western European Economies." *Economic and Industrial Democracy* 34 (4): 667–691.

Gangitano, A. 2020. "AFL-CIO: Attack on Headquarters During Night of Protests 'Disgraceful.'" The Hill. June 1. https://bit.ly/3v4AJee

Godard, J. 2011. "What Has Happened to Strikes?" *British Journal of Industrial Relations* 49: 282–305.

Gould, E., and W. Wilson 2020. "Black Workers Face Two of the Most Lethal Preexisting Conditions for Coronavirus—Racism and Economic Inequality." Report. Economic Policy Institute. https://bit.ly/3s3YZLD

ILR School, Cornell University. No date. "Labor Action Tracker." https://striketracker.ilr.cornell.edu

Jacobs, L., S. Davis-Faulkner, R. Pumarol, and M. Sneiderman. 2020. "We Want Bread and Housing Too: Bargaining for the Common Good an Intersectional Feminist Strategy." The Forge. March 31. https://bit.ly/3h2lv0Y

Johns Hopkins University. No date. "COVID-19 Dashboard." Johns Hopkins University Coronavirus Resource Center. https://coronavirus.jhu.edu/map.html

Kelly, J. 2015. "Conflict: Trends and Forms of Collective Action." *Employee Relations* 37 (6): 720–732.

Korpi, W., and M. Shalev. 1979. "Strikes, Industrial Relations and Class Conflict in Capitalist Societies." *British Journal of Sociology* 30 (2): 164–187.

Krauth, O. 2020. "How JCPS Teachers Are Standing Up for Their Black Students During Breonna Taylor Protests." *Louisville Courier-Journal.* June 6. https://bit.ly/3p4HYyX

Lee, T.L., and M. Tapia. 2021. "Confronting Race and Other Social Identity Erasures: The Case for Critical Industrial Relations Theory." *ILR Review* 74 (3): 637–662.

Madsen, J. 2020. "UC Berkeley Professors Take Action in Solidarity with Nationwide Scholar Strike." *Daily Californian*. September 10. https://bit.ly/3I4mXM9

Mallory, T. 2020. "Tamika Mallory Full 'State of Emergency' Speech at the George Floyd Presser in Minneapolis May 29." YouTube. June 1. https://bit.ly/3tLeskA

Marable, M. 2015. *How Capitalism Underdeveloped Black America: Problems in Race, Political Economy, and Society*. Chicago: Haymarket Books.

Matsuda, M. 1995. "Looking to the Bottom: Critical Legal Studies and Reparations." In *Critical Race Theory: The Key Writings That Formed the Movement*. K. Crenshaw, N. Gotanda, G. Peller and K. Thomas, eds. 63–70. New York: The New Press.

McCartin, J. 2007. "Approaching Extinction? The Decline of Strikes in the United States, 1960–2005." In *Strikes Around the World, 1968–2005: Case-Studies of 15 Countries*. S. van der Velden, H. Dribbusch, D. Lyddon, and K. Vandaele, eds. 133–154. Amsterdam: Aksant.

Milkman, R. 2011. "Immigrant Workers, Precarious Work, and the US Labor Movement." *Globalizations* 8 (3): 361–372.

Miller, R., K. Liu, and A.F. Ball. 2020. "Critical Counter-Narrative as Transformative Methodology for Educational Equity." *Review of Research in Education* 44 (1): 269–300.

Milner IV, H.R., and T.C. Howard. 2013. "Counter-Narrative as Method: Race, Policy and Research for Teacher Education." *Race, Ethnicity and Education* 16 (4): 536–561.

National Association for the Advancement of Colored People (NAACP). 2021. "Criminal Justice Fact Sheet." May 24. https://bit.ly/3sS6S60

Pessin, H. 2020. "The Movement for Black Lives Is Different This Time." New Politics. July 11. https://bit.ly/3H4ZjxR

Phillips-Cunningham, D.T. 2020. "The Long History of Black Women Organizing in Georgia Might Decide Senate Control." *Washington Post*. December 10. https://wapo.st/3BDdeKI

Rhomberg, C., and S. Lopez. 2021. "Understanding Strikes in the 21st Century: Perspectives from the United States." In *Power and Protest (Research in Social Movements, Conflicts and Change, Vol. 44)*. L. Leitz, ed. 37–62. Bingley: Emerald Publishing.

Robinson, C.J. 1983. *Black Marxism: The Making of the Black Radical Tradition*, revised and updated 3rd ed. London: Zed Books.

Schermerhorn, T., and L. Sustar. 2020. "The Movement for Black Lives and Labor's Revival." Labor Notes. October 27. https://bit.ly/3oYwZqY

Shierholz, H., and M. Poydock. 2020. "Continued Surge in Strike Activity Signals Worker Dissatisfaction with Wage Growth." Economic Policy Institute. February 20. https://bit.ly/3I4mo5i

Solórzano, D.G., and T.J. Yosso. 2002. "Critical Race Methodology: Counter-Storytelling as an Analytical Framework for Education Research." *Qualitative Inquiry* 8 (1): 23–44.

Tai, D.B.G., A. Shah, C.A. Doubeni, I.G. Sia, and M.L. Wieland. 2021. "The Disproportionate Impact of COVID-19 on Racial and Ethnic Minorities in the United States." *Clinical Infectious Diseases* 72 (4): 703–706.

Tait, V. 2016. *Poor Workers' Unions: Rebuilding Labor from Below*. Chicago: Haymarket Books.

US Bureau of Labor Statistics. 2020a. "8 Major Work Stoppages Began During 2020." TED: The Economics Daily. March 4. https://bit.ly/3LMRTTC

US Bureau of Labor Statistics. 2020b. "Major Work Stoppages in 2019" and related table, "Annual Work Stoppages Involving 1,000 or More Workers, 1947–2019." February 11.

Virdee, S. 2019. "Racialized Capitalism: An Account of Its Contested Origins and Consolidation." *Sociological Review* 67 (1): 3–27.

Wang, C. 2020. "Damaged Asian Businesses Show Solidarity with Black Lives Matter Protesters." NBC News. June 4. https://nbcnews.to/3BAJePj

Weeks, M., and M. Sneiderman. 2016. "Why Labor and the Movement for Racial Justice Should Work Together." In *These Times*. September 2. https://bit.ly/3h0SQtl

Will, M., and S. Schwartz. 2020. "'Teachers Cannot Be Silent': How Educators Are Supporting Black Students After Protests." *Education Week*. June 1. https://bit.ly/3BA1qIO

Williams, N.R. 2020. "Workers United: Intersectionality and Labor." *Labor* 17 (4): 74–77.

Yu, K.-H. 2014. "Organizational Contexts for Union Renewal." *Relations industrielles/industrial relations* 69 (3): 501–523.

CHAPTER 8

Critical Lenses in the Global South: Two Scholars in Conversation

TAMARA L. LEE
Rutgers University
School of Management and Labor Relations

NICOLE BURROWES
Rutgers University
Department of History

Abstract

This conversation between Tamara Lee and Nicole Burrowes is based on a series of verbal and written exchanges. It explores their life histories and how they started doing international research; how Black feminist and global critical race theory informs their work and approaches; and what we can learn from the Global South. Interspersed quotations add structure to the storytelling and thematic emphasis on critical theory and praxis (see, e.g., Tolliver 2022).

I mean it's been really exciting for someone like me, both in terms of the personal desires I have to remain bonded with the working-class culture and experience that I came from as well as the sort of southern black aspect of that and at the same time to be part of a diasporic world culture of ideas and to see how can there be a kind of interplay between all of those different forces.

—bell hooks (1994: 2)

Tamara: Hi, Nicole. I'm just so happy we finally got together and we're going to have this conversation. Maybe we'll just talk a little bit about who we are as scholars and what called us to this work. The reason I want to start there is because it formed the foundation of my methodologies and my approaches to the things that I study,[1] so it just makes sense for us to start there for me, and hopefully it'll do the same for you.

So I came to academia really late, like my fourth career choice. I was an engineer, and then I was a lawyer, and the thing is, when Black folks go into the professional world, there's a lot of stuff we learn in our theoretical training that doesn't really reflect back the things that were happening to me as a worker, and in relation to the folks I was trying to help (Daniels 2008).

And so, in engineering, I thought I was helping workers, and then I realized that the science was used to hurt them (Grey 1996), so then I left that work. With law school I thought "I'm gonna protect workers through the institutions and the laws." And then I think in that practice I realized that the laws seem to me to be the problem (see, e.g., Kim and Khoshgozaran 2017); they're the things that are holding us back.

And so then, I was like, "I gotta go and be part of the people who are thinking about policy, and how we create institutions and what institutions are supposed to do," and that's how I ended up in academia—like super-duper late—and most of that was just trial and error as a Black worker in the United States. Lived experiences led me to try to imagine some other way that we could organize our political economy (Iglesias 2000). And so here I am, and my major research area is to study work and institutions, capitalist institutions, and alternatives to these things for justice.

And we were talking off the record a minute ago about the tremendous loss of bell hooks this week, and I remember reading something along the way in all that education leading up to academia, where bell hooks said, you know, to be Black, and to be an educator is in itself to be radical (hooks 1994). Right? I think about that when I think about doing work outside of the United States. And I'm looking at Cuba, and I'm thinking about what "radical" means (Castro 2002)—what it means to do work there, what it means to be qualified to take an academic lens to a society that's not my own and organized differently. That came out of that chronology for me personally, as a worker and a scholar. Hopefully, all of that will make sense as our conversation goes forward, but I just wanted to give that brief intro.

Nicole: That's absolutely fascinating.

I didn't plan to go into academia either, but as an undergraduate I received a scholarship to study abroad. I went to the Dominican Republic because I wanted to learn Spanish, Caribbean history, and I grew up around so many Dominicans in New York City. In the D.R., I took a class with a historian. Her name was Natasha Calderón. On the weekends, she would take me to the *bateys*, which were the communities where migrant Haitian sugar cane workers were living at the time. And so I used to work there with her on the weekends to support those communities. She was also part of the Dominican–Haitian Solidarity movement. And she identified as "negra," not "morena" or "india," but Black. She had seven children, and she was part of the women's movement in the Dominican Republic, which at the time was working against domestic violence. And here she was teaching us Caribbean history, teaching us about capitalism and imperialism, and the *Open Veins of Latin America* (Galeano 1973). She had this very powerful and active life. She also introduced me to the work of Walter Rodney[2] and suggested that I do my first research project on Guyana, since my family was from there.

And so navigating the world of the Dominican Republic with its complicated history of race and nation—as a Black person who had braids—meant that people constantly thought I was Haitian, even though there were Dominicans who were my complexion. I had a number of really terrible experiences based on that, but the intriguing and impactful part was that this was a political entry into this world and history of the Caribbean.[3]

I didn't go into academia after I graduated from college, though. Throughout college, I was doing community organizing work in New York City, and in the South. And so, when I graduated, I continued in that vein. Around 1996, a crew of NYC organizers and I started the Sista II Sista Freedom School for Young Women of Color. It was modeled off of the idea of freedom schools started by the Student Nonviolent Coordinating Committee in Mississippi in 1964. During the civil rights movement, freedom schools were created to counter white supremacy and miseducation in the South, provide relevant education, teach people to radically question, and develop activists.[4]

I mention this particular experience because it influences my work in the academy, my questions, and approach. Those of us who founded Sista II Sista were all organizers within different movements. When we came together to launch that organization, it was because we felt that there wasn't enough space for young women of color, there wasn't a focus on them, and there weren't enough programs in the city that spoke to their needs. And here we were, Black and Latina[5] young adult women in Brooklyn starting something for teenagers. We wanted to support them to use their collective power, to think about holistic approaches to their lives, and to tackle some of the concrete issues that were occurring in Bushwick, Brooklyn.

We originally planned to do work around economic justice because all of us came from working-class or low-income backgrounds. And then one day, we had a meeting with the membership because two young women were killed by police. When we were talking about these incidents, other issues of violence started coming up, and we realized that the majority of those young women had experienced some sort of violence, a lot of sexual violence. And even though we weren't that much older than them, we couldn't ignore that, and a lot of us had experienced that kind of violence too. And so we ended up organizing around that. We were trying to figure out how to deal with questions of interpersonal violence and police violence, with a gender-based lens. We didn't use this language at the time, but we were doing abolitionist and feminist work.[6]

I just went into this long history, but that work was about building a base of community organizers—Black and Latina young women; challenging different forms violence—sexual violence, economic violence, and state violence—because we organized around policing back then; and trying to challenge a culture that told us that young Black and Latina women were not worthy of protection, support, and love. All that work informed how I ended up coming into academia later and realizing that a Black feminist lens was critical for me. I also worked in film for a long time, as well. Anyway, if you know community organizers, you know that they are some of the most serious intellectuals on the planet. We always had lots of questions, we were always studying, and we were always thinking about how to transform society, and so this work made me want to really engage some of the questions I had about how the world ended up the way that it is, in a sustained way. And you know, when we said "Black and Latina" in a place like Brooklyn, that was local, and *definitely* international.[7] And so how did we begin to work together across some of the differences in culture *and* experience?

Tamara: So this is a great point for us to connect on race and ethnicity.

The first time I went to Cuba, I was in law school. It was the '90s. And listen, I grew up in Indiana—like, a small town in Indiana—where really in terms of race and my race consciousness, if you weren't Black, you were white. I didn't have any sort of foundation nor was I surrounded at that time, in that area, by any concepts of ethnicity.

So when I visited Cuba for the first time, I actually was like "Black folks is here!"— because I had no concept, no training, and in an Indiana high school and public school system no one teaches you about the transatlantic slave trade and why Black folks are in certain locations. And this idea—my picture of Cuban people—was those are Latino, those are "Hispanic" people, and it wasn't racialized for me. So when I got to Cuba and there were Black people—Black people who look like me—who were speaking Spanish and living, this entire thing was a wake up to me on the fact that there was a part of understanding the world that I didn't know.

That was very embarrassing to me as a Black person. How did I not know that [Black] folks were here? And then connecting with Cubans from this new racialized lens, I started to see reflections of what it meant to be Black in the United States. In Cuba, I recognize poverty. I recognize subordination. I recognize some things that I think across the diaspora Black people would be able to recognize (see, e.g., Briggs 2018). I also recognize things in the cuisine! Though I had never had Cuban food before in my life, I do know about a community dumping whatever they have in a soup and eating that as a village. I know that life, right? And I started to connect and be interested in Cuba because I started thinking, "Wow, okay, here's a place with a whole different set of institutions, a whole different set of ideologies about what it means to be free and liberated—not just as Black people, but from capitalism." And then I think about growing up as poor as I did in the United States and how we also had the conditions that you would see in Cuba—[they] were in my neighborhood in the United States! And I started thinking then in the '90s on my first visit in Cuba, if I had the kind of institutions and social welfare nets that Cuban socialism has, would that solve some of the problems that we have as Black people in the United States, right?

What kinds of methodologies will enhance our understanding of their lives? Can liberation have different meanings in different cultural contexts? Can First World and Third World women collaborate effectively on feminist projects?

—Adrien Katherine Wing (2000: 13)

So that was the first entry for me into thinking about the role of institutions: Can they solve structural racism? If we fix the structures—whatever fixing it means— does racism go away? Is it impacted? What is it, what are the differences, is there still going to be subordination? And I think when we cross boundaries and look in different regions of where there are Black folks, and these different systems and institutions, different laws, that this is something that needs to be done more because it has implications for policy (see, e.g., Busey and Coleman-King 2020). It has implications for definitions and conceptualization of what the relationship is between race and power, how it shifts, how it doesn't shift.

Right. So maybe we can talk more about race, ethnicity, institutions, borders— what that all means—in terms of being an academic or an organizer, because I don't think you … did you stop being an organizer?

Nicole: That's what I'm doing right here right now, working with a national strategy team to connect birthing justice to abolition work—how do we create the kinds of communities we need to sustain people after they are born? But I think I shared some of your experience when I went to Cuba, also in the 1990s, with the Venceremos Brigade, with members of Sista II Sista. I remember thinking, "Wow, they are figuring out how to do healthcare and education differently," and, I also felt like there was progress on some of the bigger questions we were grappling with at the time. It was like, wow, despite all of their problems and challenges, a different type of system is possible. And so for me it opened up a whole bunch of doors about how we as a society can choose what we value, and that if we choose to, we could imagine something different, we can create something else that genuinely deals with people's needs.

Tamara: But even when we're going back and forth, you know, whether it's Cuba or the Dominican Republic or Guyana, we are, as researchers, as Black people, going back and forth, switching lenses on being there and being Black in the United States.

Turning the gaze back on itself may help the new comparativist inhabit the gaze differently, by recognizing that in looking at others we are always also looking at ourselves.

—Brenda J. Cossman (2000: 37)

When I go to Cuba and wonder … "Are things there working? Can they do healthcare? Can they do all this stuff?" Number one, I saw this as an example of non-white people having power to construct realities, right? So that's number one. But then it's like, it was problematic for me to even use the word "non-white" because in Cuba, whiteness is a thing. And there are some systems of subordination where folks in Cuba wouldn't be white [in the United States] but they're white in Cuba (Guridy 2010). And now I'm a Black person from the United States, trying to decide, and figure out what the racial language is, what the racial construct is, and how that relates to power and their institutions. And having to sort of, and this goes to methodologies, park my lens, my Western capitalist, Black, queer, woman—all the identities that I bring, right? And park that for a second. Really spending time and going deep institutionally to make sure that I could even understand how to describe people, especially coming from the United States and with the diplomatic contestations between the US and Cuba.

What that meant to me during my doctoral studies was, "I'ma go to Cuba, but I'm going to enroll in their university," and I actually studied at their trade union school with them. Just to signal to them that I was open minded about the way in which they see global capitalism, the way in which they see the United States and democracy, right? Because I can't write a research project on democracy and the Cuban workplace without understanding what their construction of democracy is and who gets to make decisions about the institutional rules of how they practice democracy.[8] So, to me, there was no way for me to understand that as a Black American without spending a significant amount of time embedded there and learning from their perspective. That doesn't mean I had to believe them, right? But it did mean that I had to understand them before I could write about them. At least for me, it wouldn't [otherwise] feel authentic.

And there was a tipping point. I got into year five or something, where I'm starting to be able to think like Cubans would inherently think about something, and then immediately be able to switch to how Americans would think about A, B, or C. It became like a language. The Cuban constructs and their institutions, once you're there long enough, you can start to understand their conversations. And I feel like a lot of people do work in places not their own, and we don't do a deep enough socio-structural foundation in terms of epistemologies and paradigms, and even the literature that we're engaging. Even if you don't buy it, you don't believe it, or you don't think it's persuasive, you got to know it. You got to understand why it's important to the place or people that you're studying.

Critical race theory recognizes that the experiential knowledge of people of color is legitimate, appropriate, and critical to understanding, analyzing, and teaching about racial subordination. In fact, critical race theorists view this knowledge as a strength and draw explicitly on the lived experiences of people of color by including such methods as storytelling, family histories, biographies, scenarios, parables, cuentos, testimonios, chronicles, and narratives.

—Daniel G. Solórzano and Tara J. Yosso (2002: 26)

Nicole: Yeah, I think that's a big deal. It's important to know the literature of the place that you're studying. Sometimes people assume that there is nothing written.

It's really important to do a deep dive on the local work, written and nonwritten sources, because it is really problematic—especially for people in North America and Europe, where there is such hegemony in publishing—to do work on places that have a tradition of doing work on themselves, without recognizing this. I think that's really important to highlight the need for the deep engagement that you mention. My current book is on British Guiana in the 1930s. I look at African–Indian relations and a series of labor rebellions that took place in 1935. In that particular moment, there was environmental crisis in terms of flooding; there was political crisis because British Guiana had just become a crown colony in the 20th century, which meant the curtailment of the very limited political enfranchisement that the population had; and economic crisis, because it was the middle of the Great Depression. And so I am really interested how Black and Indian sugar workers and their families led these rebellions and managed to come together when everything was stacked against them, despite the fact that they were pitted against each other for generations.

And for some historical background, indenture contracts ended in 1920. The indenture system brought a majority South Asian workforce to British Guiana in the aftermath of enslavement, as a strategy to break Black bargaining power and tie new populations to the plantation. My work shows, in the tradition of global critical race theory, that despite the fact that enslavement and indenture had ended by the 1930s, those systems had afterlives that continued in the 1930s. I was interested in how these groups who were structurally positioned against each other, who had dealt with issues of divide and rule, who had been segregated in terms of residential arrangements, who came from different cultural and religious backgrounds, who were politically disenfranchised, and who had suffered severe environmental and economic crisis—how *they* managed to mount a force against both the colonial state and private sugar enterprises. It is historical work, but it is also an intervention in current politics. The racial tensions in Guyana today, while informed by white supremacy, are primarily played out between the two largest racial groups: people of Indian and African descent.

My family is from Guyana, but I grew up in Brooklyn, which is very different from growing up in Guyana. Even though I spent time there as a kid, I didn't fully understand what was happening politically. As a daughter of Guyana, I always wanted to understand the racial tensions that existed. Before I even started working on this project, I sat with a lot of elders in Guyana and asked them about their experience and how they felt about the history and future of the country. I asked a lot of questions. One of the people who was extremely generous was Andaiye, a woman who co-founded a women's organization called Red Thread in the 1980s, which brought together grassroots women from Indigenous, Black, and Indian backgrounds to deal with issues of poverty and violence. Andaiye was one of those straight shooters, you know? Someone who told it like it was! She died in 2019, and there is a book edited by Alissa Trotz that just came out with her writing (Andaiye and Trotz 2021). She is one of the people who I think is really important if you're interested in learning about intersectional analysis coming from the Global South that takes seriously questions of work, gender, race, class, and colonialism.

Anyway, when we met years ago, Andaiye didn't know me, you know. I told her I was interested in learning more about Guyana's history, her work with Walter Rodney and the Working People's Alliance, her work with Red Thread, and the current conditions in Guyana. She sat with me and my sister for hours in her house! It had a significant impact on me. She wrote about questions of social reproduction, how we count women's labor, how to organize the "unorganized," and how to intervene in the situation of racial conflict that was created by imperialism, conquest, enslavement, and the indenture system. I think her work is important for us to think about how we continue to intervene in these areas especially now. Exxon is currently in Guyana and causing a lot of problems, not just environmentally but also in terms of this race question and governance.

Tamara: So yeah, I'm listening to you, and it took me back to … countless Cuban women, especially elders. And you know I was always blown away by the storytelling of folks in Cuba who had a much more vivid, accurate, and global knowledge of history. They understand and know colonialism and imperialism, of course, because they've been through countless independence fights from different colonial powers. As you were talking, I was thinking about this relationship—between imperialism, colonialism, and then identity formation—we're talking about constructs obviously, right? And one of the things that's really difficult, I find, about being an "United Stater" who studies Cuba is that—and especially also to be a critical race scholar—is that the way in which colonialism played out in Cuba, and most recently the '59 revolution, that there was such a strong need at the moment after the 1959 revolution to identify nationally. National identity in some ways became more salient than the racial identities that they associate with capitalism and the wrongs of society: "Once we get rid of capitalism. We're going to focus on a national identity." And they literally try to do a color-blind society, right? That was the great experiment that, I would argue, they're still trying to perfect.

But then what happens is that they, with the force of a new government, with the force of a new constitution, with the force of new structures—economic and otherwise (Zabala Argüelles 2021)—replaced or supplanted racial identities (e.g., white, Black) with propaganda and dialogue about national identity. (There's a critical juncture happening right now in terms of race and reconstruction of an African identity separate from the national identity, which is very interesting to watch.) But imperialism in Cuba led to a revolutionary national identity—the salient identity—and they try to set up their society in that way.

What I reckon with now is the sheer force of a global capitalism that is racialized—and what that means in Cuba. Do they have the ability to carve out from the racism of global capitalism and actually make good on having a color-blind socialism? But whenever they open up their markets a little, whenever they try to [respond to] severe economic conditions, what happens is, many of the Cubans who are abroad, who have money and resources to send remittances back to the island, are "white." Now we've got a whole familiar racial divide, which I think Cuba was very slow to recognize was going to be a problem for them, and now we're at the moment where, you know, there's #BlackLivesMatter. Now you see subgroup and identity formation around African consciousness. There's some overlap—homegrown and exogenous—with this racial awakening that we've had recently in the US.

So I find myself thinking, as a scholar, a lot about what decolonization means, what imperialism means, and what are the trickle-down consequences of that on institutions—domestic and global—and what consequences that has for people on the ground, whether we're studying workers or organizers, or any other type of body in another city.

Nicole: When you were talking about what happened in 1959 and Cuban identity, I think that same process was kind of shut down in British Guiana, right? In 1953, a Marxist multiracial government was elected in British Guiana, and it became the first casualty of the Cold War in the Western Hemisphere. This experiment in self-government was shut down after 133 days by the British because they were afraid that British Guiana would move into the communist domain. Then the movement that created that government ended up being split along racial lines, and that has to do with internal dynamics, yes, but it also has to do with US intervention.

And so the nationalist movement was completely torn apart, and this moment that could have led to something different was denied due to British, and later, CIA-based US intervention. People are still living with the aftermath today, which included race riots between Blacks and Indians in the 1960s, before British Guiana became an independent Guyana in 1966.

Tamara: Can you talk to me a little bit about that in particular? One of the things we share is the US imperialist relationship with the world—US intervention. So, when you're doing research … And listen, being born, raised in the United States, … I guess I was just thinking that US intervention is always looming. It's so palpable in the lived experiences and collective histories of the people in Cuba. So how does that impact, if at all, how you are as a scholar when you're engaging in research? You have to talk about US intervention, and you're from the United States. How does that impact how you move, what you do, how you approach?

Nicole: Yes, I think that's an important question. I listen to people, and I think that's kind of my way of operating in the world, period, right? I think there's sometimes hostility toward the US, but also this desire to go to the US, so the relationship to the US is complicated. Like a lot of people in Cuba, people in Guyana have family in the US. So, in Guyana, there is this love–hate relationship, sometimes depending on who the people are, their experience, and how political they are, right? But mostly for me it's really about building relationships, listening, and working to avoid making a lot of assumptions.

Tamara: Great advice for doing this work. I also feel it a lot in terms of the positionality of doing research in a place that has been colonized or harmed by the US. I have to be very careful in my analysis. You and I do this in data collection: We listen a lot, we make sure that we speak to different types of voices, right? That's part of the process. But then, when I'm analyzing data, I always have someone that I trust in Cuba read and give it to me straight, right? I don't want to be the equivalent of a "white Savior" on a global scale. I'm not going to, you know, only say good things about Cuba, or if I find myself really trying to write, and understand, and give deference to the Cuban perspective, make sure that I'm not romanticizing it. And I can't do that with my own lens. I have to give it over to somebody there to give me notes, and I think that's a practice that we could all use. Everything's not perfect in Cuba. And, you know, sometimes we need that check. Because I will sometimes look at Cuba and be like, yeah, that's really fucked up, and you know, the poverty is overwhelming and whatever, but y'all got healthcare and universal education, and those are my biggest struggles in the United States. And to me, I'm like, whoa, but you can't do that sort of comparison! I think is better if you submit your analysis to somebody from that place, and [they can] help push you to be more complicated, more nuanced, more analytically rigorous in the context of imperialism.

Nicole: I have a question. You were talking about the more recent iterations of people of African descent in Cuba or people who identify as people of African descent, building movements. How do you see that work playing out historically—because there were iterations of this before, right? How do you think about this?

Tamara: You know, listen, this iteration of it in Cuba is happening during the first non-Castro regime. It's also a critical moment in the relationship between the US and Cuba. Obama made things a little softer, then Trump came in and reversed it, and Biden is more like Trump than he's like Obama. And I feel like we think about political apertures like these—openings for revolution—or for, you know, uprising. So I think it's an important political moment for this conversation to happen, number one. Number two, I think Fidel was very much loved, and still is, by an overwhelming majority of Cubans on the island. I think under this new president, the national identity is also shifting at the same time that racial identity is reconstructing, right? Before it was easier to not have to identify racially because everyone, you know, a lot of people would say "I'm a *fidelista*." The Cuban [national] identity was the first and primary and most salient identity. Now is a political moment in which folks, disproportionately, feel as though they are being left behind or that there are racial differences that are untenable under Cuban ideology. This is not a new conversation with the government, but this is a new government, and this is a point when there's questions about what the national identity should be post-Castro and under a new constitution. So I think some folks see this as a moment.

I also think that whenever there's "a moment" in Cuba, there's US intervention that is part of this. So—and I don't want to take away the autonomy of the Cuban people and their discussion about race, which is very important, and historic—but it also has intervention by the US, who is fueling those divides. This has always been [US political] strategy in Cuba—to pit people against each other. So that they tear themselves up from the inside, right? And so the truth is that that conversation in Cuba is not free from our unclean hands. And the US has already been involved, and that's unfortunate because my opinion has always been that whatever Cubans are going to do, Cubans should do without the US intervening. So this is a moment, but also covert operations. It was wild when I was on the ground in Cuba and the US was very open about the fact that they had infiltrated the hip-hop movement in Cuba, and were fueling anti-government rhetoric that was racialized, right? We did that. Does that mean there's no real conversation that Cubans need to have about race? No, it doesn't mean that, but it does mean that we again are engaging in US intervention in a conversation that would otherwise be a [domestic] conversation.

Nicole: Right.

Tamara: So that's a separate conversation, though: the relationship between Cubans and the Cuban government and Black Cubans with African Americans, two separate conversations with separate consequences. If I'm invited to observe and listen and learn from that conversation that they're having, I think it will improve my research and the way in which I talk about Cuba. But that has to be a conversation that I'm invited to. I don't think I have the judgment to tell Cuba what's racist and not racist and who's Black and who's not Black.

Given CRT's sociohistoric origin in the United States, we caution against the use of US theories as dominant frames for thinking about race and racism. Black anti-racist and decolonial theories have been, are, and will continue to be generated from the Global South.

—Christopher L. Busey and Chonika Coleman-King (2020: 5)

Nicole: One of the things you point to is a level of humility. I think that is an important quality in order to really do some of that research that we are talking about.

I think the other thing that came up for me, too, about being a US-based scholar, is related to this situation where ExxonMobil is in Guyana ... where they have pretty much built what stands to be one of their largest centers for fossil fuel production in the world. They started exploring there several years after they got kicked out of Venezuela. Now they have found enormous oil deposits, and they have set up this enterprise at a time when the world is saying no to fossil fuels. For some Guyanese, it seems like this grand opportunity to use oil money to lift people out of poverty. Guyana used to be called one of the poorest countries in the hemisphere. But this oil extraction is extremely dangerous for the entire world because the rain forests in Guyana serve a critical role in absorbing greenhouse gases. And so here is Exxon, this company that has been flouting environmental laws in Guyana and beyond, and talking out of two sides of its mouth. As a US-based scholar, I feel some level of responsibility because we're allowing these companies that are based here to go around the world and do all kinds of damage.[9]

Tamara: So, what is our responsibility as people in the US, as US scholars, as people who are paying attention to these questions of race and labor and gender and imperialism and even in language, right? Part of our responsibility is to push against the way in which US scholars talk about other countries. I was listening to you about Exxon and global exploitation. One thing that happens a lot with me when I'm in Cuba is that things that are happening to them, the rest of the world doesn't even read about it. Nobody knows about what Exxon is doing in Guyana more than the people who are there, right? So, what is your role as a scholar in trying to fit that into our literature and journals, and how do we describe it? In labor and employment literature, we talk about "emerging economies," which is the new "Third World nation." But can I just call them "exploited nations" instead of "emerging economies"? There's a reason why they're poor that doesn't entirely have to do with choices that they have made—that Exxon could have the power to do these things, and whatever Exxon does put those folks in a situation where they must decide between these rights and those rights and how they set up their systems. There's an exogenous force that's always happening. So how do we give weight to this when we're trying to write in our journals and we have a 30-page limit to just get to it?

Nicole: I think one of the things that we do is a lot of translation.

Tamara: Circling back to bell hooks, I think one of the things we have to do, which doesn't get done a lot because we, especially in the US, hide behind this false neutrality of social science is to admit that researchers are not politically neutral. There is no political neutrality. To even decide that translation is necessary, how much backstory to give, and whether to call it an "emerging economy" or an "exploited economy" is a political decision. And I feel like that's one of the things I learned from bell hooks is that we are lying to ourselves if we think knowledge is apolitical. And it's my role to step in there and do some translation. That's a choice and that doesn't always sit well with social science methodologies.

Nicole: I think that the same is true of the humanities, right? And definitely with history, where sometimes people frown on politically engaged work. But the truth is, you are choosing a side when you are "neutral."

Tamara: Yeah. And if we *don't* do it, we've chosen a side. Yeah, absolutely. If you don't make political choices, you are doing something to our collection of knowledge. *Not* engaging and *not* understanding what's happening in terms of imperialism and Western hegemonic theories is to continue those hierarchies and become an eraser of the agency of the place and people we're writing about.

Nicole: I am also thinking about the politics of citation—lifting up people who have shaped our thinking and citing them. I think lifting up their voices and highlighting their work when we have an opportunity, and sometimes deliberately doing partnerships with people in the Global South, is also important.

Tamara: You just described is what organizers do all the time.

We have to think again, all those of us who do not want to build careers. We need, first, to identify the world we want to build, not in the old language of "isms," but in a new language that has clarity and purpose. In sum, my commitment to the global campaign to count women's unwaged work comes from the fact that my goal is a world which values caring labour because, as Selma James has put it, it values caring as the essence of the relationships among people.

—Andaiye and Alisso Trotz (2021: 18)

Nicole: I have one more question for you. How do you feel like the work that you're doing around Cuba impacts scholarship in the US and the movements here?

Tamara: Yeah, I mean, you know, there's always been a very big love for Cuba in the US Black liberation movement. I mean, you can see—we're on Zoom right now, and for the record, my living room has a graffiti picture of Assata Shakur, who is still now in Cuba and has been housed and protected there by the revolutionary Cuban government. So, for me, Cuba is always a model for movements that want to say a "fuck you" to the American government. Like, somehow this small island nation has frequently and consistently fought back against the United States and the US government. And for those of us in the US labor movement, social movements, and civil rights movements, a lot of what people are fighting against—our institutions, governments that they feel that don't care or are intentionally harming us enslaving us, Jim Crow-ing us ... I mean, we're still arguing about voting rights in 2021—this relationship between the state and citizens is always an important one.

I think Cuba also represents, like I would say about the Global South and anywhere else that's not a mature neoliberal capitalist state, that another world is possible. It's another model to the way in which we think democracy should work, the way in which we think a political system should work. And that is a question at the very heart of any society: What is democracy?

I also think Cuba has done a lot with respect to showing what a society looks like when it lifts up culture and the arts. If your government, if your society values culture and the arts, it changes what your society is and where it's going. There's no meeting in Cuba, there's no conversation that's important in Cuba, which doesn't start with children doing some sort of performance that opens our hearts and our minds to get to the business of the day. So I often bring that back with me when I come back into the United States, and we're just in such a rush to do all these things, and we're so policy forward—and it's so disconnected from my cultures and my identities in particular in the labor movement. So I think that Cuba values culture and storytelling and history, and those are some things that I feel are sometimes missing from traditional labor and employment discourse on movements.

And also, the commitment and the role of an organizer and the role of a lawyer in Cuban socialism. I will tell you, I left the practice of law in the United States, because in the US a lawyer has to swear to uphold the laws and constitution. And when you wake up and realize that the laws and constitutions are the problem, but you're still sworn to uphold them. This was like an untenable situation for me. In Cuba, the role of a lawyer is to transform society. So a lawyer is inherently an activist. In the US, an activist lawyer is a bad thing. For some reason, we get penalized for wanting institutional change. And if we advise our clients to break the law to bring about institutional change, we can actually lose our license.

And so when I think about the role of an educator, pedagogy, all that stuff, to me Cuba really has some clarity that I think gets clouded when you bring it into the capitalist world, especially when we think about Black liberation. What are we fighting for as Black Americans? Are we trying to be Black capitalists? Because capitalism doesn't really bring us all up, we know. So, what is liberation? And I think that we can look to Cuba, we can look to other places, for imagination. What do we want? What does freedom look like? What are different notions of abolition? [Cuban] folks have been doing it for 60-plus years, and they've had failures, but they've had some successes. And I think, you know, that's what we need to look at.

What about you?

Nicole: I mean, when you were talking about what freedom looks like, and what liberation means, I think another question that helps us learn from the Global South is "What does solidarity mean?" We can especially learn this from Black and Brown women—how they conceptualize, how they engage, how they build community. ... Some of the lessons are that we can't paper over difference, nor ignore how communities are targeted differently; that we have to know and study each other's histories, life experiences and stories; that we need to pay attention to positionality and overlapping oppressions; that we have to incorporate *and* challenge culture; that we need to center those who are marginalized; that we need to build relationships; and that borders are a problem (see, e.g., Alexander 2006, Andaiye and Trotz 2021, Boyce Davies 2007, Hosein and Outar 2016, and Trotz 2000). We don't always make these kinds of connections in terms of what people have been doing for generations. I think it is important to highlight some of the voices from the Global South around questions of solidarity because wherever there was genocide, colonialism, racial capitalism, and continuing imperialism, fractured societies were left in their wake, right? And so people in the Global South have done a lot of work trying to figure out how to deal with the real-life aftermath— the racial division, the gender oppression, the economic consequences, the lack of sovereignty—that were produced. And I think we have a lot to learn with them for our society here, and thinking about what a more just world would look like, and how to build solidarity beyond these borders.

Tamara: I think that's a wrap.

ENDNOTES

1. "I came to theory because I was hurting—the pain within me was so intense that I could not go on living. I came to theory desperate, wanting to comprehend—to grasp what was happening around and within me. Most importantly, I wanted to make the hurt go away. I saw in theory then a location for healing." (hooks 1994: 59).

2. Walter Rodney was a Marxist and Pan-Africanist scholar and activist from Guyana. He was active as a teacher and activist across the globe, but particularly in Jamaica, Tanzania, the United States, and Guyana. In Guyana, he was a leading member of the Working People's Alliance. He was assassinated by the government of Guyana in 1980 because of his work for democracy, multiracial class-based alliance, and socialism. His written works include *A History of the Guyanese Working People, 1881–1905* (1981), *How Europe Underdeveloped Africa* (1972), and *A History of the Upper Guinea Coast, 1545–1800* (1970).

3. For discussions of the dynamics of race in the Dominican Republic and the relationship to Haiti, see Eller (2016), García-Peña (2016), Mayes (2014), Ricourt (2016), Sagas (2000), and Wright (2015).

4. For background on Freedom Summer 1964, see Dittmer (1995), Hale (2018), and Payne (1996).

5. "Black and Latina" was how we came to identify ourselves, but as we know, "Black" is a diverse identity, and most of the Latinas in the organization identified as "Afro-Latina."

6. For more about Sista II Sista, see Burrowes (2018), Burrowes, Cousins, Rojas, and Ude (2017), and Sista II Sista (2016).

7. Members of Sista II Sista came from many backgrounds—American, Latinx, Brazilian, Dominican, Puerto Rican, Jamaican, Nigerian, Trinidadian, Chilean, Venezuelan, and Guyanese—to name a few.

8. For anti-imperialist understandings of Cuban democracy, see Fuller (1992).

9. For more information, see Juhasz (2021) and Trotz and Bulkan (2020).

REFERENCES

Alexander, M. Jacqui. 2006. *Pedagogies of Crossing: Meditations on Feminism, Sexual Politics, Memory, and the Sacred.* Durham: Duke University Press.

Andaiye and Alissa Trotz. 2021. *The Point Is to Change the World: Selected Writings of Andaiye.* London: Pluto Press.

Boyce Davies, Carole. 2007. *Left of Karl Marx: The Political Life of Black Communist Claudia Jones.* Durham: Duke University Press.

Briggs, Anthony Q. 2018. "Second Generation Caribbean Black Male Youths Discuss Obstacles to Educational and Employment Opportunities: A Critical Race Counter-Narrative Analysis." *Journal of Youth Studies* 21 (4): 533–549.

Burrowes, Nicole A. 2018. "Building the World We Want to See: A Herstory of Sista II Sista and the Struggle Against State and Interpersonal Violence." *Souls* 20 (4): 375–398.

Burrowes, Nicole, Morgan Cousins, Paula X. Rojas, and Ije Ude. 2017. "On Our Own Terms: Ten Years of Radical Community Building with Sista II Sista." In *The Revolution Will Not Be Funded: Beyond the Nonprofit Industrial Complex.* INCITE! Women of Color Against Violence, ed. 227–234. Durham: Duke University Press.

Busey, Christopher L., and Chonika Coleman-King. 2020. *All Around the World Same Song: Transnational Anti-Black Racism and New (and Old) Directions for Critical Race Theory in Educational Research.* Beverly Hills: Urban Education.

Castro, Fidel. 2002. *War, Racism and Economic Injustice: The Global Ravages of Capitalism.* New York: Ocean Press

Cossman, Brenda J. 2000. *Turning the Gaze Back on Itself. Global Critical Race Feminism: An International Reader.* New York: New York University Press.

Daniels, David C. 2008. "Critical HRD (CHRD) and Critical Race Theory (CRT)—Theory Building and Suggested Methodologies from the Voices of Descendants of the African Diaspora." https://bit.ly/3hkD3Wo

Dittmer, John. 1995. *Local People: The Struggle for Civil Rights in Mississippi.* Urbana: University of Illinois Press.

Eller, Anne. 2016. *We Dream Together: Dominican Independence, Haiti, and the Fight for Caribbean Freedom.* Durham: Duke University Press.

Evenson, Debra. 2003. *Law and Society in Contemporary Cuba*, 2nd ed. The Hague: Kluwer Law International.

Fuller, Linda. 1992. *Work and Democracy in Socialist Cuba.* Philadelphia: Temple University Press.

Galeano, Eduardo Hughes. 1973. *Open Veins of Latin America (Las Venas Abiertas de América Latina): Five Centuries of the Pillage of a Continent.* New York: Monthly Review Press.

García-Peña, Lorgia. 2016. *The Borders of Dominicanidad: Race, Nation and Archives of Contradiction.* Durham: Duke University Press.

Grey, Christopher. 1996. "Towards a Critique of Managerialism: The Contribution of Simone Weil." *Journal of Management Studies* 33 (5): 591–612.

Guridy, Frank Andre. 2010. *Forging Diaspora: Afro-Cubans and African Americans in a World of Empire and Jim Crow.* Chapel Hill: University of North Carolina Press.

Hale, Jon N. 2018. *The Freedom Schools: Student Activists in the Mississippi Civil Rights Movement.* New York: Columbia University Press.

hooks, bell. 1994. *Teaching to Transgress: Education as the Practice of Freedom.* New York: Routledge.

Hosein, Gabrielle Jamela, and Lisa Outar, eds. 2016. *Indo-Caribbean Feminist Thought: Genealogies, Theories, Enactments.* New York: Palgrave Macmillan.

Iglesias, E.M. 2000. "Global Markets, Racial Spaces and the Role of Critical Race Theory in the Struggle for Community Control of Investments: An Institutional Class Analysis." *Villanova Law Review* 45 (5): 1037–1074.

Juhasz, Antonia, "Exxon's Oil Drilling Gamble Off Guyana Coast 'Poses Major Environmental Risk.'" *The Guardian.* August 17.

Kim, Eusong, and Gelare Khoshgozaran. 2017. "Mari Matsuda: Founding Critical Race Theorist, Activist and Artist." Blog Entry. *Contemp+orary.* April 30. https://bit.ly/35fpcOz

Mayes, April J. 2014. *The Mulatto Republic: Class, Race, and Dominican National Identity.* Gainesville: University Press of Florida.

Payne, Charles M. 1996. *I've Got the Light of Freedom: The Organizing Tradition and the Mississippi Freedom Struggle.* Berkeley: University of California Press.

Ricourt, Milagros. 2016. *The Dominican Racial Imaginary: Surveying the Landscape of Race and Nation in Hispaniola.* New Brunswick: Rutgers University Press.

Rodney, Walter. 1970. *A History of the Upper Guinea Coast, 1545–1800.* Oxford: Clarendon Press.

Rodney, Walter Rodney. 1972. *How Europe Underdeveloped Africa.* London: Bogle-L'Ouverture.

Rodney, Walter. 1981. *A History of the Guyanese Working People, 1881–1905.* Baltimore: Johns Hopkins University Press.

Sagas, Ernesto. 2000. *Race and Politics in the Dominican Republic.* Gainesville: University Press of Florida.

Sista II Sista, "Sistas Making Moves: Collective Leadership for Personal Transformation and Social Justice." In *The Color of Violence: The INCITE! Anthology.* INCITE! Women of Color Against Violence, eds. 196–207. Durham: Duke University Press.

Solórzano, Daniel G., and Tara J. Yosso. 2002. "Critical Race Methodology: Counter-Storytelling as an Analytical Framework for Education Research." *Qualitative Inquiry* 8 (1): 23–44.

Toliver, S.R. 2022. *Recovering Black Storytelling in Qualitative Research.* New York: Routledge.

Trotz, Alissa. 2000. "Red Thread: The Politics of Hope in Guyana." *Race and Class* 49 (2): 71–130.

Trotz, D. Alissa, and Arif Bulkan. 2020. "Guyana's Political Tragedy." *Stabroek News.* June 30. https://bit.ly/3Itz1XI

Wing, Adrien Katherine. 2000. *Global Critical Race Feminism: An International Reader.* New York: New York University Press.

Wright, Micah. 2015. "An Epidemic of Negrophobia: Blackness and the Legacy of the US Occupation of the Dominican Republic." *Black Scholar* 45 (2): 21–33.

Zabala Argüelles, María del Carmen. 2021. "Desigualdades por color de la piel e interseccionalidad: Análisis del contexto Cubano 2008–2018." https://bit.ly/3powV3P

CHAPTER 9

Democracy Reconstructed:
The Promise of Southern Black Workers[1]

ERICA SMILEY
Jobs With Justice

Abstract

Based on an analysis that democracy is not just a political practice, but the fundamental role everyday people have in governing themselves economically as well, I discuss the role of organizing and collective bargaining—particularly efforts led by southern Black workers—as a primary pathway toward building a multiracial democracy. Anchored in the historic framework of the Radical Reconstruction, the last nationwide attempt to codify democracy, as well as more modern examples of union campaigns catalyzed by events that went far beyond traditional shop-floor issues, I argue in this chapter that strategies to combat white supremacy are central to democratizing employment and other economic relationships. Finally, I outline the approach of the Advancing Black Strategists Initiative to invest in and elevate the creative efforts of southern Black workers in ways that proliferate a new school of thought and ultimately design a roadmap that centers workers in reconstructing democracy in the United States.

This was not merely the desire to stop work. It was a strike on a wide basis against the conditions of work. It was a general strike that involved directly in the end perhaps a half million people. They wanted to stop the economy of the plantation system, and to do that they left the plantations.

—W.E.B. Du Bois (1935)

INTRODUCTION

Let us start with a set of ideas that many southern Black people understand without having to read a book by Thomas Piketty.

Democracy is not just a system of political practices. It must be applied to participation and decision making in all aspects of our economic lives as well. Without one, the whole system of democracy is compromised. Collective bargaining is fundamental to democratizing the economy. Collective bargaining, at its best, is a system by which working people can exercise collective power in a way that directly confronts the owners of capital and in a way that reclaims portions of that capital back to working people and their communities. But the 20th-century mechanisms that protect collective bargaining have been eroded and even perverted into limitations to the democratic activities of the working majority—often peeling off elements of the working class by race, gender, and national origin. So the way we apply collective bargaining must be broadened to all economic relationships and account for the ways in which the economy (and workers' experience of it) has shifted, ultimately changing the very nature of what a union contract covers—broadening what individuals can negotiate over and who they can negotiate with—from their direct "boss" to the individuals with concentrated power in their sector or community. Confronting the system of white supremacy and movements for white nationalism must remain a central element of this overall strategy to prevent the opposition from dividing workers and weakening their collective power.

Most Black workers have long been ready to get behind a democracy worth fighting for. Repeatedly throughout history, southern Black workers go out of their way to call unions in to support them—not just on the basis of combating exploitation but also of actualizing democracy. And when unions step up to the challenge and do not shy away from the centrality of combating white supremacy, they win. So, instead of leaving the wisdom and power of arguably the US labor movement's most militant base of workers untapped, our task is to invest in and elevate the creative efforts of southern Black workers to imagine a multiracial democracy—politically and economically—that works for all of us.

THE HISTORIC PROMISE (AND THREAT) OF A MULTIRACIAL DEMOCRACY

The political economy of the United States is increasingly characterized by right-wing populism and how motivated or disgusted you are by it. A resurgence of right-wing populism has grown in numbers and boldness both in the United States and globally throughout the past decade—emboldened by authoritarian leaders like former US president Donald Trump, Vladimir Putin of Russia, Brazilian president Jair Bolsonaro, and Boris Johnson of Great Britain. The reckless rhetoric of these administrations, and their antagonistic relationships with facts, has emboldened the most racist, xenophobic, sexist, and homophobic elements of society.

Perhaps nowhere was this more apparent in the United States than during the insurrection on January 6, 2021, when the Confederate flag made its first public appearance in the US Capitol since the Civil War. The act was a symbolic reminder of what we are up against. Flawed as they were, the periods of the Great Reconstruction following the US Civil War were marked by consistent attempts to build a multiracial American democracy in all aspects of society. The questions before us are will we formally transition into a racially "pure" authoritarian country, or will we finally step up to meet the challenges of our ancestors—to build a powerful, inclusive democracy?

Historian Eric Foner elaborates on how Reconstruction-related policies sit at the root of modern-day conflicts in his most recent book, *The Second Founding: How the Civil War and Reconstruction Remade the Constitution* (Foner 2019). The early Reconstruction periods were, by many accounts, marked by attempts to build a multiracial American democracy in all aspects of society. The 13th Amendment to the Constitution abolished slavery and all forms of forced labor. The 14th Amendment guaranteed citizenship to those born in the United States. And the 15th Amendment guaranteed the right to vote to Black men. All represented efforts to fully actualize democracy.

Democracy, imagined

Our movement has spent the past 150-plus years attempting to expand on these ideals and make them real in practice. Many of the gains made by progressive social movements since then were anchored in the promises of these constitutional amendments—women's suffrage, the New Deal, the Civil Rights Act, and the Voting Rights Act. And these same gains have been targeted by conservative judges and elected officials who have intentionally, systematically rolled them back, many to pre–Civil War interpretations of the Constitution. Best put by Barbara Fields, who appeared in Ken Burns' documentary series *The Civil War*, "the Civil War is still going on. It's still to be fought and regrettably it can still be lost" (Burns 1987).

However, the social justice movement and our institutions are not without responsibility for our current predicament. Moderates and progressives have done their share of limiting our understanding and practice of democracy—limiting ideals of democracy to voting, the supposed choice to spend your money at one place or another and, maybe most important, to be left alone (i.e., "Don't Tread on Me").[2] Over and over again, Black workers call unions and political leaders in to wage the struggle for democracy with them, only to be rejected for not fitting a narrow "winnable" framework defined by leaders in New York, Washington, or Los Angeles.

Democracy depends on our active, collective participation in all areas of the economy, and it should be based on the culture and experience of working people in their communities. Working people must have enforceable, not just advisory, roles in decision making everywhere to have a healthy democracy. This broadened view of democracy is not a new concept for many southern Black workers.

US SOUTH: EPICENTER OF THE FIGHT FOR A MULTIRACIAL DEMOCRACY

In 2021, Amazon workers in Bessemer, Alabama—mostly Black—called for help in their bid to form a union with the Retail, Wholesale and Department Store

Union. Many workers shared how radicalized they were after the murder of George Floyd in Minnesota by former police officer Derek Chauvin, having participated in 2020 summer uprisings for racial justice that gave them the courage to speak out about their own conditions during the COVID-19 pandemic. During the Alabama Amazon workers' campaign for a union, the Georgia state legislature provided an illustrative backdrop of the anti-democracy climate that these workers were operating within when it passed its most undemocratic, regressive set of voter restrictions in years targeting Black voters. The workers ultimately lost the union election after an intense intimidation campaign by Amazon that included sending workers four or five emails a day from the company to discourage unionization (Green 2021), attempting to bar workers from voting by mail—despite actively opposing the Trump administration's effort to curb mail-in ballots during the political election (More Perfect Union 2021a), and even asking Jefferson County to change the traffic lights (More Perfect Union 2021b) so workers have less time to talk to people in their cars about unionizing.

While the Bessemer workers lost their first union election, their experience and ongoing struggle highlights the momentum built when organizing efforts focus far beyond narrowly defined workplace issues. Workers are inspired to act when our institutions don't cower away from their full lived experiences—including their experience with racism and white supremacy.

Practicing democracy

These fights are too often siloed from the other struggles that workers carry, turning all other aspects of a worker's identity into "allies" instead of approaching them as whole people. Meanwhile, corporations are building their business models off of exploiting those *other* identities workers carry, intentionally creating a downward pressure on labor standards, knowing they can prevent their overwhelmingly southern Black workforces from organizing successfully.

For example, transnational auto companies such as Nissan and Volkswagen have focused their US manufacturing growth on the southern part of the country, where the remnants of Jim Crow and extreme limitations on union representation remain particularly virulent—in some places making it almost illegal to form a union. The impact of weaker labor standards and organization in the South make it difficult for midwestern autoworkers to maintain gains won over the past several decades—conceding to increased numbers of temporary and contract workers, regressively tiered wages, and cuts to healthcare.[3]

And the auto industry is not alone in milking this trend. All forms of manufacturing, logistics, service, and agriculture sectors have taken advantage of the southern region's regressive ecosystem.

You would think this to be the perfect set up for a robust national campaign highlighting the auto industry's active use of Jim Crow–era political climates to suppress the standards of its entire workforce. But to date, few such union campaigns have been framed in that way. And, not surprisingly, most of them have lost. In 2014, Volkswagen workers organizing with the United Auto Workers (UAW) lost their bid for union election against a (publicly) neutral company and their rabidly anti-union political allies. Those same workers lost another bid for unionization with a now publicly and privately anti-union company in 2019 (Brooks 2019). That same year, Boeing workers in South Carolina lost their union bid with the International Association of Machinists. Nissan workers in Mississippi lost their 2017 attempt to make UAW members out of the last two nonunion plants in their global production chain—the only two plants predominantly run by Black workers.[4]

Such outcomes have led many national union leaders to see the South as too difficult to invest in, despite ongoing lip service. Sending a few organizers to the region for a hot campaign here and there does not amount to the ongoing infrastructure needed to wage a sustained effort to organize southern workers, especially in such a hostile climate. In contrast, our institutions must establish long-term, multiyear efforts that invest in local leadership and leverage the power we have in other less-hostile environments to support workers in winning.

What happens to democracy denied? It explodes

While some movement leadership may still be figuring this out, southern workers— particularly Black workers—have long been ready to reimagine a democracy worth fighting for—politically and economically. Repeatedly throughout history, southern Black workers go out of their way to call unions in to support them. And when unions step up to the challenge and prepare for the fight in ways that do not shy away from the centrality of combating white supremacy, they win.

In her book *Putting Their Hands on Race*, Danielle T. Phillips-Cunningham discusses the often-integrated strategies of Black and Irish domestic workers in the late 1800s, when the Irish had yet to be defined as white. While much of the original news sources kept silent on it "to protect the public from scorn," many accounts acknowledge that Irish domestic workers stood with fellow Black laundresses during the strike of the Atlanta Washing Society in 1881. Phillips-Cunningham later notes that "African-American and Irish women molded race through their resistance to labor exploitation in domestic service" (Phillips-Cunningham 2019: 65, 115).

In the late 1960s, Memphis sanitation workers came to be freedom fighters because of the inhumane treatment they experienced not simply as workers, but as Black people. Neither the economic system under which they labored nor the political system that defined their rights as citizens recognized them as full and equal human beings—and that's what drove them to take desperate, dangerous steps to change their fortunes. And yet union leaders were initially reluctant to support the Memphis sanitation workers. P.J. Ciampa, director of field operations for the American Federation of State, County and Municipal Employees (AFSCME), was quoted as saying, "Good God Almighty, I need a strike in Memphis like I need another hole in the head!" (Honey 2007; Memphis Public Libraries 1968). But over time, the determination of the workers forced them to change their tune. Walter Reuther, president of UAW, eventually donated $50,000 to support their cause, and AFSCME provided organizing support, ultimately representing them when they won.

In another example, this time from coastal Virginia in the late 1970s, workers built a multiracial coalition to win a democratic union to represent them with Tenneco, a shipbuilding and dry dock company based in Newport News that contracted with the US Navy. Black workers had long been stuck in the dirtiest, lowest-paying jobs. Lane Windham describes the organizing drive with the United Steelworkers in her book *Knocking on Labor's Door*, stating how after an 82-day strike, they would "build a union that remained active on civil and women's rights issues for decades" (Windham 2017).

It took workers at Smithfield, a North Carolina pork processing facility, over 15 years to form a union with the United Food and Commercial Workers in 2008 (Burgdorfer 2008). Lidia Victoria worked at the plant after immigrating to the United States from the Dominican Republic and shared:

> There were a lot of different kinds of people in the plant. It was diverse. Men and women, whole families. Black people, White people, Native Americans, and Spanish-speaking people from all over. …[Management] told other people that the Spanish-speaking people were there to steal their jobs. White people were mostly in maintenance at that time. Maintenance was very important to the company because, you know, they keep the line running. Maintenance workers sometimes had an easier time getting what they wanted from the company back then. Most of the African-Americans were already in favor of the union, and I was helping them win support among more of the Spanish speakers. But less of the White people were with us at first. We knew we eventually needed everyone on board to win. (Smiley 2019)

Workers eventually built a strategy that consistently centralized the fight against white supremacy, including its impact not only on Black, native, and immigrant workers but also white workers. That, together with consistent pressure on the buyers of Smithfield hams and a corporate campaign—both waged by partners like Jobs With Justice—led to victory in 2008.

Again, when workers—especially southern workers—center the fight against white supremacy to build a multiracial strategy to organize and collectively bargain, they win. And they win efforts that to most seemed impossible just before they succeeded.

CENTERING SOUTHERN LEADERSHIP TO WIN FOR EVERYONE

Black workers, especially in the US South, remain central to rebuilding a labor movement that will challenge modern-day reactionary forces—and not just as a "strategic ally." Black workers are *active participants* in the movement to expand organizing and collective bargaining power for all people and, perhaps, its salvation. This may be because so many Black workers have long lost (if they ever had access to) the 20th-century protections that changed the lives of so many during the New Deal—despite leading many of the democratic struggles that led to it. The Brotherhood of Sleeping Car Porters of Black rail workers that was led by A. Philip Randolph, for example, took courageous actions in the midst of violent repression from the Pullman Company and its allies. Their efforts led to amending the Railway Labor Act in 1934, expanding democracy far beyond their one union.[5] The six-week, multiracial organizing drive of over 600,000 mine workers in the early 1920s made Alabama the state with the highest union density in the South well before the passage of the National Labor Relations Act and even of its weaker predecessor, the National Industrial Recovery Act.[6] And these are just a fraction of the Black workers in motion during this period that led to changes in the law that many of them would later be excluded from.

For this reason, defining the mechanisms that would guarantee working Black people a dignified life goes far beyond getting back to any glory days of yore. We still remember the promise of Reconstruction, a promise not yet achieved and still to be imagined.

We, too, dream of democracy

While the specifics of such a society should be worked out collectively, it would likely include pathways to organize without the legal and economic restrictions currently making it difficult for so many Black workers—in other words, a 21st-century commitment to the freedom of association. It would include the ability to negotiate fair compensation over the labor that we own in an environment where workers are encouraged, even incentivized, to combat exploitation through collective bargaining and collective action. Voting would be accessible and mandatory for everyone, even if that vote is an abstention. There would be exponentially more decision-making positions to run for election to at all levels, and democratic consultation would happen in all neighborhoods and regions of the country. These are just the limited musings of an organizer and public intellectual. A true multiracial democracy would outshine many of our wildest dreams.

To tap into this creativity and achieve this dream requires a strategy that centers the southern Black experience.

As of the last Census, most of the Black population in the United States remains concentrated in the US South (US Census Bureau 2001). States in that region have been increasingly written off and abandoned by national progressive actors since the New Deal—excluded from 20th-century protections for the ability to vote and negotiate with capital, whether explicitly from Jim Crow and right-to-work laws pushed by southern property owners and businesses or implicitly by the Right's systemic disenfranchising of formerly incarcerated people in states with large Black and brown populations[7]. The Economic Policy Institute released a report in June 2016 outlining that people of color will become the majority of the American working class by 2032, based on projections of the Bureau of Labor Statistics and other trends—sooner than what was projected by the Census Bureau at that time (Wilson 2016). And Black workers, particularly Black women, have long been more likely to form unions than any other demographic (US Bureau of Labor Statistics 2019).

I emphasize again that southern Black workers have long lost (if they ever really had) most 20th century protections for the ability to vote and negotiate with capital. And because of this, they have an appetite for building 21st-century infrastructure that does not mimic or make the mistakes of our past. This is not simply about fixing the exclusive compromises of the New Deal, the shortsightedness of Operation Dixie, or the mass incarceration of Black workers still being leased out to multinational corporations on the cheap. Sure, we want that too.[8] But southern Black workers have long been ready to fight for 21st-century frameworks for economic democracy—and frankly are tired of dragging movement leaders kicking and screaming to the region to help. Why do we think the laws are so skewed against unions in the South? Because that is our most potentially militant base of working people. Why keep leaving all that power on the table?

Democracy, restrained

Change cannot come fast enough for many Black people in the Deep South who have lived through segregation, vast inequality in wealth and income, harsh right-to-work laws, stark under- and unemployment, and excessive policing and incarceration. But the shift in demographics alone won't get us there, and southern workers know it. They will not stick their necks out for a union in the absence of a winning approach. Any sustained effort must have organizing and institution building in the South as a central component of its strategy.

Many movement leaders are just starting to take notice of the growing power and clout of Black progressivism in the South. Election victories in Alabama in Fall 2017 and the new slate of liberal and progressive Black gubernatorial, legislative, and mayoral candidates in 2018 and 2020 awoke many to the possibilities of fundamental change in a part of the country they had once only pejoratively viewed in the past. Emboldened by uprisings and social movements such as the Movement for Black Lives, Black workers yet again are calling unions in to help be a part of the great democratic project.

Some of the most exciting and militant upsurges are happening in southern states. From the organizing drive among mostly Black Amazon workers in Alabama, public sector mental health workers in Virginia, construction workers in Texas, agricultural workers in Mississippi, rubber tire manufacturers in Southern Carolina and Georgia, and many others, the region is wide awake with activity. Working people throughout the South have come together to struggle against the existing power structure, often demanding far more than a return to the old system of organizing, bargaining, or even voting. Movements in this region, many already led by Black workers and community leaders, may hold some of the most potential for building our 21st-century democracy.

For this reason, Jobs With Justice has partnered with the International Comparative Labor Studies Program at Morehouse College, and others. Having surveyed the landscape, we realized that by combining our resources to nurture the skills, thoughts, and experiences of Black labor and economic justice scholars, intellectuals, and other students of social movements, we can change the political economy of the US South and thus change the relations of power nationwide—setting the foundation for a healthy 21st-century democracy.

The Advancing Black Strategists Imitative (ABSI) seeks to accomplish this in three ways.

First, ABSI recruits and then accompanies a cohort of Black students, year after year, through a series of courses, seminars, internships, visiting scholars, and other experiences—eventually counting them in a national network of ABSI members who are schooled in and continuing to develop a shared analysis for society. Second, ABSI will support a cohort of worker–leaders who seek to expand their skill sets through a Movement Fellows Program—placing them on Black-led southern worker campaigns as apprentices for 15 months. Last, ABSI acts as a container for active Black strategists in all forms of work, who analyze and learn from the experiences of Black workers and their campaigns, elevate those learnings into public discourse nationally and globally, and apply lessons into the development of sharper theory via direct feedback loops.

Such a project is not completely unfounded.

Contemporary scholars such as Duke University historian Nancy MacLean in her book *Democracy in Chains* (2018) showed us methodically how past conservative intellectuals using academic institutions as their basis for credibility sought to alter both the rules and the role of government in a last-ditch attempt to preserve the power of the white elite in the wake of the *Brown v. Board of Education* decision. In response to the widening of American democracy, Nobel Prize–winning political economist James McGill Buchanan became the principal architect in developing a brilliant, even if diabolical, plan to undermine the ability of the majority to use its numbers to level the playing field with the wealthy in all areas of life. Corporate donors and their right-wing foundations then and now were only too eager to support these efforts, teaching a generation of libertarian strategists (think Paul Ryan) how to divide America into "makers" and "takers."

As opposed to simply standing in fear or awe of these efforts and tactics, the ABSI sees a roadmap for working with unions, community organizations, higher education institutions, philanthropy, and key allies to reclaim what has been lost. Together we promise to make sure what is created is intersectional in its analysis of race, class, and gender. And unlike Buchannan and his protégés (bless them), our ideas are popular. So, there is no need to be stealthy about it.

We are building a program where Black institutions can act as incubators for the future of Black scholarship and applied research on race, class, gender, and economic justice in the South—anchored within the historically Black institutions of the Atlanta University Center Consortium. Partnering with other institutions that are already thigh deep in tackling the great problems of our day, ASBI will accompany a network of leaders, organizations, and Black-led campaigns on a journey toward the multiracial democracy our ancestors dreamed of.

As we've seen in the past four years, our success can be fleeting. Our opposition is fighting equally hard to put democracy in chains.[9] Today, our task as a movement is to leverage the resources of our current institutions in ways that boost existing and new southern worker organizing strategies. Doing so will infuse new energy into the national agenda to build a multiracial democracy, breathing new life into the democracy-oriented constitutional amendments. We have an opportunity to fulfill the promises of Reconstruction, intentionally choosing campaigns that align the shared self-interests of white workers, Black workers, and all workers of color against systems of white supremacy and corporate control. Partnering with others who are already thigh deep in imagining 21st-century structures of governance that would work for all of us, the Initiative is on a journey towards the multiracial democracy our ancestors dreamed of.

A democracy, reconstructed

ENDNOTES

1. A version of this first appeared in the *New Labor Forum,* September 2021.

2. Put more eloquently by Martin Canoy and Derek Shear, "Democracy was limited to suffrage and consumer choice. The workplace was governed by the laws of private property, not the Bill of Rights. … Economic democracy is a crucial ingredient in political democracy and vice versa. Under the capitalist organization of production, political democracy is an imperfect concept and can be achieved in practice only through a democratization of the economy" (1980: 12, 131–132).

3. A fairly detailed outline of the UAW's last contract with General Motors, Ford, and Fiat Chrysler can be found in Jeffrey S. Rothstein's *New Labor Forum* article, "The New UAW Contract: A Somewhat 'Clear Path'" (2015).

4. As of this writing, the National Labor Relations Board is reviewing these and other unfair labor practices by the company. Some or all results of the election could still be overturned. The workers are still in an active organizing campaign.

5. The amendments of 1934 added a new section to the Railway Labor Act which created

what is in effect an industrial court for the adjudication of disputes involving the interpretation or application of wage and rule agreements of rail carriers. It is known as the National Railroad Adjustment Board (Cornell Law School, no date).

    6. For further discussion on this fight, see Goldfield (2020).

    7. For a thorough discussion of the influences, motivations, and impacts of increased incarceration on inequality, see Petach and Pena (2020).

    8. A major critique of those who led Operation Dixie in the 1940s was their often refusing "outside help" by groups in the Black community and thus failing to build a locally sustained movements to support workers who were sticking their necks out, instead depending heavily on an inside strategy with temporary allies in the federal government. For further discussion on the criticisms of Operation Dixie, see Press (2021). Also see Goldfield (2020).

    9. Yes, this is a nod to Nancy MacLean's 2018 book, *Democracy in Chains*. Important read for anyone who believes in democracy.

REFERENCES

Brooks, Chris. 2019. "Why the UAW Lost Again in Chattanooga." *Labor Notes*. June 14. https://bit.ly/35U4lR6

Burgdorfer, Bob. 2008. "Workers at Huge Smithfield Meat Plant Vote for Union." Reuters. December 11. https://reut.rs/3sJAjbC

Burns, Ken. 1987. *The Civil War*. Directed by Ken Burns. Florentine Films.

Canoy, Martin, and Derek Shearer. 1980. *Economic Democracy: The Challenge of the 1980s*. Armonk: M.E. Sharpe.

Cornell Law School Legal Information Institute. No date. "45 U.S. Code §153–National Railroad Adjustment Board." https://bit.ly/3Cid9wb

Du Bois, W.E.B. 1935. *Black Reconstruction in America: An Essay Toward a History of the Part Which Black Folk Played in the Attempt to Reconstruct Democracy in America, 1860–1880*. New York: Harcourt Brace.

Foner, Eric. 2019. *The Second Founding: How the Civil War and Reconstruction Remade the Constitution*. New York: W.W. Norton.

Goldfield, Michael. 2020. *The Southern Key: Class Race, and Radicalism in the 1930s and 1940s*. Oxford: Oxford University Press.

Green, Jay. 2021. "Amazon Fights Aggressively to Defeat Union Drive in Alabama, Fearing a Coming Wave." *Washington Post*. March 9. https://wapo.st/3hI5az6

Honey, Michael K. 2007. *Going Down Jericho Road: The Memphis Strike, Martin Luther King's Last Campaign*. New York: W.W. Norton.

MacLean, Nancy. 2018. *Democracy in Chains*. New York: Penguin Random House.

Memphis Public Libraries. 1968. "This Week's Profile: P.J. Ciampa." February 15. https://bit.ly/3KmFmVA

More Perfect Union 2021a. "Alabama Amazon Workers Could Make History with Union Vote." YouTube Video. February 2. https://bit.ly/3HJf5Pu

More Perfect Union 2021b. "NEWS: A Jefferson County Public Official Has Confirmed That Amazon Asked for the Traffic Light Patterns to Be Altered Outside Its Alabama Warehouse." Twitter Post. February 16, 5:25 p.m. https://bit.ly/3vHQ98G

Petach, Luke, and Anita Alves Pena. 2020. "Local Labor Market Inequality in the Age of

Mass Incarceration." *The Review of Black Political Economy* 48 (1): 7–41.

Phillips-Cunningham, Danielle T. 2019. *Putting Their Hands on Race: Irish Immigrant and Southern Black Domestic Workers.* New Brunswick: Rutgers University Press.

Press, Alex N. 2021. "The Alabama Amazon Union Drive Could Be the Most Important Labor Fight in the South in Decades: An Interview with Michael Goldfield." *Jacobin.* February 19. https://bit.ly/3sLR1qE

Rothstein, Jeffrey S. 2015. "The New UAW Contract: A Somewhat 'Clear Path.'" New Labor Forum. December. https://bit.ly/3HMahsC

Smiley, Erica. 2019. Interview with Lidia Victoria. North Carolina, March 12.

US Bureau of Labor Statistics. 2019. "Union Membership Rate 10.5 Percent in 2018, Down from 20.1 Percent in 1983." TED: The Economics Daily. January 25. https://bit.ly/3vFWbqc

US Census Bureau. 2001. "Majority of African Americans Live in 10 States; New York City and Chicago Are Cities with Largest Black Population." August 13. https://bit.ly/3pHMG6d

Wilson, Valerie. 2016. "People of Color Will Be a Majority of the American Working Class in 2032: What This Means for the Effort to Grow Wages and Reduce Inequality." Economic Policy Institute. June 9. https://bit.ly/35yNIKT

Windham, Lane. 2017. *Knocking on Labor's Door: Union Organizing in the 1970s and the Roots of a New Economic Divide.* Chapel Hill: University of North Carolina Press.

PART II

CALL TO ACTION /
HOW TO

CHAPTER 10

The Intersectionality of Liberation

HAVEN MEDIA

TAMARA L. LEE
Rutgers University
Department of Labor Studies and Employment Relations

Abstract

The following is an edited transcript[1] of a virtual panel discussion titled "The Intersectionality of Liberation" hosted by Haven Media, Inc.[2] on November 20, 2021, and moderated by Tahira Benjamin. From a myriad of identity-forward and intersecting experiences, the participants shared the many ways in which they are reimagining capitalist models, empowering communities that the system disempowers, and creating and experiencing joy through self-expression in a world that creates, perpetuates, and amplifies obstacles for Black, Indigenous, and People of Color (BIPOC), and particularly those holding intersecting marginalized social identities.

PARTICIPANTS

From bios in their own words, the voices include the following:

Tahira Benjamin: Community manager of Haven Media.

Danielle St. Luce: Chief investment officer for Matriarch Technologies. She holds a bachelor's degree from Cornell University in industrial and labor relations.

Alejandra Pablos: Reproductive justice community organizer, storyteller, and writer, at the intersections of mass incarceration and immigration.

Jamie Pandit: South Asian woman and content creator who shares beauty, fashion, and her experiences living openly as a trans person, all with a bit of humor and sass.

Kristina Gisors: Has lived many lives; in her first, she was a fashion stylist for magazines. Then a visual merchandiser manager for Kenzo, and world traveler.

Ella Dior: Eighteen-year-old Black, Queer, and nonbinary activist from Brooklyn, New York. They have organized on-the-ground actions to amplify the voices of Black people.

Ericka Hart: Black, Queer Femme, activist, writer, highly acclaimed speaker and award-winning sexuality educator.

Ren Fernandez-Kim: Nonbinary, Korean, and Peruvian American artist, anthropologist and educator.

So much of our education is designed to silence us, to deradicalize who we are. I realized that through the work that I do as a sex educator, that yes, we could talk about vulva and penises and pleasure orgasms, but there is an intersection of race, class, gender, and ability that often times doesn't get addressed.

—Ericka

Tahira: When Haven started speaking about what we wanted today to be about, we envisioned a conversation on the many ways Black, Indigenous women and nonbinary folks of color are dismantling oppressive systems and replacing them with ones in which our identities are fully respected, humanized and celebrated. So, today's going to be a huge celebration of all the amazing work you folks are doing in our communities of color! One by one I want to know your pronouns, where you are joining us from, and parts of your story: what you're doing in your communities, who you are at the core.

Ren: My name is Ren. I go by she/they. I'm currently in Los Angeles, California, and I'm so happy to be here with you. Most of the stuff that I work on is on social media. The topic that I focus on is more of decolonized education and trying to make that accessible to everyone.

Danielle: My name is Danielle St. Luce; my pronouns are she/her. Currently, I've been working in my community and supporting small business owners. Particularly, owners who are BIPOC and folks who are usually from lower-income communities to help them better understand how to access finance for their businesses.

Ericka: Hi, everybody! Thanks so much for having me. My name is Ericka Hart. My pronouns are she/they. I am a sexuality educator, and my focus has been on racial and social justice as well as gender disruption and dismantling the gender binary. I'm also a breast cancer survivor, so my work is also focusing on medical racism and uprooting that structure.

Tahira: Hell YES to all of that.

Alejandra: ¡Buenos Dias! My name is Alejandra. I use pronouns she/ella. Sometimes folks call me Ale. I'm a community organizer, [but] first and foremost I'm a storyteller. I always want to get people to talk, talk, talk … because I think we don't do enough of that personally … like interpersonal talk and sharing stories.

But I do that because I've been informed by my own deportation case. I've been fighting deportation for about 11 years now. So, what I do now is let other people know they can fight back, and they don't have to take that, and we can build pathways of protection for one another.

Kristina: I'm Kristina. You can use the pronouns she/hers. I'm French originally, but now I'm living in Amsterdam. Now I'm in the Netherlands. I own a book club that celebrates the Black community and its diversity through literature. So, my goal is to create a greeting culture within the community.

Jamie: Hi, everyone! Thanks for having me, by the way. It's just crazy that I'm even using my voice and talking to everybody. I'm just so excited and thankful. I'm from Toronto, and I'm South Asian. I was born in Bangladesh. I moved to Canada when I was 11. I'm also a woman of transgender experience, meaning I was assigned male at birth. My pronouns are she/her. I'm a content creator. I started creating content last year with fashion and beauty and then eventually, I came out officially in public. It sounds so weird saying "officially in public." Publicly—to the world. I've been living in stealth. Meaning I've been hiding my identity for over half my life. I'm 33 now, so I came out at 15 to my parents, hid my identity until I was 32, last year. I came out publicly through my social media, and my content does talk about fashion and beauty, but I've also switched up my gears and talk about my experiences as a trans woman. It's not about just creating awareness; for me, it's creating conversations and dismantling stereotypes and transphobia. It's wild using my voice. I'm getting used to it.

Tahira: Yessss, we love it!

Ella: My pronouns are they/them. I'm currently based in Brooklyn, New York. I'm a part of an abolitionist collective called For Liberation. There, we focus on organizing Black people and Black communities by giving them, and creating alternatives that they can rely on other than the systems that are oppressing them. Meaning mutual-aid projects, tools that can radicalize them, etc.

We are going to use the term "community role" because we're reimagining and redefining what the capitalist world of "work" is.

—Tahira

Tahira: Today is a really tough day. We are coming together as a community to talk about all the amazing work that all these amazing folks are doing, but it would be crazy to not acknowledge what has been going on in our countries and communities: the heartbreaking verdict[3] that we've been watching. So, we're half heavy today.

It's really difficult to be people of color in this day and age, even though it's the best time for us to be here doing all the amazing work that we're doing. There is so much we have to dismantle, and we at Haven completely envision dismantling and abolishing the oppressive systems that are keeping us tied and that are harming people.

You are all working in different realms, but at the same time, the goal at the end of the day is to dismantle what is and replace it with more representation of really being humanized as people of color in this system. There is always this catalytic moment that everyone experiences that brings them to their community role. We are going to use the term "community role" because we're reimagining and redefining what the capitalist world of "work" is. In your community role, I want to know how you got your start and what that looks like day to day.

Ren: We'll have to go back to just me being born. Coming to the United States as an immigrant meant that I would have to become the voice for my parents, and I had to become their advocate as well as my own advocate and become my own voice. That in itself led to a lot of education— not only for myself but for the people around me and that I was in a community with, went to school with, went to church with, etc. There were lots of moments where I had to sit with myself, read the room, and understand why people were in certain positions or why I was in a certain position, as well as the social dynamics of what was going on at a very young age. That led to my love for education.

At the end of the day, we are human beings, and yes, there are privileges that people may have over me, or I may have over other people, but at the same time we have to be able to sit down and talk to each other and work together through these systems of oppression that do exist. I may not have had the vocabulary as a child, but as an adult, I definitely do. I've always been an educator and I continue to be to the people around me. With my social platform now—I'm able to reach more people. I feel like the real impact that happens is when you really get down to a personal level and reach out to people like that.

Danielle: I would have to start with my parents who are small business owners. And seeing them be successful in their business. Living in a community in south Florida where pretty much everyone has their small business, I've grown up seeing examples of success and examples of what failure looks like when you are a person of color versus when you are not, and the barriers of entry that existed.

With graduating recently and working within the nonprofit space, I saw and learned how bigger white institutions got money, how they ignored the community. I got into small business finance, nonprofit finance, and then I learned the ways in which that was also messed up: how when you are in a capitalistic society and you are mimicking these institutions that have now declared a pathway for people of color to gain access, but there is never as much support, never as much money, never as much care in the outcome. How *that* community can also be dangerous and how not all skin folk are kinfolk. That was a very big lesson that I learned.

Now I've moved into a space where I can explore ways in which we can democratize finance as much as you can in a capitalist system and different options and structures of financing that exist for small businesses, but also for individuals trying to bring the community into the concept of work, which isn't usually something that's generally done.

Ericka: Well, for one, definitely my ancestors. I think it was already divine that I would be an educator. A lot of my family are educators, so it was already passed down. And with sex ed, I went to an abstinence-only school, and a lot of my friends were having sex. And they were coming to me about it because I was the only one willing to go toe to toe with an adult, even though it was very scary to ask questions that we were very clearly being told that we shouldn't ask.

From there, so much of our education is designed to silence us, to deradicalize who we are. I realized that through the work that I do as a sex educator, that yes, we could talk about vulva and penises and pleasure orgasms, but there is an intersection of race, class, gender, and ability that often times doesn't get addressed in a conversation of sex ed. When we're talking about consent, there's never a conversation around how the thievery and theft of stolen lands connects to how we are living in a country that is based on a foundation of no consent, and how that informs how we relate to each other. If it's four years old, all the way up to 84 years old, it makes a difference for me to collaborate and have a pedagogical approach that isn't dominating. Because even in education, it could become a space where you are having this power dynamic that is often just not helpful.

Tahira: How does it interact with your journey of healing and liberating yourself? Especially in what you do, I can imagine that there's so much that *you* go through and unpack from within yourself as you're educating others on their bodies and sexuality.

Ericka: My partner always says that just because we educate on racial and social justice doesn't mean that it's not happening to us in real time. I think having a very public presence online has people assume that we have it all figured out and that racism and transphobia and classism, misogynoir, ableism, etc. doesn't happen to us because we have all the language for it, and we know how to get beyond it. But that is just so far from the truth. I am nothing without community. I'm nothing without the people who have lifted me up and continue to have me survive and thrive in these spaces. This is not a one-femme show. It is collaborative.

So I always have to do a nod to community for the healing that I've done. But also, my therapist asked me this really rude question the other day where she said, "When have you had the time to heal?" And I was like, "Wow, sis. *Wow.*" Cuz it's true! I mean, if it's just trauma, trauma, trauma, trauma, trauma, when do we have time to heal? I'm sitting with that question. I'm not healed. Healing is not linear. There's always something that I'm working on.

Alejandra: Shout out to therapists! My therapist also was like, "So, are you never going to have peace because prisons exist?" And I'm like, "Damn."

Ericka: Why are they all reading us this week?!!

[all laugh]

And the answer is *yes*.

Alejandra: I think the way I show up in every conversation each day is different: how I'm feeling, what I'm going to share—I get to pick, right? When I got incarcerated, when I first pleaded guilty to something that I should have never pleaded guilty to—cuz that's how the court system makes it to be, all of our people have gone to court—I remember lying to my mom. My mom never knew I was going to court for some serious shit that I literally didn't know that could impact my life forever. I remember I got arrested and I was taken by ICE. I didn't know that whatever I pleaded guilty to later can have border patrol picking me up and taking me to this immigration prison. And I remember I was willing to take it. I was willing to take it. And a lot of people are willing to take what the system and the government place on us.

And that was the moment when I was sitting inside thinking, "I'm a legal permanent resident. I don't know, this must be a mistake. I'm different than the people here." It changed my life forever. 2011 changed my life forever. I fell in love with people all over again, I woke up to what was happening. They dumb us down through our education. They dumb us down through the media they feed us— these labels. I was in there, and it was just such an awakening, and then I realized I'm the chain breaker in my family. For so many reasons. Not only was I here to resist that, but I'm resisting misogyny, sexism within my family. I'm okay with leaving every time and being like, "Y'all are not going to be transphobic and homophobic and sexist when I'm around." If I hear something, I'm always going to interrupt. If the revolution don't start at my house, I'm not going to be part of any revolution outside in the streets. I've always been breaking those chains, from my body hair—I've been apologizing for my body all of my life, I've been apologizing for so many things. I've been challenging that.

I'm Mexicana, a Mexican from the southwestern land. I'm speaking to you all from the Tohono O'odham lands right now and fighting deportation on stolen land. It's such a mind fuck, you know? For me, every role that I take now is about power, is about access, and knowing that I have it. Nobody has to give it to me. I'm going to have it. I'm going to own my own production. So, even facing deportation, I found out that I could own every single part of what I do.

—Alejandra

Just being able to share my story, talk to other people, self-fund all my work, mutual-aid organizing, all that shit. And yes, I still want to work on policy because policy is directly creating barriers and legalizing the way that the police and the system treats us, but I also believe that we have to be creating new joy, fun communities, everything. I do interpretation because if we're not having conversations in the language that your most comfortable in, that's not power. For me, all the roles of breaking the chains and planting seeds with other people— you can do it. You can interrupt in your family. You can do all of this. I'm that *tía* that you want your family around.

Jamie: I just love your energy.

Tahira: When you said if the revolution doesn't start in my house, I'm not going to be a part of revolution in the streets, wow.

Alejandra: It needs to be said. The first thing organizers do—they don't deal with their family. They want to organize and be abolitionists in nonprofits and in our communities and fundraisers, but at home they can't even interrupt racism and anti-Blackness.

Jamie: I feel that so much.

Kristina: It's so different for me because I'm French also, West Indian, raised by my mom. If anybody knows about the story of West Indies, it's still now a colony. White people still have the power. My country, Guadeloupe, is still a plantation with owners and everything. So, in the end we still have racism, but we have a different way of—French, European people maybe have a different way to express it. I feel like Americans are more frontal; European is more sneaky, and it's difficult because when you grow up you think you're crazy. You think everything that happened to you is in your head, and they all make you believe that it's in your head. So, it's really difficult when you grow up into that kind of country.

I feel like I was born outside of The Matrix. Right now, I'm being Morpheus and trying to give everybody I meet in the street a red pill. I always have been aware of what's going on in the world. I've always been aware of racism, sexism, misogynoir, everything, but I find it really difficult to express that because of my surroundings and the fact that I was a Black woman but in Europe. As you may know, French is a difficult language, but it's also a language that's stuck in history. I feel like English is moving, like you have new stuff, new words, but French is really strict. Everything is stuck in the history of the country, and you cannot move things. So, when we have new words, they don't really understand.

For me, the real cataclysm was when I left my job. I was visual department manager at Kenzo for six years. I was lucky to have my boss. He was Indigenous American and Indigenous Mexican, but he was white passing. But lucky for me, he helped me make my way in the company. If I had a French boss, it would never happen. When I got this position, I made my goal to only hire people that look like me and people of color. My team was Arabic, Asian, Blacks, because I felt like if I get there, everybody has to get there. I always had this mentality to have my community doing stuff. But when I left my job in 2019, I felt like I had time to think and stop for a moment.

I felt like the weight of racial stuff made me think I was lacking in vocabulary. So I started to read. I fell deeply in love with the discipline. I felt spiritual enrichment. Reading instantly became a form of liberation. I learned the importance of reading Black and brown stories, I discovered the value of reading about the whole Black life. Because also I felt like what they push in French is just books that talk about Black struggle, slavery, all that stuff. I didn't want to read only just books about when our lives intersect with white lives. I wanted to read about our joy, sorrow, family, grieving, success, triumph—all of that. I realized the invisibility of Black culture and brown culture. So I wanted to offer books that feature Black and brown characters by Black and brown authors. So that's why I created the Blackletter, which is really a bilingual book club that celebrates Black and brown community and diversity through literature.

When I quit my job, I was a bit lost. COVID gave me a lot of space to stop and think about what I was doing and really rethink work and job—what is it exactly? Capitalism made me think my life was supposed to be work, you know? I was kind of depressed for a moment because I didn't have a job. I felt like I was doing nothing because I didn't have a job. And then I realized by the fact that I was posting, writing, doing stuff, I had a lot of people coming around and saying you helped me to realize this, or you make me think about this, or because of you I read this book. I was like, oh, I have an impact even though I'm not working. I said, okay, doing other things, reading, sharing, talking, it's also having an impact on people and community.

Tahira: I think that interacts with everything that everyone here is doing, whether we're being paid a ton of money to do it or not, which in most cases we're doing the real work that needs to be done. But it's such valuable, meaningful, community-driven work.

I was working in fashion. It was kind of like my armor to keep it together, I guess. I didn't make too many friends. I kept to myself. Because again I was so afraid of people finding out my identity. Eventually I moved to Toronto. I met this wonderful man. We're in a relationship. Five years later, or four years later, he proposes to me. We're about to get married. …The pandemic hit. I lost my job. Like even that itself, the fact that I'm trans. I found love and I'm married, I cry about it every single day almost because it doesn't happen to people like me. And it's something worth celebrating.

—Jamie

Jamie: It's transgender day of remembrance, and I just woke up feeling very emotional and sad and just feeling lucky that I get to sit here and use my voice. That itself is healing for me. But something earlier that Ren said—the moment that you're born, you feel like you have to advocate for yourself—I really felt that because I feel that the moment I was born, I had to fight for my existence, truly. And I still do, of course.

My body is not seen as a real woman's body. My body is not seen like it should exist. Since I was born, I didn't understand why my sister was wearing saris and pretty dresses and I was being dressed up as a boy. I didn't really understand who I was. Living through that and then going to school, having kids throw rocks at you, making fun of you, bullying you, getting beat up, and I don't know why. I'm just being me. I don't understand why I'm different, but then I realize that I am different because I'm not a boy, I'm not a girl. How I was feeling wasn't really making sense to how I was presenting at the time. And I had no word for it to describe my experience.

And then when we moved back to Canada back, I still didn't know what the word "transgender" meant because obviously in Bangladesh it's not something that's really talked about. Coming out to my parents and having no support from my family, running away from home, being homeless, living in a shelter, living on the streets. It just kind of changes you, and you have to advocate for yourself. And it's really hard out there. It's a really, really cruel world.

I started transitioning when I was 15, 16, and I realized that I had passing privilege. I already experienced hate and discrimination as a brown person and now a brown woman, and now this identity. Like, no thank you, sir. No thank you, ma'am. No, not for me. So, I just went on stealth mode. I moved to a different city, and I just lived like a cisgender girl. But I realized that obviously there's parts of me that felt like something was missing in my life. I was hiding my identity. My boyfriend obviously knew that I was trans, but his family didn't know, none of my friends knew. I had friends for ten years that didn't know. Living like that was really difficult because you have to constantly feel like you have to lie. I realized that I wanted to help people like me because there was no conversation, there was no awareness.

I put myself through university. I still wasn't ready to come out because I was scared, and that's the truth. I was scared because—it's weird to say this, but I feel comfortable saying this—I feel like the world was progressed when it comes to being gay, being lesbian, in some ways. There has been some progression. But when it comes to gender identity and being trans and now I'm nonbinary. Nonbinary people have always existed, but I feel like people are giving more space and are comfortable talking about it now because there are more resources, more education. But yeah, I just kept hiding myself.

During that whole time, I was working in fashion. It was kind of like my armor to keep it together, I guess. I didn't make too many friends. I kept to myself. Because again I was so afraid of people find finding out my identity. Eventually I moved to Toronto. I met this wonderful man, we're in a relationship. Five years later, or four years later, he proposes to me. We're about to get married, last year happened, so it's 2020 now. The pandemic hit. I lost my job. Like even that itself, the fact that I'm trans. I found love and I'm married, I cry about it every single day almost because it doesn't happen to people like me. And it's something worth celebrating. Sorry, I don't know why I'm so emotional today.

Tahira: Emotions are welcome here, by the way.

Jamie: Yeah, thank you. It's a very heavy day for me because I feel very blessed.

Last year too with Black Lives Matter, seeing so many Black trans women being murdered for who they are. Just a lot of different things happened last year. I got this fire in me; I can't keep quiet anymore. I didn't see someone like me growing up. There was no representation. There was no visibility. I made this life and I have privilege and I want to use my voice to help other people that don't have a voice, or don't feel comfortable to have a voice. And it doesn't mean that I'm the voice of the community. I'm just one voice in the community.

I didn't identify with my identity until really last year. Before that I was like I'm a cisgender girl, I'm "normal," don't talk to me, I had my blinders on. Last year, I came out through a YouTube video publicly. It was definitely one of the scariest moments of my life. I don't think I would have done it if the pandemic didn't hit. In a way, it was a blessing for me because I felt safe at home. My job was very public, living and working downtown Toronto, working with so many people, being a manager and managing so many people. I didn't feel safe to come out because I've had instances where people wanted to kill me, people wanted to hurt me because I was trans.

I came out, and it's helped me find my voice, it's helped me heal, and I'm talking about my experiences in a way that feels authentic and that feels real to me. There's so much history of trans people that I don't know. There's so much I'm learning about myself that I never even wanted to address. It's been a year of growing.

[everyone claps in support]

Tahira: You almost brought me to tears, too. We're so proud of you. Thank you for being you and just for being out about it and sharing your journey.

Even though I'm a content creator, friends don't want to work with someone like me because I'm trans. They're scared of what their followers will think. Because I pass, some brands don't want to work with me because they want to have their token trans person so their followers can see, okay, you're trans, so this brand must be inclusive. It's performative. There are so many things that I'm experiencing, but I'm talking about it all in my community because it's important to, not just be aware, but to create these conversations and unlearn and learn.

—Jamie

Tahira: What is your definition of liberation, and how does your role seek to accomplish that and really liberate communities of color?

Ericka: My definition of liberation would look like existing without structures of oppression; that white supremacy actually goes away and is dismantled, and the most marginalized Black, fat, trans, disabled folks get to actually exist in their bodies without contest and get to have access to healthcare without any sort of struggle, get to do any sort of gender-affirming surgeries without worrying about how it's going to get paid for, houselessness no longer exists, everyone has access to homes, prison systems are completely dismantled, the ways in which we surveil and disregard activists through the nonprofit industrial complex goes away, medical racism goes away, reparations are given to descendants of the transatlantic slave trade in the United States in ways where we can actually … actually have generational wealth, period. So, that is my definition of the freedom from environmental injustice, as well as the end of gentrification and redlining. That's what freedom looks like to me.

Ella: I had my taste of how the system works at a very, very young age. I knew that it was flawed, I knew that eventually it would wither away, but I did not know the community that I had with me and the soldiers and my comrades who were with me to help fight against that. I didn't really know the source of what is killing my people is not just one party, it's not just one white supremacist. It's capitalism. And, finding that out, I felt even more alone.

If I'm the only one who's going to go against capitalism, they might kill me, just like they killed my ancestors. But I was able to finally see the power of the people. Because I'm very young and I haven't been able to live through other revolutions, I was able to see the power of the people globally last year during the uprising. I was able to work, organize, and strategize with people who had the same beliefs, where we could all agree on the same political lines and with the same passion—people who loved and protected one another no matter their race or sexuality or their gender. And I had never had that sense of community before. With them, I was able to believe that we could do anything, and I am willing to sacrifice to be able to at least get a taste of that liberation that we want to see. And if not me, then I want to make sure that the next generation is able to do that too.

My role right now—we are currently trying to empower Black people by creating alternatives that they can use instead of the system that is oppressing them. What does that mean? That really means being able to give them housing, being able to find out ways to give them food other than one little table with a few granola bars. Being able to understand what mutual aid is. That means making sure that we're learning from each other, and knowing that is about community building; it's not charity.

That process will take years. I know that. We have to include all of our siblings in it, which is why I said once we have Black liberation, then all people will be liberated, because Black people are struggling all over the world. We have Black Palestinians, Haitians, Africans, Brazilians who are fighting every global struggle. So I believe once we are able to come together and organize and mobilize under that struggle, we will finally seek the liberation and build a new world where everybody has a chance, no matter if they're incarcerated, no matter if they're trans, queer, no matter if they're disabled. I believe that all Black people have a chance. And that inevitably means all marginalized people, too. Because again, once Black people are free, everybody is free.

—Ella

Kristina: It's good to see someone who is optimistic for the future and everything. I'm always waiting for the asteroid to come. I'm done with human beings. I'm done with this planet. Nothing is going to change. Asteroid, just come. It's time now. I'm ready to die. I think it's good to see someone young, so optimistic to think we can change the system. Because I always believed that when I was younger. I always thought if we come all together, we can change everything. But there's always someone that we thought that was on our side that in the end is not on our side: so greedy to have the money, the exposure or the token whatever you want to call it, there's always somebody like this that makes us not reach our goal. When you learn about white supremacy and you learn after that a lot of people of color, a lot of BIWOC—oblige to the white supremacy system, you're like, man, seriously. I don't know what to do anymore.

Alejandra: We're going to dismantle the presidency. There's going to be a board of matriarchs. Ella is going to be leading.

I am somebody who focuses their work on Black liberation and centers Black people in a world where diversity and inclusion is very important. They don't want you to center Black people in diversity and inclusion at all. It is so painful to essentially talk about your own traumas, the things that your community experiences, and then to have it diminished because white people are violent. I don't even want to say it's a discomfort. It's just violence. It is disheartening. It's like, "What am I doing wrong where? I'm getting so much pushback?" But it's pushback from people who are not interested in your existence.

They're interested in, literally, you dying. They're not interested in you living your will at all, especially living and calling out white supremacy.

—Ericka

Ericka: My ancestors spoke the truth; I'm going to continue to speak the truth. I know if I speak the truth or not, I am not safe as a Black, queer, nonbinary person in this world. I'm just not. I've been dealing with navigating folks wanting to eliminate and disregard my work while keeping my stress levels low. Because stress is trying to take us out, okay? Stress is deadly. So, really trying to lower my stress levels, continuing to go to acupuncture, therapy, masturbate, talk to my friends, have regular sex, have access to pleasure. All of that is also liberation to me—feeling good on my own terms and having the access to that, but also having the access to want to do those things. If you're fearing for your life, you're not going to necessarily want to have an orgasm. Navigating that is kind of what I have been dealing with. Again, not something I really talk about publicly because the Internet can't hold this shit, right?

Ren: For me it really comes down to generational healing, and I think it started with my father. He is a Spanish literature professor, as well as a professor of colonization. He's from Perú and my mother is Korean, so I like to say that I am aggressively Koruvian. It comes down to what he started teaching me from a very young age, which was to question everything and to be open to interpreting things from different cultures. Because I am multicultural and we were living in the deep south of Louisiana, in America, there are a lot of complexities and small niches that I didn't understand. I continued that education with studies of cultural and forensic anthropology and following in my father's footsteps of the study of colonization. Because my mother's Korean, she has her own understanding of colonization through Japanese and US imperialism still in our country.

Danielle: The work that I do sometimes supports my healing, but a lot of times it exacerbates all the bad things I'm working through because I'm constantly working with folks who are minorities who have been targeted, taken advantage of, who don't know all their options and resources in the community. So, working in the nonprofit space, working in community space and dealing with folks in the community who are taking advantage help put you in that space of—Kristina said it—I just want to leave the planet, I'm past it, I'm over it.

It can get very difficult, especially when you're talking about finance and in America the impact that one bad decision has on the next decade of your life. A lot of people just don't realize this credit score system is inherently racist. It's barely older than me? It wasn't necessary, and it prioritizes having enough assets and debts to have a history that a bank is willing to lend to you. Knowing that people get to a place of bad credit very young for things outside of their control is heartbreaking because the options aren't there, the assets aren't there. I tell people this all the time; one of the first assets that banks used to collateralize loans were enslaved Black people. So we're dealing with institutions that from the very beginning did not see certain people as economic tools in the capitalist system. We weren't people, we were collateral.

—Danielle

It's hard to wake up every day and try to introduce people to these financial tools that you know are and were being used against them. So, one of the biggest things to help with that is taking a step back, involving myself in other communities are a lot more liberationist, anti-capitalist, and anti-white supremacist than the ones I work in. And also lots of therapy, building a community of people around me.

I work in finance, and people think you have it together, and just because I understand the tools of oppression does not mean I've mastered them or I know how to navigate through the system that exists on my own. So one of the things I tell people is that you have to invest in a community of people who are invested in you, whether that's a therapist, a good accountant, an attorney when something happens, or a financial advisor when you start to get the place to grow an individual income. These services are not cheap—that's part of the work I'm doing. How can we get these systems in place for people where it's not going to be prohibitive for them and where they don't have to dip into their savings to get access to tools that white folks have been using for centuries to get themselves ahead.

Thank you for being honest about it. There are very few people who are willing to detach themselves from an industry that they work in, and it can be very hard to look at yourself in the mirror and say, "Am I part of the problem or am I part of the solution?"

—Tahira

Jamie: There is so much divide even between marginalized communities. It sometimes feels like Black versus LGBT versus brown. It really doesn't make sense to me. Going back to Ericka and Ella and what they were talking about before: we all can't be free if Black people aren't free. We all need to be free for us to feel free. So marginalized communities must work together.

Alejandra: Even in the nonprofit world, I'm still in the industrial complex, and it's like "Is this a charity for people or are we really changing conditions for people?" A lot of people want to help formerly incarcerated people. It's a thing now to want to be closest to the people that are closest to the harm who are closest to the solution. So, it's a thing to have us involved— impacted people. But even when we do fund, it's just those programs that are going to inform and support our mission and goals as nonprofits instead of what it really looks like to go sustain yourself and look holistically so you don't have to keep begging from us or being our story or being a member in our org for us to help you. So that's what I'm struggling a lot with. We need to be out there challenging these nonprofits that think they're actually helping when they are actually keeping us begging. And that's what power looks like for me right now. For people to actually be divested from their nonprofits, their budgets, to really invest into us. To really help us to be free on our own, not because we are tied into this nonprofit world.

Tahira: This conversation about white saviorism and how that can even live within POC. I think we can make a whole other panel about it. Kristina, how do you feel about how your community role impacts your healing? You talked about how creating the Blackletter and reading helped you on a spiritual level to liberate yourself. Break it down for us.

Kristina: I thought I was reading for liberation, but at the same time it doesn't heal. Healing and liberation are not the same to me. In liberation, you start to understand the element, the western structure, what you have outside of this and how you can understand the complexity of the world. For me, healing is something else. Based on where I am right now, for example, right now in the Netherlands, I feel like our healing cannot come from a country that has been so violent against our people. So my goal before was to go back to Africa—I don't know which country because I'm West Indian. And so this should also be a formal healing—to know exactly where I'm from to start my healing process. It is difficult because the more I know about this, the more I'm unapologetically myself and that scares people--being Black and brown and being proud of it scares people (even Black and brown people). I even think about the LGBTQIA community, it's the same. If you're proud, people think you're too loud now.

Jamie: Definitely struggling with that. They are like, "Why are you talking about it so much?" Because I'm trans!

Tahira: Kristina and I are friends, and we met in Paris. I'm in Paris right now, and I'm privileged enough to have left the US. I told my family from when I was really young that this was my intention. I'm a first-generation American, my family is Caribbean from Jamaica and St. Kitts. All of the time, inside and outside of my family, I'm asked when I am going to come back. And, I'm like, "Guys, I'm really not coming back" for this exact reason. My healing, my liberation, my mental health, my physical safety.

I don't feel safe when I'm in America.

—Tahira

And I think I lived a very privileged experience in America. But I still did not feel safe within that privileged experience. To have found a little bit more safety, freedom, and joy than I did when I was living in the States is incredible, but it really comes with then learning the society that you're part of now and what does your assimilation to it look like, or how can you join that society? And people may look at me and say, "Who do you think you are questioning our society?" The fact is I would be sad to watch any country become like my country to the point where we're not liberating ourselves as a society, and really looking at ourselves and saying, "Is the system working for people?" and "Is it working for all of us?" I've had a very interesting experience in France, but I can say overall that leaving your home country is 1000% part of a healing and liberation journey. Alejandra is getting her papers [in the US] so she can leave! Like, yes! There're so many other places, and I think I was lucky to grow up with family who traveled, and they never made me feel like the US is the end all, be all.

Jamie: I want to say something about traveling and leaving the country, too. For me, traveling is something that gives me so much anxiety because until I was 25 or 26, my IDs were not congruent. Even though I had transitioned and I was living as a woman, my IDs didn't match and limited me from doing things like going to a restaurant, going to a doctor, going to anywhere—just traveling in general. Even though I passed, there was this fear that "My God, what if somebody finds out? What if somebody picks up on something?" Recently I went to Jamaica—and please tell me if I'm being offensive in addressing this topic at all. I wasn't nervous to go to Jamaica, but there is an LGBTQ+ law that literally can put you in prison, right? There is a lot of homophobia and transphobia. It's the reality. It is what it is. So traveling, I was very nervous. While I was there, even though I was having fun, it was wild. I would stop having fun because it's like, Jamie, don't have too much fun because people are going to notice you, and what if they look too closely and figure it out? I feel like being traumatized day after day, I literally have to put a smile on my face and work through my feelings every single day. It's a struggle, and it's harder when it's not coming from white people, but other marginalized communities. We should know better how it feels to be excluded.

Tahira: 1000%. For me, I don't take offense to anything you shared. As a cisgender woman who is not Jamaican—my mom was born in Jamaica—so, I view it from this lens of I wasn't even a person who lived in, grew up in the country, and has a good idea of what that looks like, the anti-LGBTQ+ hate. It's really embedded in the culture. You hear it in the music. We would be so stupid to not address it in this conversation. So I'm happy that you brought it up.

Jamie: I've been reading a little bit on it. I'm not super educated on all of these topics, but I've read that slavery and ancestral trauma affects people's way of thinking. But where we are now, ... I really do think that we need to use these different experiences as an explanation, and not an excuse anymore. When you've been taught to hate yourself, your skin, the way you look, and then you've been taught to be a certain way, anything different than that is, "No, cannot accept this." And I think this is what is happening with LGBTQ+ people, not just in Jamaica but everywhere. Even within the brown community. I grew up in a family where I've heard my family say that white, Black, brown, Asian people all experience racism the same way. Can you imagine that? I'm laughing, but I'm not laughing. It's embarrassing for me to say that. If you think we all experience racism the same way, how can you understand what LGBTQ+ people go through? It's difficult to heal when that type of narrative is so ingrained in your minds.

Alejandra: I think that is the work of everybody here in this space. It's understanding that we have so many centuries and centuries of unlearning to do.

Ella: I feel as Black women and femmes, people expect so much from us, while also disrespecting us and killing us. It takes a lot out of you spiritually, mentally, and physically. This is coming from my light-skin, cis-passing experience. I've noticed that it's mostly Black matriarchs who have the movement on their backs. It's Black queer and Black trans people who continue to have the movement on their backs, and people expect so much from us without letting us take a break. So I had to put it upon myself to realize that I can't please everybody. I can't prove myself to everybody. If I can't love and care for myself, I can't care for my community.

Black queer femmes are always expected to be strong, endure trauma, and then continue to fight without thinking of taking breaks—or else be portrayed as weak. We deserve rest, we deserve care, we deserve love because the whole system is working against us. Even when I thought I could move forward after experiencing a traumatizing situation, I had to stop and realize that I shouldn't feel guilty for taking some time because I have the privilege to do so versus many other comrades in different countries who can't go home.

—Ella

Kristina: I always feel so tired and just realized after years that I'm tired because of this, like my mental health. The system was taking all my energy. All of the oppression that you are surrounded with makes you depressed, tired. Part of the system is to drain our energy.

Tahira: It keeps us dumb, busy, and distracted. Uneducated, not getting the resources in our schools to know what the system is and why it functions the way that it does. Because knowledge is power. If we have the knowledge about something, we can work to dismantle it. We have to work to live. We are not capitalists; we are the means for capital.

Danielle: The more I decenter whiteness in everything I do, especially in my rest, the easier it is for me to restore my pleasure because now I have references for people who look like me, identify like me, and have my struggle being able to find happiness and peace. Changing consumption to prioritize that healing is important.

For me, happiness is a moment. It is a very short definition of time. Joy is something you have to choose. It is a state of being. It is a state of mind. Choosing joy versus chasing happiness has to come from within, of my own autonomy and volition. It has to do with decentering whiteness. Use that whenever you are exhausted. Use that whenever you are tired.

—Ren

Alejandra: For me, organizing is more of lifestyle. I'm organizing all the time because abolition is about creating the things we need once we shut all this other shit down, right?

Jamie: It's different every day. Sometimes being alone, sometimes talking with friends, to make myself feel seen … it really depends on the day. There is no formula to my personal joy. But I realize that activism is joy, too. We need to celebrate being happy. That is a form of activism.

ENDNOTES

1. This transcript has been edited for length, content, and clarity. The full audio and video are currently available at Haven Media's Facebook page: https://bit.ly/3DCM9YX.

2. Haven Media, Inc., is a 501(c)(3) organization co-founded by Tamara L. Lee, one of the editors of this LERA volume. It is a collective for and by Black and Indigenous women and nonbinary folks of color (https://www.havenmedia.org).

3. The November 20 acquittal on all charges of Kyle Rittenhouse, who shot and killed two people during protests against the shooting of Jacob Blake by a white police officer in Kenosha, Wisconsin.

CHAPTER 11

Race, Power, and the Path to a Just Transition: A Conversation with J. Mijin Cha and Larry Williams Jr.

J. MIJIN CHA
Occidental College

LARRY WILLIAMS JR.
UnionBase

MODERATED BY
MAITE TAPIA
Michigan State University

Abstract

The following is based on two recorded conversations over Zoom in June 2021. The Zoom meetings were attended by J. Mijin Cha, Larry Williams Jr., Maite Tapia (co-editor of this volume), and Joy Milner (undergraduate student at Michigan State University). The text has been edited to fit within this volume. In this conversation, J. Mijin Cha and Larry Williams Jr. talk about their own story and their work around "just transition"—particularly, how, as people of color in these white spaces, they have broken through barriers and how they think about just transition in terms of critical race theory and intersectionality.

PARTICIPANTS

J. Mijin Cha is an assistant professor of urban and environmental policy at Occidental College and a fellow at the Worker Institute, Cornell University. Dr. Cha's research focuses on labor/climate coalitions and just transitions. She is a part of the Just Transition Listening Project research team convened by the Labor Network for Sustainability, which was the first effort of its kind to interview over 100 individuals on their experience with industrial transition. Along with her colleague, Dr. Manuel Pastor, she developed a novel framework for developing just transition policies and conducted a four-state study of what is needed for a just transition and how to build progressive power at the state level. She is also a member of the Labor Leading on Climate initiative at Cornell University's Worker Institute that supports several state-based climate jobs efforts.

Larry Williams Jr. is founder of UnionBase.org and co-founder of Progressive Workers Union (PWU). UnionBase is the first secure social networking and education platform for unions and union workers. It is regarded by *Forbes* and *Fast Company* as the leading digital platform for a new generation of workers. PWU is a growing and powerful national union for nonprofit employees that was started at the Sierra Club, America's largest environmental organization.

Maite Tapia is an associate professor at the School of Human Resources and Labor Relations at Michigan State University. Her research focuses on worker voice within the workplace, as well as worker organizing and movement building within the broader society, paying specific attention to workers' social identities and structural racism.

Maite: Thanks, Mijin and Larry, for being here! To start us off, you have both done a lot of work around just transition. What is your own story within that work and particularly your own story as a person of color?

Mijin: I grew up in Wyoming in, as you can imagine, a very white space. Since then, I think I've just always wanted to live in big cities where there's a lot of diversity. So you're invisible in a different way, right? There's the invisibility that comes with when you're the only person of color in a room. And then there's the invisibility that comes with when you are more of a majority. So you can just relax and be. But there have been a couple of times doing this work where I've been kind of jolted out of it. For instance, I was meeting with a solar expert, and we're having this perfectly normal conversation about rooftops. And he stops me in the middle of it and asks me, "Oh, where are you from?" Which you know, I really hate this question. So I said, "I'm Korean," to which he responds, "Oh, my wife and I, we sponsor this little girl in the Philippines." Great. One, not Filipina. Two, has nothing to do with solar. And three, I have no idea [how] I should respond to this. In some ways, I think a lot of people would say, "Oh, they're just curious about you," but what it actually does, it's really disruptive and your mindset of "I'm an expert in this field" has suddenly distilled down to "Actually, no matter where you go, you'll still be this somewhat odd-looking, foreign-looking person."

Larry: Wow. Thank you, Mijin, for starting us off from a real place. I was about 21 years old when I got this temporary employment opportunity at the Teamsters. I was the youngest person there, and definitely one of the first Black employees in the Organizing Department. I could tell because of the initial apprehension when I was hired by some staff. In my first week employed, a friend of mine named Abdur, who was also African American, and I became friends. He's 6'8", I'm 6'2". So imagine these two tall, young Black men walking down the hallway. People were thinking, "What the hell is going on in the Teamsters?" So one day our manager calls us into her office, and she says, "Hey, I want to let you guys know you're doing a great job. But we got a notification from another department that you guys are roaming the halls." My response was "What?" We have two 15-minute breaks a day and a one-hour break because this is a union job, right? And we take off to get a break and we walk outside, we're talking about how grateful we are to be working for this union, and then somebody profiles us in our own jobs. So that was my introduction to working in the labor movement?

Maite: When you are in these white spaces, what have you done to break through those barriers?

Mijin: To be honest, for a long time I just made myself small. I felt like what I had to do was make people comfortable. When you're Asian and you have an opinion and you're a woman, people feel a way about that. And so to be honest, when I first started, I just played dumb a lot. And now that I'm old and angrier, I don't care.

Larry: That's interesting you say that because, first of all, you're not old, okay?

[laughing]

Mijin: Skincare regime is very important!

[laughing]

Larry: You should share some tips! But I actually did the opposite when I was young. Teachers always assumed I didn't know or punished me for speaking, so I made it my ultimate goal particularly to show white people that I knew what I was talking about. I would almost perform.

Mijin: Yeah, I know. I definitely think it has also to do with our societal positions. People see you, they think a certain thing, and they see me, and they think a certain thing. So we both have to negotiate that white space from our different poles.

Maite: Thanks for sharing this. Now talking about your main work on just transition, what does this concept mean to you and the people you talk to and work with in your communities?

Mijin: The closer you get to people on the ground, the more that they're like, "Can you please go away with this lingo?" Which I totally understand. But when you're talking to them, what they want is a just transition. There are internal conflicts as people say I work in an oil refinery, it's a very good job, and I care about climate change, and I have children. But there is no other alternative for me, right? If you ask me to willingly leave—I just cannot willingly leave this job for nothing and let my family starve. This is why organizing has to be central to everything. *Because what we're hearing from workers is that they feel largely abandoned. So when you tell them that we're going to transform our energy system and stop using fossil fuels, they're just like, "I can't even go to the dentist. And you want me to believe that we're going to have a whole new system with millions of green jobs?"*

Larry: Yeah, there's just transition in the context of workers when a plant is shut down. What happens to those workers in that community? Are they repatriated to new jobs, moved to a different facility, offered retraining? There is just transition in the context of a community that wants to move away from fossil fuels themselves and wants to be a part of that planning process. The idea of community benefits agreement in legislation that brings funding to local communities, specifically for the purpose of transition. There is just transition in a sense of people fighting recidivism, people coming back from prison and being able to have skills-based work that's environmental work and union solar jobs. And then there's also climate transition, economies going off fossil fuels and how communities have a say in that process and how it impacts them. So understanding [the] contexts in which people are talking about is important.

I did some work in Nairobi, Kenya, with a couple of grassroots groups named Save Lamu and Decoalonize. They fight for those who live off fish and off the land. They looked me in the eye and said, "Just transition—we like the concept. But what does just transition look like for us? What are we transitioning to? We live off the land. We live off the fish. We live a very natural, low-impact life. So what are we transitioning to? We're not going to go work in an office somewhere." That was a really emotional and interesting moment for me because I was like, *"Wow, you can't tell people who are in the 'hood who never had the opportunity for any of the basics that all of a sudden now they need to go work a construction job or something. They should be granted the decision making that guides what they want to build their community into."*

Mijin: Well, 100%, I think this is a mistake some members of the environmental movement made by saying that coal miners will become coders or solar installers, right? I just don't think a just transition happens without tackling the systems of injustice that we have now. So for instance, we need to revive a lot of these rural regions. That's not going to happen under our neoliberal capitalist model because there's just not a lot of profit there (in investing in rural regions). You're going to need a 10- to 20-year period where it's just investments so that you can grow the next economy.

Maite: How can we think about just transition in terms of critical race theory and intersectionality?

Mijin: As my colleague and mentor Manuel Pastor would also say, *Just transition is a transition to justice because in some sense, these extractive practices that we've been talking about, it's not just resource extraction.* It's the prison industrial complex, it's the nonprofit industrial complex, it's predatory lending. And climate injustice is just a manifestation of existing extractive systems. So we actually need to change these existing extractive systems. This means we have to really start thinking about systems change. *These injustices and inequities are arising because we have unjust systems and will just continue to arise. So just transition is about if we were to envisage a just society, how would we be in relation to each other? How can we grow a shared sense of commitment, a shared sense of responsibility that could help tackle what is a shared problem?*

Larry: To me the book *Black Reconstruction* by W.E.B Du Bois was one of my first introductions to understanding how work has evolved in the United States as it shows the historical exclusion of Black people from labor laws, jobs, employment, or the economic system. *So if you don't liberate Black people particularly—we are at the bottom of economic ladder, which is now being replaced by people from Latin America—you can never have a completely fair system, and you're going to exclude a class of people just by proxy. The same goes for Native American people. So this has to be a guiding principle of just transition.*

Mijin: I'm also seeing more adjectives before transition. I just saw one today that said a "just, equitable, and fair transition." And in theory, if a transition is just, it is both equitable and fair. So I feel like the more these terms come in, the more you're just looking for metrics. The justice part is being lost. And you know, to Larry's point, if you center the most vulnerable, then you actually help everybody, right?

Larry: I struggled with the Sierra Club having a kind of shallow definition of "just transition" that was segmented by a campaign, Beyond Coal. This campaign was responsible for shutting down a large percentage of the coal plants in the country, but they are very metric driven because they're funded by Bloomberg. So they never reached out to the workers or to the union. Even though, within the environmental movement, you have environmental justice groups. These grassroots organizations were often started by Black activists in the '80s and '90s, and they organize with very few resources. But then you have green groups which are sometimes funded by multibillionaire corporations that have conflicting interests.

Maite: What are some of the tensions between the labor movement and environmental organizations around issues of just transition?

Larry: One of the differences between their perspectives is simply time frame. Local unions and the labor movement are always thinking about the next contract and the next bargaining session. They have an almost quarterly view on things. And they have to, because they're thinking about their members. Whereas environmentalists might think on a hundred-year time frame, right? That realization, even though it's a very simple thing, is very important because you can't have a conversation with groups working on different time frames and expect them to come to a working solution unless you find a shared interest or enemy.

So there's the everlasting battle between the environmental groups' priority of shutting things down, and then the economic ramifications that are just completely adversarial to the labor unions. The unions are thinking about their members today, tomorrow, next month, next year, and then the factory or whatever is being shut down. The environmental groups are thinking about climate change, 10 years, 15 years. But it's like, *you can't tell a Black person who is at threat of getting shot every time they leave their home that they should be thinking 50 years out. You just can't see that far.*

Mijin: Watching the unionization campaign in Bessemer, it's disheartening to see that we don't make a bigger deal about the fact that when we have unchecked corporate power—that is disastrous for everybody, but particularly for the climate, right? *If you cannot check corporate power, you cannot address the climate crisis.* I really wish that more big environmental organizations would come out and say, "Worker power is the only counter we have to capital." It's true, right? And until we really develop and hold worker power and expand it, we are at the mercy of capital. And if we're at the mercy of capital, we will never solve the climate crisis, will never be able to address it, because capital will always win.

Larry: My co-worker used to use the analogy of "Game of Thrones." We're all in our own little kingdom fighting amongst each other, and then the white walkers are over there behind the wall just heading towards us. But nobody can pay attention.

[laughter, then five-minute side conversation about the horrors of "Game of Thrones," but then we got back on track!]

Larry: And then there's a big disconnect between the outcomes because, for the environmental groups, it's cool to shut down coal plants. Great, we shut the plant down. Victory. We get to have a nice e-mail post or whatever. But then, are there jobs left there? When you left, did you talk to the union? Did you communicate with any of the workers in the community and find out what they wanted? When you got that hundred-million dollars to actually go into that community and work, did you actually work with the Native tribes there? So that question you asked at the very beginning, the defining of what just transition is, should actually be decided by the community and by the impacted people. For example, there are companies that have made solar panels in prison. So you're doing something billed as clean energy, but you're still exploiting a worker in that, right? Same thing with Tesla. We got these beautiful clean energy cars, but people get paid pennies and have terrible racist experiences while they're making the cars. For example, a Black worker just successfully sued Tesla and won a $137 million dollar judgment for the racism they endured and the company condoned.

Mijin: Another important difference between the labor movement and the environmental movement is that the labor movement is very comfortable talking about power. And needing to build power and taking power. Whereas a lot of enviros tend to think that's unseemly. So they talk more about science-based targets. There is the thought that if you have the perfect solution, people will come on board. Nobody gives a fuck about the science, okay? It's somewhat uninspiring to talk about science-based targets, and it doesn't prompt a lot of people to action. Whereas labor is based in organizing, they understand power and power dynamics and the messiness that comes with trying to build power. And I think that is a big lesson that the environmental movement could learn from the labor movement.

Larry: It's almost like their Achilles heel in a way. Imagine if those two movements truly work together. It would be literally unstoppable. *That was always my vision that you will have people both having union membership but also being members of environmental organizations, getting joint training on how to make your workplace fair, how to make your community resilient.* And I think you need unique collective power, collective organizing power mixed with that amazing ability the environmental movement has to mobilize people. The environmental movement can get a thousand people to do a march at two o'clock on a Wednesday. It's crazy, I saw them and I was like, "What?" The labor movement can't do that unless they pay all those people.

Maite: How can we envision or reimagine a new society then?

Larry: If we're talking about the labor movement, it's crazy because I feel like I've always been the youngest person in any room. Being in it for ten years, I'm still the youngest person in most of these rooms, and I'm still being talked to like I'm five years old and I don't know what's going on.

When I launched my company UnionBase in 2015, I sent out an email to have 20,000 or 30,000 emails from labor leaders. And you know, when you start something, it's a process iteration. You put it out there, you get feedback, you iterate. It's not going to be perfect. You move fast and break things. But one of the emails I got was from an old-time labor leader who said, "You have too many mistakes, you need to go back to the drawing board." So I responded to him: "Hey, thanks for the feedback. Not everything is going to be accurate. This is the first thing of its kind, but this is the process we go through to iterate." He responds, "It's not ready for prime time, try again." The arrogance of that, that's a very common thing that I see from these old labor guys; they think that everybody else is stupid. Now, not only do you have this attitude, which is bad enough, but then you have the whole infrastructure of leadership in the labor movement that coddles them and doesn't want to offend them. So you don't have real conversations in the labor movement.

Mijin: What Larry is talking about is just so fundamental because you cannot change the world if you perpetuate that rot, right? I'm sure that if we went on a lot of big organization's websites, in fact, I would bet my money—that I don't have much of, I'm an assistant professor at a liberal arts college.

[laughing]

But for sure they have a DEI—diversity, equity, and inclusion statement, right? 1000%, I'm sure they say, "Racial justice is climate justice," all of that. But what are we asking for as a movement if we are saying that we care about racial justice, but people of color have really mixed experiences in some of these places. Some nonprofits become this extractive industrial complex. Until that changes, until we stop this internal rot, I just don't care what you say because I've seen what you do.

So when we see all this verbiage around diversity, equity, and inclusion, what do we actually see in practice? It would really mean power-sharing, right? You need to take power from one group and give it to another group. But what we really see is this inability to share power and this inability to change direction.

Maite: Those are really good points and powerful stories. These institutions clearly need to change also from within. Who should lead these organizations? How would they change? How can we reshape, reimagine these core institutions?

Larry: We're going to have a white female president of the AFL-CIO, which yes, that's progress—that's great progress [*update: this now happened!*]. But why is it so out of the question to have a Black woman lead the AFL-CIO? Can you imagine? At the same time, however, there's also a risk here where, whenever we get people of color into powerful positions, we think that that's going to change everything, like President Obama, for example. There's surface and then there's a deep change. If they're a person of color, if they're a trans person, whatever background that they have, they should also have the type of analysis that's radical and that is progressive—and that actually talks about intersectionality as opposed to a person as a figurehead who you put a bunch of people around them that really prevent them from actually changing anything. This is the pattern that I see in every space.

Mijin: Yeah, I think that's so spot on. And if we're talking about the AFL-CIO, for instance, they refused to kick out the policing union. And you just think, "What is solidarity? What does that mean if this union literally terrorizes Black and brown communities?" I just think you cannot say you're committed to racial justice. On the one hand, you're talking about how important it is to support and protect communities of color. On the other hand, you support police unions. These two things cannot coexist.

And similarly in the just transition space, people say "Well, we're up against this timeline and equity takes time." So there's this tension. And to me that is fundamentally wrong. The environmental justice movement has been doing this advocacy work for decades, so why don't you just join them and their efforts? Share your power with them? The issue is that you want to own it. You want it to be your idea, you want it to be your campaign. That's why you think there's this time constraint when in fact you could just put those resources into something that is already happening and help that along. And I think that's the fundamental issue—people don't want to give up power and resources. And until that changes, until we can understand what really shared governance, shared prosperity means and really internalize it, I just don't see it changing.

And I think that this is actually the point—neoliberalism needs these big institutions that don't really push the needle. You need the big institutions to give cover so that we can continue business as usual, while also saying we need to change. Carbon capture is a great example of this. Some unions support it, but the whole point of carbon capture is that we will continue burning fossil fuels. We get big environmental organizations on board, we get big labor unions on board, and then we just continue our neoliberal way of being.

Larry: Right! I also visualize a more decentralized labor movement. I work with so many groups of workers who are organizing themselves without any other union leading them. I'll use the PWU [Progressive Workers Union] as an example. We've organized staff at many of the green groups, such as the Sierra Club, Greenpeace, the Union of Concerned Scientists, and 350. But the way we did that was by focusing on the paradigm that racial justice should be at the lead of fighting the climate movement and the economic justice movement.

I was the first president. The second president was a South Asian woman, and the third was an African American man. The logo is a black hand and a brown hand embracing each other, and the central idea was centering the most vulnerable people.

We realized that decentralization actually packs a lot of power. The traditional labor movement is very centralized—there was this paradigm: the bigger, the better. But what that really means is the bigger you are, the less power the workers tend to have because now there's a chain of people who can decide whether you're going to go on strike, how far you're going to go, whether or not you have the ability to negotiate certain things. Whereas we had a group of very motivated people who believed in centering vulnerable people. For example, Black women are a major part of the reason we got the most outstanding contract in the nonprofit world probably ever. Because one of the first things we did was a pay equity analysis and found out that Black women, particularly, were making between 8 % and 13% less than anybody else in the organization.

Maite: Great to hear the work of the PWU! Well, we've come to the end of our conversation, would you like to add a final comment?

Mijin: I think it's cool the format that you're using because this starts to decolonize some of these structures, right? So the fact that it's an academic publication, that's not just, "Here's my 500 citations," and the idea that knowledge can also take different forms. The closing thing I would say is that to me, the sign that things have actually changed and that there is a racial reckoning is that Larry and I can have this conversation and it would just be about how he was valued or how I was valued or how there wasn't backlash when we challenged systems of power. So I look forward to the day that we can have this conversation again and just talk about how things have changed and how we, as people of color, no longer have to do this emotional and other forms of labor. Until these stories of people of color trying to make change are not met with violence or oppression, I just don't know what a racial reckoning will look like.

Larry: Mijin, you're like Noam Chomsky with the hope you know? He'll have a thousand words and then by the end, he's like, "By the way, we're screwed."

[laughing]

Larry: But you're being honest. A lot of times, unfortunately, that's where I'm left. When the whole George Floyd movement happened, a lot of people in our movement were excited, saying, "Oh, it's our moment." I was exhausted. I've been thinking about this stuff as long as I've been here. I was happy to see Black Lives Matter come along. But sometimes it feels like these things come as a wave and then people are like, "Okay, we're cool now," "All right, Trump is out, we got Biden now." It's so exhausting how we tend to think that we won already. And I think the labor movement definitely needs to represent more than 10% of the national population. Within the climate change movement in terms of race, I think that it is finally slowly becoming part of the conversation around just transition. Also questions about funding are important— who's going to fund just transitioning? I don't want it to be solely funded by people like that who are very self-interested.

I want just transition to be the number-one conversation. I'm still waiting for it to be the number-one conversation in the world. It's not yet, and it really should be. I'm happy, though, that we're having real conversations like this. That's probably the bright spot for me.

Mijin: Yes, I should say that the existence of this conversation in this edited volume is hopeful.

Maite: That should be the last line of our chapter.

[*laughing*]

Larry: Seriously, though.

ACKNOWLEDGMENTS

We thank Joy Milner for her help transcribing the original conversations.

PART III

PRACTITIONERS

"Many Faces, One Voice"

By Heen Shawat (Water Woman), Kasi Marita Perreira (Łingit), 2011

Gunalchéesh sh yáa awudanéix'i. Gunalchéesh Duwamish, gunalchéesh Muckleshoot, gunalchéesh Coast Salish. Yak'éi yeexwsateení aan yatx'u saani. Heen Shawat yoo xat duwasaakw. Dłeit káa x'eináx Kasi Marita Perreira yoo xát duwasáakw. Ch'aak naax xát sitee. Hoots hít áyá haa naa kahídi. Tdleité yádix xát sitee. Cháanwaan dachxán áyá xát. Cháanwaan áyá ax daakanóox'u. Xutsnoowú kwáan dáx áyá xát.

Features Bear (House clan), Raven (creator, trickster), Salmon, and Orca (connecting Seattle and Alaska). Original is full color, paper stencil on wood, in oil and acrylic paint. Inspired by working people, artists, the land and life of the Pacific Northwest—a gift to honor past, present and future members of the United Food and Commercial Workers union.

In September 2020, Kasi Marita Perreira was named director of racial and gender justice, a new staff position at the Washington State Labor Council, AFL-CIO, dedicated to leading the council's work in challenging all of Washington's labor movement—union leaders, staffers, and rank-and-file members—to understand our collective responsibility and stake in advocating for racial and gender justice. In addition to this education work, Kasi is also flagging problems, including problems within the movement as well as between organized labor and other social movements.

Kasi is an organizer, artist, loving partner. and mama of two. She joined the Washington State Labor Council after 15 years of organizing working people from the Bay Area to North Carolina with the United Food and Commercial Workers union and a lifetime of advocating for social justice. As organizing director at UFCW 21, she focused on member-led, equitable leadership development and helped to bring thousands of members into the union.

"Many Faces, One Voice"
By Heen Shawat (Water Woman), Kasi Marita Perreira (Łingit), 2011

Chapter 12

"The Strategy Is Love": Womxn Speak on Innovative Strategies and Leading in Labor During Unprecedented Times

WILL EMPOWER

SHERI DAVIS-FAULKNER

Rutgers University, Center for Innovation in Worker Organization and Department of Labor Studies and Employment Relations

We are in a world, a society, a time frame that is absent of radical love. [If] I love you, I am going to practice truth, and transparency. If I love you, I will secure your safety. I will protect you. I am going to work for your benefit. In love, I can face enemies and challenges: enemies that are big bogeymen and challenges that seem insurmountable. ... We have to begin to employ strategies that include the issues that real people, the people we swear to God we try to help change the world, ... [have] and figure out how they see themselves, not just [in] the results, but in the strategy. So I just think that the moment calls for us to have **love as a strategy**.

—Stacy Davis-Gates, executive vice president,
Chicago Teachers Union

Abstract

This chapter presents excerpts from a virtual plenary session titled "Leading for Innovative Strategies in Unprecedented Times" as part of the first Womxn's Labor Leadership Symposium hosted by WILL Empower (Women Innovating Labor Leadership).[1] The symposium was sponsored by a cross section of unions, worker centers, community-based organizations, and foundations. We invited Sarita Gupta, director for the Ford Foundation Future of Work(ers) program and a leader working to shape a future of work that puts workers and their well-being at the center, to moderate this session. Gupta, formerly the executive director of Jobs With Justice for many years, is a founding member of the WILL Empower Advisory Council. We began the session with a video of questions posed by leaders from across the country within the WILL Empower network.

WILL EMPOWER (WE) NETWORK QUESTIONS
Katrina Peterson
Emerging Leaders Cohort; Washington State; Power Switch Action–
Puget Sound Sage

Hi, my name is Katrina Peterson. I use she/her pronouns. I'm the climate justice program manager at Puget Sound Sage, which is located on the unceded, stolen lands of the Duwamish people and other Coast Salish Tribes. I completed the WILL Empower Emerging Leaders Cohort. My question for the leaders table is "Given the climate catastrophes that are increasing in frequency and intensity, what is holding the labor movement back from exercising their full power to fight for a livable and healthy planet?"

Keani Christianson
Emerging Leaders Cohort; Texas; Service Employees International Union

Hi, my name is Keani Christianson. Pronouns, she/her. I work for SEIU as a national security campaign director, and I'm based in Houston, Texas. I completed the WILL Empower Emerging Leaders Cohort. My question for the leaders table is "Given the current climate that we are in with southern governors working hard to restrict voters' rights and women's rights, why aren't unions joining together to support southern regional organizing by providing sustainable resources, such as funding and boots on the ground. Thanks."

Angelina Cruz
Executive Leadership Cohort; Wisconsin; Racine Education Association

I'm Angelina Cruz, president of Educators United. As a woman of color labor leader in Wisconsin, I'm proud of the educator members of our local union who organized around safety in school buildings. These educators came together to keep school buildings closed until March 2021 to ensure the safety of both educators and our students. We are less than a month back to school, and the learning loss and achievement rhetoric is causing an unnecessary sense of urgency. While kids, families, and educators are all hurting and grieving, we are expected to make up for lost time because our kids are behind. Which begs the question "What are we even measuring against?"

All of society is still firmly planted in the midst of a pandemic. While our school district has overtly expressed a deeper commitment to social, emotional learning, and equity training, as a result of what we experienced last school year in the pandemic—[which are] things we should have already been doing particularly in a demographically diverse school district—[when you couple] this with an increased emphasis on data points and testing, [it] proves that this is a superficial commitment at best. It seems all too many, including workers and including educators, are eager to go back to normal. My question to you all is this: "How do you lead through pandemic fatigue?"

Sarah David Heydemann

Emerging Leaders Cohort; Washington, D.C.; National Women's Law Center

Hey everyone! My name is Sarah, I use she/her pronouns. I'm a senior counsel on the workplace justice team at the National Women's Law Center, and I'm in Washington, D.C., which is the traditional territory of Anacostan and Piscataway people. I completed the WILL Empower Emerging Leaders Cohort, and my question for the panel is this: "Women, especially women of color, have been on the front lines of this pandemic-induced recession as domestic workers, as essential workers, as breadwinners. How would this moment have been different if the New Deal had not denied rights to domestic workers, agricultural workers, workers with disabilities, and so many more? Thanks so much!"

MODERATED TABLE DISCUSSION

Sarita Gupta: I'm so excited to be moderating this panel with amazing leaders. Those were terrific questions, [and] we are all set to find out what it means to lead in uncertain times [including] everything from a global pandemic to the economic crisis we are all experiencing to the real racial tensions and reckoning that is happening in our country to the attacks on voting rights, attacks on reproductive rights, attacks on housing security, and much more. And those fabulous questions that touched upon climate crisis, and how we actually lead us through exhaustion, and how women are being impacted on the front lines. All of these are questions that I think many of the leaders today on this panel have been grappling with as well.

The invitation is to dig in and learn a little bit about what it means to be leading in this moment. How each of you, as panelists, are helping to build a thriving and sustainable labor movement and really responding to the opportunities—because the truth is, crisis is always lined with opportunities, and we are in a really great moment of immense transformation and opportunity. So I want to start with a question for all of you: What is keeping you up at night, given the unprecedented moment we are in?

Lauren Jacobs (executive director, PowerSwitch Action): So, what's keeping me up at night? Many things. I will not talk about the to-do list at my house or taking care of an elder parent or those things [*laughs*]. Our work is thinking about what are we called to do in this moment. We are living in a moment of immense opportunity and immense risk. I do not think in my entire life—yes, the gray hair is duly earned—that I have seen a wider consensus that the present system is not working. We can see that in the strikes, the job actions that are happening, without formal organizations being involved. We saw that in the uprising last summer and continued sparks that are happening at any given moment, across the country, and frankly, globally. We cannot control what the proto-authoritarian right is going to do, [and] I think that is one of the risks out there. We can control and think about what we will do.

I worry about the pace of our organizing. I think about not letting our uncertainty about the future, of not being able to see [what] the new thing is, trap us into being so nostalgic for old models that were compromised at the time they were engaged. Things are shifting and changing—I want us to. It is scary, but we need to embrace it. We need to say that the old system had its problems, I will not fight to go back to the thing that kind of was not totally serving me in the first place. But think about what is ahead—I worry about nostalgia; it is seductive.

I worry about balancing our need for short-term wins against being deeply committed to have our people in power. Having us run the joint. Right? And not giving up on that. Finally, I think for our movement—I do worry about all of us really, deeply, heart, soul, brain, embracing that ending white supremacy and ending patriarchy is fundamental to transforming the economy. We ain't going to do it unless those go as well! That's my list! [*laughs*]

Sarita Gupta: That's quite a list, Lauren. I knew you were the right person to start with to kick us off. I would love to invite Cindy to tell us what is keeping [her] up at night these days!

Cindy Estrada (executive vice president, United Auto Workers): All the things we are worried about we can solve if we have people who care and empathize and care about community, and workers, and gender and race, so what keeps me up at night is whether we are going to be able to organize on a large scale. It takes capacity, which everyone on this call does not have enough of. [It takes] skill to find organizers that want to be part of this movement, mentors for those organizers, and women that want to be mentors for the women. It is [not only] capacity [but] whether or not the labor movement, at this moment, is going to put [in] the resources that are necessary and also realize that the great thing about this moment, of all of us being so small and having lost so much, [is the recognition] that we all need each other to win.

There is this really great opportunity, and having a president who speaks about the labor movement and an administration where you are hearing about workers and workers' issues and working families and unions [is great], but [will] we be able to come together? I know we can. It's time to all come together to say we will not allow those on the right [to present us] with this false choice of climate or jobs, climate or community. Really, together we have to show that we are not going to fall for that. It is both: It is a moment when it is not just for us [unions] here. It is not just about the plant—it is what happens in that community outside of that plant. What are the environmental issues facing those communities?

Whether it is air quality, whether it is access to jobs, schools right by these plants breathing in that air—it is this intersectional moment and will we, as leaders, take the opportunity to have those hard conversations at the table with one another. I always tell workers, [who] I am working at organizing, that you do not have to like each other [because] I find that through a campaign, people [actually] tend to find they like each other more than when they walked in the door because they get to know each other.

Sarita Gupta: That is great, Cindy! I'm so glad you raised this point about how we should not fall into the trap of having a White House and an administration that is talking about workers suddenly means our job is done.

Veronica Mendez-Moore (co-executive director, Centro de Trabajadores Unidos en la Lucha): Two things I will name. One is deeply informed by the context that I live in here in Minneapolis, and George Floyd was murdered ten feet outside my office. The amount of weight and trauma that that creates for my staff, for my members—we have members and staff who were out there 24 hours a day [and] were sleeping in our office, who were working with figuring things out with the local gangs that were trying to keep the peace. It was an incredibly intense experience on top of everything else with the pandemic. For me, one of the things that I'm deeply concerned about is our people and how can they be sustained through this? How can we support our staff and members? How can we do right by our community in terms of healing, in terms of rest, in terms of the right amount of work that people are even able to do? The amount of emotional labor people are able to commit to—that is something I worry about a lot. It is a difficult thing for us to keep our finger on the pulse, and everyone wants to keep fighting through it, right? That is one big thing.

Another thing is in this moment, where we know there is so much money coming from the federal government, part of me and the leaders that surround me, our instinct is we have to get that money into the right places. We have to build organizations and institutions; otherwise, developers will get that money and say that they need to build condos, or whatever, and none of them will be affordable, and [they] will use nonunion labor. How do we make sure that we are both doing this short-term drive to get that money—because our commissioners on a state level, they are all in it—while at the same time thinking about the need to be building our long-term solutions. This is also a moment where we have a real opportunity, especially in the city of Minneapolis, where we have entire small-business corridors that were destroyed in uprisings. This is a moment for us to build institutions and do that in a different way. It cannot just be about getting money; that balance between what is too much [short-term] or too much [long-term]—it really keeps me up at night.

Sarita Gupta: Yes. Such great points. This is a moment to think about how to transform our institutions, right? That is so important and necessary. I just want to extend a huge thanks to you and the leadership of you, and your team, in this moment in Minneapolis.

April Verrett (Local 2015 president, Service Employees International Union): I am more determined than ever after surviving the last 18 months. We have paid so much lip service to the status quo not being good enough, not wanting to go back there, that we have to reach for equity. But I am all about how we are operationalizing that.

What does it mean to practice equity? How is it not just a buzzword that corporations are quick to use in their branding and marketing tools? [*laughs*] How do we really learn together, how to define equity? And how are we not settling for the status quo? And how are we as a labor movement and folks who work every day to build powerful workers not settling for the status quo in our part of the world? Because it is certainly not delivering for people who look like me, who come from the southside of Chicago, … who live in Mississippi where my family is [and] who live in South LA, where I am now.

We act like collective bargaining is the greatest thing since sliced bread. And the end-all be-all. It is the manna from heaven that will deliver for workers [*laughs*]. I just challenge us to be real about the limits of the labor movement we have. It is a labor movement that was built for [the] 20th-century economy. That has gotten us a long way. We are deeply in the middle of the 21st-century economy, with 21st-century workers. What does [it] look like to meet the crisis that we are all experiencing together?

Sarita Gupta: Great, April. I'm glad you brought this really important view around these questions of real equity and understanding how we envision the 21st-century labor movement.

Liz Perlman (Local 3299 executive director, American Federation of State, County and Municipal Employees): Besides my teenagers [keeping me up at night] [*laughs*] … I think one of the things I feel as the obstacle is our own sense of bravery. Whether or not we are demanding and asking for the rest of the labor movement to say we need to support Black and brown women in leadership in this movement, full stop, period. We need to share the power. We need to have people who understand the experience and understand what the solutions are [*laughs*]. I am fully honored I get to be in the space. I also recognize the labor movement, and part of the reason there is no change, is because people who are running things—it is not their goal [to share power]. To be honest [*laughs*]. We have to be proactively dismantling white supremacy [*laughs*]. That is the problem.

The other thing that keeps me up at night is both the need for militancy, but also whether or not my institution and organization and others can say that I'm going to actually engage in long-term planning and strategy, with my allies, and start with the question of [asking] what are you fighting for and how I will incorporate that into my fight and say that this is what our folks are fighting for. How can we create a multi-organization, multi-industry, multi-community leader partnership to fight for big, big systemic changes, fully funded, like, class-size caps in California, [changes] that make K–12 to higher education completely fully funded? Are we actually going to lay down the tracks to really do that big work? We can do it.

Sarita Gupta: Thank you, Liz. I just want to say there is a lot in the [Zoom] chat. Sarah [who submitted a video question] wrote, "This whole conversation chills. It feels like an exhale to see so many things I am thinking about all the time." I'm glad she wrote that because that is the whole point of answering this question and continuing to appreciate all of you in your honesty.

Andrea Dehlendorf (executive director, United for Respect): The risk is that the Right, which is more resourced, more organized, in some ways more powerful, is going to succeed at giving a massive, massive power grab for concentrated corporate control and [for] financial sector and right-wing white supremacist patriarchal agendas.

I am deeply concerned that we are missing the moment. I do agree that there has been some evidence of people taking action, [but] it has been a minute since that has happened, I think since last summer I have not felt this. It feels like there was a moment of spontaneous strikes and the mass #BLM uprisings, but it has petered down. I think it's a combination of both the organic appetite to take action—I think we know why ... people are exhausted, people are facing so much crisis. It is so hard. The fact [that] it is not happening means that either it is not spontaneously happening, and those of us that are in organizations are not succeeding in organizing for it either.

I think it is creating a vacuum where we are not tilting the balance of power in the way we need to. We have not really figured out how to let go and harness more distributive leadership models of organizing. We do not necessarily have the resources, and the [human] resources we do have—it is harder because people are really struggling. Even our highest-capacity people are dealing with so much personal stuff right now with the crisis that [it] makes it really hard. We have to figure out new ways and new models. I do not think it is clear what that is and what the path is.

Sarita Gupta: Those are all really great points, Andrea. Thank you! How we really build leader-full teams and institutions is a critical question. As I pivot to Stacy, I want to acknowledge that all of you so far have been putting aside [your] personal stuff [to say], "Here is what I am dealing with." Which I think is fascinating! I want to challenge you not to do that. We want to be whole people. So I would love to continue to probe this question and invite you to share personal stuff, but I would also love for you to share with us, given the many tensions and contradictions we are sitting with as a movement in this moment, what strategies are you employing to expose and work through these tensions? What makes them innovative? You have certainly been an incredible leader innovating on many fronts.

Stacy Davis-Gates (executive vice president, Chicago Teachers Union): The strategy I am employing in this moment, quite frankly, is to love all human beings and I want that to land. Because we are in a world, a society, a time frame that is absent of radical love. When I say "love," I'm not telling you that I want to give you a hug, or pat you, but if I love you, I am going to practice truth and transparency. If I love you, I will secure your safety. I will protect you. I am going to work for your benefit. Right? In love, I can face enemies and challenges, enemies that are big bogeymen. And challenges that seem insurmountable. Because that is what we do when we love. The strategy is love.

Then the work comes behind that love. In Chicago, we are back in our classrooms. My union has been very clear about a couple of things. One, loving on the people who not only are in the school but in the community. We practice coming to bargaining, not just because it seems cool, or this is a way to get strategies in, but we practice it because there is no other way to practice unionism when you educate children in spaces that ain't never loved them. That being said, we lost two moms that are at an elementary school in the west side of Chicago that had 11 classes out of 17 classes in quarantine. An elementary school! The question becomes "How do you practice love, continue to practice love, as a union dealing with poverty, racism, white supremacy, patriarchy, a caste system in Chicago, and in the west side and [the] south side of Chicago, that seem unrelenting and closed to transformation?" That means you have to figure out how to collaborate with the people who are in that space. Hear them, take direction, work with, and organize for the things that you collectively agree makes sense.

You have to give up some of your power as a union, as an institution, to hear and be with other people, and then you also have to slow down a little. This is where I get into trouble all the time because I am like, putting the gas pedal on the floor. I get in trouble all the time. Because I want people to be at the end of the book, but they might be at the first chapter. My impatience with poverty and my impatience with the way our structures work, I'm on ten; some people might not be on ten because surviving prevents them from being on ten. It does not prevent them from being as pissed off as I am or from seeing and experiencing the injustice, but it may prevent them from saying that this becomes the priority over time. What does that mean for us as a movement or people who work in community? It means we have to figure out a co-governing model, a co-leading model, that respects the fullness of the impediments to transformation. White supremacy and patriarchy are real impediments if I have to work two jobs.

We have to begin to employ strategies that include the issues that real people, the people we swear to God we try to help change the world, [have] or need to be able to cling to and figure out how they see themselves, not just the results, but in the strategy. And in the work of it. And that is difficult because some of us see a thing and want it to change instantly. Not realizing that there are short-term and long-term [strategies]. Not realizing that real people have to grapple with this, and the real people we want to be in coalition with have other things there.

So I just think that the moment calls for us to have love as a strategy. The moment calls for us to both be impatient and patient at the same time. The moment calls for us to understand people. And to be with you. And to do everything that we can to make it work. For people.

Sarita Gupta: That is beautiful. Thank you so much! I love this framing of the need to center love, and radical love at that. And patience. It is a helpful way to think about the moment we are in and how we make meaning of it. And have impact.

I want to stress for you and all of you that I would love to hear about how you are bringing a real feminist analysis into the work, and strategies you are developing. A tall order of questions, take it away!

Andrea Mercado (co-executive director, Florida Rising): We have a governor [Ron DeSantis] trying to kill us [*laughs*]—you all know, not trying to take the pandemic seriously. Miami has passed LA in terms of not being an affordable place to live. Our housing crisis is extreme. He [initially] refused to take $800 million from the federal government for food for our kids, food stamps for children. He finally relented after some pressure. So Florida became the very last state to accept that money. It is bleak! The Right is out here running circles around us, co-opting organizing strategies, co-opting our service strategies, building off of our work to contest for people's hearts and minds and really stoke the flames of fear and division, [and] at the same time, they are cutting the checks for the corporations. Right? Cutting programs and cutting big checks for all of their friends. That is all happening, and at the same time, what gives me hope and keeps me in it is I see all the ways that we are winning.

We have an all-women county commission in Orlando. Okay! Challenging corporate power. We have the first woman [and first Jewish] mayor of Miami–Dade County, reclaiming the largest county in the state for progressive forces, and just this week, we passed the most progressive budget we have seen for decades [*laughs*]. That includes wins on climate and wins on housing and wins on labor and wins for women!

It is always hard for me to separate this question about how we are bringing feminism to our work. I have always organized with bad-ass women of color. That is true for me today. [They] are organizing parades, cultural events, and claiming unapologetic progressive Latina people from politics in the heart of conservative, Hispanic territory. Women like Angie Nixon, who was a labor organizer for many years and decided to run for office. I hold on to the fact it is always darkest before the dawn. This has been a challenging period, but also a period where there is innovation happening.

We are asking questions. We are asking the right questions around how we want to pace ourselves and the kinds of campaigns we think are needed, and how we are developing the next generation of leaders that we really need. Not just here in Florida but across the country, [we are] increasingly ... owning our power, owning our voices. I am actually in a hopeful and reflective place and really inspired by so many of you in this conversation.

Sarita Gupta: Andrea, I want to see if you had any quick thoughts on the question around southern organizing and resources around southern organizing, and what is needed, given where you are placed in Florida.

Andrea Mercado: The South is very diverse, even within southern states, we are very diverse. Some of us, like Florida [and] Georgia, have a battleground situation where these political sandcastles were built in two months. Ungodly amount[s] of resources pour into the state, and then they disappear a week later. In a way, which I think is a challenge in long-term organizing, we have done a lot of work to build collaborations with a set of people who are committed to transforming the state. To disrupt that dynamic or the ways that makes people feel used [*laughs*] and really commit to show up to [engage] people year-round. And be knocking on their door, in January, February, the year that is not a hot election.

There are other states that are starved for resources where they are doing incredible work and have been advancing against all odds, but not getting the kind of investment that is needed. Brilliant organizers, Black and Latina women doing the thing and fighting the fights, and winning campaigns, but are starved for resources. I am hoping we will see some shifting of that [to] the work that is being led across the region, the diversity of work, the super grassroots locally based work, the union organizing, the statewide power building. We need ecosystems. It is challenging too for us partner ... when we do not have our own communication's infrastructure or policy infrastructure that is really in the state. [The outsiders] do not understand the dynamics of what we are dealing with. It's challenging to figure out how we help these ecosystems in the South really flourish.

Sarita Gupta: I love that notion of ecosystems. I have been privy to take part in conversations with labor unions and philanthropy, thinking about how to support southern organizing. That language of ecosystems is being held and centered in those spaces. Thank you for bringing that in. Which makes me want to pivot to Cindy. Part of your strategy is organizing in the South ...

Cindy Estada: We are focused a lot [on] the South, and the auto world. A lot of those nonunion assembly companies are located in Georgia, South Carolina, and

Alabama. Alabama will be the third-largest auto state, and it is mostly nonunion, which means that workers are working very similar to [the] service sector. They are lucky if they make $15 and full time in some of those plants. We are taking an approach of how we build an auto industry committee—not just a one-plant approach, which never worked anyway.

In terms of a longer-term plan, that is the challenge. To me, that means you have a five- and a ten-year plan. You are there until workers have formed unions. We are doing that now and working with 19 different autoworkers from 19 different plants. I do not want to oversell this. It is hard work. We are trying to look for more organizers and making sure that organizers, if possible, are from the South, not only helping with having a better organizing program, but it also helps the burnout factor, which there is a lot of COVID fatigue. Some workers want to go [forward] with an election. They may get a contract, [but] even if they do, it will go away after a few years. So really trying to get them to understand if they want to form a union, they need to do it together and by striking.

Also, how do they develop relationships within that community? Some may already have them, but how do we have workers organizing around issues that are important to that area or to that state? That is where we are finding a lot of help that is needed because [for] a lot of organizations, the resources are not there for them. Right? They have great ideas, great vision, great plans, and no money. Trying to connect with people [so] we figure that out together, with other unions, progressive groups, or foundations, because I think that plan has to be built together. I think the full-on plan has to be done with other organizations at the table [and] with those workers at the table. We are struggling with it, but it is exciting. Workers understand it; it does not make sense for a group, even if it is 2,000 workers, to go forward in the state of Alabama, unless there is help. Right? They know what is coming for them once they get some power. They get that. So … anyone interested in Alabama, reach out to us [*laughs*].

Sarita Gupta: We will leave the South for a moment, and we are going to shift over to you, Veronica. I would love to hear from you about this question about strategies and how you bring an intersectional analysis to the work. CTUL [Centro de Trabajadores Unidos en Lucha] has [for a long time] worked with immigrant workers and worked at these intersections. How have your strategies evolved in this moment?

Veronica Mendez-Moore: Yeah, thank you. Because of this intense moment of isolation, it has become incredibly clear to us that what we need to do is build movement. We need to build ecosystems, we need to build across organizations, we need to think intersectionally. We know that was true, and also, we all know that siloing is bad and that we should un-silo and figure out how to work together; we know that intellectually and in our guts. But in this moment, where every structure and system around us is crumbling, people's health in the pandemic, people losing their jobs, evictions, education, police violence, gun violence in our communities, with all of that happening at the same time, it does not make sense anymore [to think] this issue versus [that] issue. It can't. I think that while our infrastructure is crumbling, [this] is a major tragedy—it provides an incredible opportunity for us to rethink how we partner.

Over the last couple of years here in the Twin Cities, CTUL has been building connections and partnerships with a set of ideologically aligned organizations that organize and are led by people of color, women, and working-class communities. We call this alignment "tending the soil." It is not a coalition—we are not a coalition fighting about an issue, and once we win, we form some other coalition. This is a long-term ecosystem alignment that invests in each other and practices radical solidarity. It is organizations that are workers' organizations, there is housing justice, racial justice, immigrants' rights.

These organizations are partnering behind the scenes in terms of infrastructure building. I always thought it was a privilege for big white institutions to get training on how to be a manager or how to be a director. I never heard of that in our communities! We are building that for each other, and with each other, because it should not be a privilege, and it should be the way we are building our institutions. We should have access to that. But now with the pandemic and George Floyd and the uprising, we built a campaign together and started doing public work together. It is a multifaceted campaign called the Rise Up campaign, working at the intersections of the different issues and different communities, particularly communities of color, and looking at the role of women in these communities as leaders.

It is a campaign that is about taking advantage of the moment. Where our city needs to be rebuilt. We want to shift who decides, rather than going back to the standard of who normally decides [like] big corporations, developers, and whatnot. We are fighting to make sure that communities aren't displaced, that construction is done by responsible contractors, that we are prioritizing BIPOC small businesses and creating alternatives to policing all as a part of one campaign, I might have dreamt of five years ago but would not have felt it any way possible. Right now, it is actually possible. It has been a really exciting moment for us to think across all these intersections, not to silo and build a long-lasting narrative. This is not something that hopefully in two years we win this campaign. We are clear that this is my lifetime. This is in my lifetime campaign. [It] is about changing who decides in our city, changing the assumptions of who is allowed to decide, who is worthy of deciding, who is smart enough to decide, and shifting that balance of power. For us, this is our best solution= building this alignment, this aligned campaign.

Sarita Gupta: Great, seeking alignment. I want to dig into that a little bit more. Lauren, it would be great to see how you are seeking alignment across racial and economic justice movements and working with diverse worker organizations to build powerful campaigns.

Lauren Jacobs: I think dovetailing on Stacy's very powerful framing of love as the strategy. I think loving our people is about wanting them to see how precious and amazing they are, to be fully aware of their own capacities, so by doing powerful alignments of movements, which is what affiliates [of Power Switch Action] do in space and place, [try] to bring together movement forces that may not talk to each other normally.

Going back to Cindy's climate [or] jobs, we reject that—it is both. And power building as a city, as a town, as a people. It's not something you can do by yourself. It is a team sport. You do it as a community. How do we take on fights? Yes, I'm a labor person. I believe in the benefits and power of collective bargaining, but it was a means to an end. I think the lesson we should hold from that is that it was a part of power, of bargaining power, it was *not* societal power. Our goal needs to be societal power. How do we think about taking on fights where we cannot see the end? Cindy is pointing to this with the auto workers—if you take on the whole industry, and imagine wall-to-wall, all of it, and really tying the environment and climate to the communities, to the job quality, you are stepping out on something where we do not know what the solution will be.

The work we are doing with others around Amazon is completely that. We have a theory [that] this is a company that cannot exist if we are to have a functioning democracy. You cannot have immigrant surveillance, surveillance of Black and brown communities, punishing extraction of working people, putting so many hundreds of thousands of people in the path of this virus with impunity and not worrying about it.

In terms of [the] strategy, there is a strategy of fights that seem bigger than we can take on, and [we must be] figuring it out together, and being really rigorous [about] not leaving each other behind. So I will not grab this and write off women in a settlement; I will not write off the workers in the settlement; I will not write off the environment. It is really understanding that if we love our folks, we love them into 24 hours of their being and their lives. And fight for all the things they are dealing with and confronting.

Sarita Gupta: I love that framing of societal power. Andrea, let's bring you back into the conversation. Tell us how you are thinking about the ways to seek alignment right now and build powerful campaigns.

Andrea Dehlendorf: None of us has a pathway to build power to make the changes we are seeking on our own. Our purpose as an organization is to transform working conditions and build power in the retail sector which put us up against Walmart, Amazon, private-equity Wall Street. We are not just trying to make the jobs a little bit better, but we are trying to fundamentally change so that we do not have the situation where the largest employment sector in the entire country is dominated by the richest people on the globe who are making their billions and trillions of dollars extracting from the labor of women and BIPOC folks who do the work.

We really agree with the framing of ecosystems as well. How do we really bring together or come together with all of the different constituencies in the communities that are impacted by these megacorporations and be a part of building a table that is reflective of the broader vision and theory of change? Athena [a broad coalition of local and national organizations challenging companies such as Amazon] [is an example of] where we have tried to do things really differently, as a collective, than what we had done with Walmart. With Walmart, workers organized and there was community support, and the workers supported communities, but it was this 20th-century model of how we do that work versus what we are trying to do with Athena, which is to say that everybody gets an equal voice at the table in terms of bringing an agenda and the campaign.

Also doing work with Jobs With Justice and others on how it's essential to bring people together, not a coalition but rather to build an ecosystem. Bring people together to be in relationship with each other because what we are doing and fighting for is connected. We all have a stake in everybody else's [issues], bringing organizations that might be a national group like ours [and] a very local group who are all part of a collective conversation, and trying to build a similar infrastructure around private equity. How do we really look at the source of the money that is creating so much disorganization and erosion of standards and rights for people? Bringing a much broader group together of both workers that are impacted but looking beyond workers to connect to the housing fight where the same people whose jobs are being destroyed by private equity, their housing is being destroyed and becoming unaffordable because of private equity. We have to create those linkages and get people into relationship with each other. That is how we approach this. We cannot win this alone. We need to do it as part of a movement ecosystem.

Sarita Gupta: I love that, Andrea. April, tell us how you are seeking alignment, and how you are thinking about movement building and movement framing at this moment, given where you are located in California.

April Verrett: I think it is important at this moment for me, and for my organization and the movement that I want to build to be unapologetic, intentional, explicit about being antiracist. About owning and telling the truth about the legacy of slavery, of the genocide of Indigenous peoples, of how this country came to be, and what that means, and place where we are in that context. Because I think we cannot continue to talk around it. We have to think about systemic and structural change as a way to move us forward to a different place.

If we are really intentional about talking about anti-Blackness, and how it has contributed to where we are [and] how all of us are affected by anti-Blackness. We cannot get to a different place, as my sister Stacy talked about, without loving ourselves enough to tell ourselves the truth. And all of us have a role to play in being antiracist. We cannot move forward without truly, in my opinion, centering those of us who have suffered the most. And when you center us, it is not just, and this irks me to my core, about giving me a figurehead seat at the table and calling it power and influence. When it is people that do not look like me who continue to make all of the decisions and are the so-called strategists. I think in the strategies and in the building the movement that gets us to the next place, let us be really thoughtful about what it means to center people of color. To create space for some of us, move the hell out of the way so that those of us impacted, who need a seat at the real decision-making table, the real places of power, can get in there.

Because we will not move workers in the South. They do not trust us [*laughs*]. They do not trust institutions; they do not trust government. As long as we continue to show up the same way we [unions and labor] have always shown up in the South, with domestic workers and low-wage workers, with immigrants, we will not change the paradigm. We will not change the game.

Sarita Gupta: That is wonderful, April. Such important points. We have got to confront anti-Blackness, and we have got to confront our history and unapologetically, exactly the way you put it.

Andrea Mercado: I'm really happy to see the amount of long-term planning. I am seeing people bringing what we need to do not just this year or the next three months, but the conversation around where we want to be in 10 years, or 20 years and how are we going to get there. For us in Florida, that has been a game changer. To really talk about April's point of confronting history and white supremacy, what it will look like to break the back of Jim Crow in Florida and to reimagine public safety and expand democracy and seize power and co-govern in a way that is centering Black and brown communities and working-class communities. I think that is what I am excited by [and] I want to see more of because if we do not have a clear North Star, if we really [don't] know where it is we are trying to go [*laughs*], we will be going in circles.

It is a time where we might be able to make some giant leaps forward. But we need to be really clear on our shared purpose and a vision. I'm seeing that, not just here in Florida, we are doing that work not just [at] a state level but at the county level. In Duvall where Jacksonville is, in Leon, in Tampa Bay, in Miami–Dade or in Broward, we are bringing people with different perspective[s] to the table—labor, community organizations, faith-based organizations—to talk about what our theory of change is. Where do we want to be in 10 or 20 years, and how will we get there? Different organizations might choose different paths. We will not agree on all things. But at least having a roadmap and a space for us to really discuss it and to be in shared practice I think is really essential.

Sarita Gupta: That is great. I love that you made that point [about getting] down to the county level. It has to be local. I know all of you as leaders are always managing this tension of local to state to national, and some of you transnational—that is a lot to be sitting with. Which makes me want to go to Liz. How we are seeking alignment, thinking about the movement framing in this moment, and building opportunities?

Liz Perlman: I think so many folks are doing incredible experimentation around truly being ecosystems, thinking about building societal power not bargaining power, shifting our cultures and ourselves to be truly antiracist and actually sharing power in our institutions. And I think about all of our respective unions clinging to the color of the t-shirt, to be honest. I think there is a lot of collaboration, but there is also a ton of money there [and] [*laughs*] a ton of power there, [and] we have to be challenging each other and challenging the white male patriarchal structure of our labor movement because there is a lot of money there.

What were the real failures of things like Change to Win? To be honest a white left model, naming that type of strategy and thinking and infusing the new ways we are thinking and doing things, and then pushing and challenging our own unions to be figuring out how they take off the color of their t-shirt. I personally struggle with that, which is why I am so appreciative, and I show up to this space. I am trying to figure out how can I strike at the same time as UTLA [United Teachers Los Angeles], that is my obsession. I'm looking at April—how can I support her in her struggles in California? How can I do that so that we can be some of the models we are looking for, frankly, from across the country leadership, but also push for more than that. I know it is easier said than done. That would be my biggest vision.

Sarita Gupta: That is great. Stacy, there's been a lot said about strategies and movement building, I want to see if you want to add anything into the mix that we should all be holding and sitting with as we begin to close out!

Stacy Davis-Gates: In a lot of ways, we get in our way, so we will have to figure out how to get out of our own way. If we talk about this panel, the number of individuals that we represent and are adjacent to our leadership, we should already be in power and in control. We should already have the thing that we think we need or know that we need. So I am just always thinking through what are the impediments to our ability to actually operate the institutions, transform the institutions, radically dismantle the institutions that are causing the oppression and pain in places where we both work and live. We practice in our systems the same types of patriarchy and white supremacy that is practiced outside of our institutions that are oppressing us. Right? Work has to be both inside and outside. The same vigor in which we fight it for members or in our common-good bargaining spaces—how do we fight those same things inside and not destroy each other? I'm talking about something sustained and that creates the institutions and transforms the institutions that we need to get to equity, self-determination, to get to antiracism. That is on my spirit today.

Sarita Gupta: Thank you so much for those amazing words. I want to thank this amazing panel, [and] I want to lift up the themes I heard. Ecosystems, radical love with the caveat of what Stacy just gave us, patience and impatience, societal power, tending the soil, building the alignment for longer-term, unapologetically antiracist, confront anti-Blackness, place where we are in a longer context. We need a clear North Star; we need to get out of our ways and reaffirm our humanity. I do not know about you, but if that was not a dose of some serious energy from these amazing leaders, I do not [know] what to do for you [*laughs*]. They really offered some incredible insights. Thank you all so much.

ENDNOTE

1. The symposium was hosted virtually on September 30 and October 1, 2021. A description of WILL Empower is available in the "About the Contributors" section at the end of the volume. The excerpts have been edited to fit within this volume.

CHAPTER 13

Negotiating Stories from the Bottom

JAVIER MORILLO

Rutgers University
Center for Innovation in Worker Organization

Abstract

Javier Morillo is not only a former union president, he is also a celebrated, Moth-trained storyteller. In this chapter, Morillo recounts his experience of very intense bargaining sessions where he was the lead negotiator for SEIU's Justice for Janitors campaigns in Minnesota. Local 26 in represents one of the most racially and ethnically diverse janitor locals, which grew to 8,000 members under his leadership. Morillo provides a behind-the-scenes look at how they set a new bar for the kind of victory that "stronger together" could win.

Weeks into negotiations with our employers, the bargaining committee of janitors and members of SEIU Local 26 were by now used to brusque treatment from the attorney the janitorial companies had hired to negotiate with us. This lawyer had a reputation for "breaking" the SEIU healthcare local in Minnesota and—despite his lack of experience with the property services industries—the Twin Cities Janitorial Contract Association hired him, presumably to give us a taste of his adversarial approach to contract negotiations. Three years earlier, janitorial contractors seemed taken by surprise that Local 26 of the Service Employees' International Union (SEIU), a union that did not previously have a reputation as rabble-rousers, had mounted a big, ultimately successful public campaign to win major improvements to our master contract.

As the president of SEIU Local 26—today a union of janitors, security officers, airport, and other service workers in Minnesota—I was our bargaining spokesperson whenever our largest bargaining unit of over 4,000 janitors was in negotiations. On this particular day, I admit, Mr. Lawyer was getting on my nerves. He had been exceptionally rude to our language interpreters; in a bargaining unit with large numbers of native Spanish, Somali, and Amharic speakers, simultaneous translation was critical for our bargaining committee to understand the proceedings to negotiate the contract under which they would be working. Speaking slowly enough for interpreters could be a challenge for both sides. Rapid verbal sparring in English and Spanish comes very naturally me—Puerto Ricans are notoriously fast talkers in any language we learn—and the opposing attorney also had to be constantly reminded that the proceedings involved a large, multilingual committee. Several times, our Spanish language interpreter had asked each side to slow down so that she could effectively do her work, and several times he snapped at her. My annoyance was compounded when Mr. Attorney gave us a healthcare counterproposal that was, to our eyes, clearly regressive. We would need to go over this carefully with the bargaining committee, in multiple languages, in caucus, and so I called one. "We're going to need a break. We're going into caucus. Just ... just ... get the hell out of here." Mr. Attorney became irate at the disrespect I'd shown him and his employers and yelled, "I will not be treated this way!" as I kept saying "We're in caucus, please leave," which set him off more. Caucuses, of course, are when each side meets by themselves, and either side can call them at any time. Mr. Attorney threw papers and slammed his binders, raising his voice more and more—and our bargaining team became increasingly agitated in response. Brian, a janitor at the Minneapolis–Saint Paul airport, screamed, "Strike!" while others started yelling in Spanish as the lawyer and employer bargaining team finally rushed out of the room.

They had barely closed the door behind them when the committee burst into applause. The room felt filled with adrenaline, and I was proud I'd given the pretentious snit a taste of his own medicine. I was reminded that members expected me to fight, to use my role as bargaining lead to go toe to toe up against their employers in ways they often could not do for fear of being disciplined or losing their jobs. Our pre-negotiation agreements always included a commitment to speak with one voice; we can and must disagree in caucus, but in front of the other side we spoke as one. But I was proud of the collective response and outburst to the attorney's behavior.

The words of a bargaining committee member sitting to my right, spoken almost under his breath, brought me down from this high. "Si lo tratan a usted así, imagínese como nos tratan a nosotros en los edificios." *If they treat you like this, imagine how they treat us in the buildings.*

***

This was my second time leading bargaining for a union I had, unexpectedly, come to lead in 2005. I had been working as a political organizer for SEIU in Minnesota for less than six months when my boss, Jon, pulled me aside at a national union meeting and began talking to me about one of the Minnesota locals to which I was accountable, the union of janitors. Local 26 was at the time led by a kind man who could have come from central casting to play a German Minnesota grandpa. This local president, my boss told me, was looking to retire; he had not built leadership to succeed him, neither among the membership nor staff. Moreover, during his tenure, the union's demographics had shifted dramatically: over decades, membership had shifted from being predominantly white, with many of Eastern European background, to being largely of Latin American descent, with a growing number of East Africans. "The national union is looking for someone to lead that local. It has to be someone who speaks Spanish, preferably someone who is Latino, and they're having a hard time finding someone in the union willing to move to Minnesota," Jon shared. I thought he was asking me to help him find someone and, having been in SEIU only six months, I thought, "I can't help you here." But instead Jon said, "and we think you can do it."

You're high, I thought. Just a year before I had been teaching history and anthropology at a local college when I decided to leave academic life behind to try to do something that felt more relevant, more practical and applied, to change a country that at the time was heading into a disastrous war with Iraq. I'd begun volunteering on political campaigns after that academic year ended and, when SEIU hired me as a political organizer, I thought this was going to be a first job in politics, not a step toward becoming a labor union leader.

It did not feel right to lead a union where I had not been a rank-and-file member. I met with a Left labor historian colleague, one who has written dismissively of "union bureaucrats in suits" and who I thought for certain would talk me out of taking on the role. Over coffee, he heard me out and said, "Well, it's clear the union is going to be led by an outsider either way. So maybe you should think about what you would need to do differently so that the union is not in the same predicament when it's time for you to leave." That is what I set out to do.

Although I was anxious about the reception I would receive, I quickly learned that for many members, their top priority was a union that worked for them and stood up to the boss; who had the title of president was not unimportant, but it was secondary. We diversified our all-white executive board and changed member meeting dates from Mondays at 5 p.m. (the exact time thousands of janitors clocked in to work) to Saturdays, when people could actually attend. I began leading meetings in Spanish that were translated into English. Later, as more East African members became engaged in the union's work, English had to serve as a lingua franca as long as we also had two or three interpreters in every meeting. As the union woke up from its slumber—a colleague once described 26 as "it had to work really hard to not be considered asleep"—I also learned a lot about myself.

I quickly dispensed with the deep-seated and common graduate student self-perception that I had no skills other than reading books and writing about them. As a child, my penchant for arguing every point to the ground had my mother believing I'd grow up to be a lawyer. I did not, but it turned out that someone who loves to argue and hates to lose comes to bargaining with very two helpful skills. The first time I successfully argued a grievance and won a fired janitor their job back, I felt a very different sense of accomplishment than I had ever felt earning a grade for a well-researched paper. And often, as in that moment at the bargaining table, I was reminded that centering my voice might feed my ego but cause me to miss the real story that needs to be centered: the janitor who could often receive abuse from their supervisor while working second or third shift.

***

Our union grew as we added security officers to our ranks, first downtown, then in the suburbs. Once in negotiations with security officers, a talented young organizer ran through an exercise with our bargaining committee that I came to adopt in all our bargaining. On a piece of butcher block paper, he asked members to come up with a list of "what we deserve." Once that list was full, leaders were asked to consider on another sheet "what do we have the power to win?" Bargaining, we learned together, is the process by which we move items from the "what we deserve" list to the list of items we had the power to win in negotiations that cycle.

As I adopted this exercise in subsequent negotiations, I was always struck when I asked the question "what do we deserve?"[1] to a room of low-wage property service workers. Invariably, the first word on the page was "respect." This always pained me—that what should be a baseline workplace value was *always* named as both missing and desired, and always first. I always remembered that, especially when on the first day of negotiations, an employer-side attorney would invariably start in on a rap about "interest-based negotiations" where "everybody wins." When power is so imbalanced that the worker side's top concern is respect for their dignity as human beings, how is such a thing possible?

Once we had put up wages, healthcare, retirement security, and other worksite issues in the "what we deserve" column, I'd ask leaders, "What about vacations on the beach? Do we deserve those?" The "what we deserve" list, we'd eventually agree, should be long, imaginative, joyful. There would be plenty of time in negotiations to figure out the real-world version of that list—the shorter list of things we were actually able to win in that contract cycle. Bargaining should be a moment of collective dreaming, of stretching the definitions of what is possible for ourselves as individuals and, especially, as a collective.

***

Negotiations, like stories, have an arc—a beginning, a middle, and an end. Some see this story as a cheerful one, and it can be. Two sides can, in theory, get together and leave with equal wins. But what if the power imbalance is so great between two parties that one refuses to come to the table to negotiate, because they can?

The Justice for Janitors movement breathed life into SEIU and the labor movement not just by serving as a model for community engagement and centering the voices of the most marginalized of workers but also because it served as a blueprint for organizing disaggregated sectors of the economy (Lerner and Shaffer 2015). Justice for Janitors campaigns were not simply a tactical use of public escalation to bring the public to the side of workers; they were also a sophisticated answer to the question "How do we organize in a subcontracted industry that big real estate owners transformed when they ceased hiring janitors to work directly for buildings and began hiring subcontractors to do commercial office cleaning?"

When janitors are at the bargaining table, they sit across from these middlemen and -women, contractors who, in very real terms, have no power outside of the checks paid to them by building owners who can claim to have no interest in contract negotiations because "they're not our employees." While the National Labor Relations Act does not allow in most cases for janitors to insist that the truly powerful—the building owners who write the checks—be a part of negotiations, they can instead use the tools of public storytelling to bring the powerful to the table. Often that requires creating discomfort. During my first contract negotiations for Local 26, we attempted to engage the Building Owners and Managers Association (BOMA) of Minneapolis. We emailed, sent letters, asking them merely to hear the union out on the proposals that we were presenting to contractors—proposals that they would have to live with. We even resorted to a tongue-in-cheek delivery of a Christmas decorative arrangement to their annual holiday party. We always got the same response: We wish the parties well, but the janitors are not our employees. Unsaid: "Yes, they clean our buildings and without our checks their employers could not pay them, but—legally and technically speaking—we have nothing to do with them."

Our final escalation came when a few dozen janitors and supporters invaded a posh country club in the Minneapolis suburbs to publicly call on BOMA to meet with the janitors. That effort had entailed a staff researcher scouting out the location, posing with my partner as an engaged couple looking for a wedding venue. Building managers were shocked to see that some of the tie-wearing attendees they were sharing tables with were pastors and other community leaders, there to support the janitors who rushed in to call on BOMA to meet with them. For years after that direct action, indeed for as long as I was president of the local, when I met with a downtown building manager or owner, they would often bring up that moment, which they saw as an affront to civility. "We don't appreciate your tactics," I heard many times, and I'd always answer the same way: "You refused to meet with us then. Now you do."

***

The next time we entered into negotiations for the janitorial master contract was at the end of 2009, as the global financial crisis rocked markets across the world and the foreclosure crisis meant hundreds of our members had either lost or were in danger of losing their homes. In the US culture of class, the way our siloed lives can intersect in surprising ways became clear when a bargaining committee member, Rosalina Gómez, shared her story with the rest of the committee. Rosalina was losing her home because she could no longer afford payments on a house that was now valued almost two hundred thousand dollars less than the loan she took on to buy it. One of the banks holding her mortgage was US Bank, one of the largest owners of real estate in the metro area and a homegrown bank. Its CEO at the time, Richard Davis, was often featured in glowing profiles as a man concerned with community because he cultivated an image of himself and US Bank as the good guys in the finance and banking worlds. Rosalina's home was not her only connection to US Bank, she told us. Not only was she a janitor who worked in the corporate offices of that bank, her nightly responsibilities included cleaning the personal office of Richard Davis himself.

US Bank pushed hard against the union as Rosalina went from telling her story to her co-workers to sharing it with local and national media (St. Anthony 2010). We planned a direct action where Rosalina was going to directly ask Mr. Davis for help with keeping her house at a luncheon where he was receiving an award as CEO of the Year. We called off the action at the last minute when US Bank, through the then-mayor of Minneapolis, who back-channeled messages and demands between us, agreed to help Rosalina keep her home.

US Bank later complained that we had unfairly targeted them in our campaign. Just as subcontracting exists to make the world more complicated for workers to organize against an employer, the Byzantine processes through which bank loans are processed, sold, and resold meant that US Bank was not the formal holder of the loan. *The New York Times* reported:

> Steve Dale, a spokesman for the bank, said the union was attacking US Bank even though JPMorgan Chase was the bank servicing Ms. Gómez's mortgage. US Bank, he said, was just the trustee, holding the loan for a mortgage bond.
>
> "We did not service the loan," Mr. Dale said. "We did not originate the loan, and we were not the financial entity that placed it into foreclosure. Do you understand what a trustee does?" (Greenhouse and Story 2010)

In the end, Rosalina's story was more powerful than the bank's nitpicking about which other bank was *really* the bad guy. But lest we read this as an admission that we had the wrong culprit, on the day we called off the direct action, it became immediately clear that the bank had more power than portrayed in the story that their spokesman later peddled to the *Times*. That afternoon, I sat with Rosalina in a meeting with US Bank where they got JPMorgan Chase and everyone else they needed to get on the phone to make the problem go away. I watched in awe as the bank that told us their hands were tied, through the course of the meeting, seemed to make hundreds of thousands of dollars of unpaid debt vanish into thin air. We had the right culprits; we just had to force them to the table to reach a resolution.

Rosalina's story was not simply about herself but about her co-workers and the entire union. The message we intended to send through that direct action was clear to the building-owner community: We will not let you get away with pretending you are not a partner in our negotiations, even if a silent or seemingly invisible one. We later heard the business community was quite rocked by the *potential* disruption and what it might mean for them if union members followed through on the that strike members had authorized. That weekend, our bargaining committee won a fantastic contract, at a time of economic disruption where all forces were telling us to settle for less, not ask for more.

***

Contract negotiations are times of stress, sometimes relief, and sometimes even joy. The third round of contract negotiations I led for the janitorial division were, for me, spiritually draining. I had begun to experience feelings I had not yet resolved, encapsulated pithily by a friend, the president of the national community organizing network People's Action, when in a conversation he said, "I'm so tired of having to work so damn hard to make shitty jobs slightly less shitty." This round, there was a new lawyer who also started out trying to convince us that janitorial contract companies and janitors have shared interests. I was feeling exhausted by the enormity of the task of not just winning for our now 8,000 members—double the number when I took over—while being keenly aware of the bigger problem: that our labor movement was ill equipped to win for all workers. We are nowhere near the scale we need to ensure that more of the "what we deserve" column for working families moves over to the "what we have the power to win" list.

These third janitorial negotiations had, as prior ones, dragged on for months before we set a very public deadline. We were starting to negotiate on a Friday, and we said we were willing to stay as long as we had to but that, if by the end of the weekend we did not have a contract, the following week we would strike. We started negotiations on a Friday morning at 10 a.m. and ended up bargaining for 27 hours straight.

When contracts are open, I often hold tension around my neck. No amount of physical therapy seemed to help, and muscle relaxants clouded my brain, so I had to use them sparingly. Around midnight that Friday, I left our caucus room to go into a room in the hotel we were bargaining to put my neck into a traction machine. While I was gone, our bargaining committee, which was already large, about 30 people, started calling their co-workers who were still working in the office buildings, telling people to come down to the hotel. Little by little, more and more people started to arrive at the hotel. By the time I came back in, there were about 200 people in the room. The atmosphere was festive, especially for that late hour of the night, and after a day that the bargaining team had spent at the table and their co-workers had spent at work. Someone had brought a guitar and sung a Latin American folk song to the room. From another corner of the room, a group of women answered back with an improvised Somali fight song. It was loud, it was boisterous, and it was joyful.

Around two in the morning, we came out of caucus, and our employers came back into the room for another round of across-the-table negotiations. They were looking tired, haggard in fact, as they came into a room packed with over 200 janitors who were looking fresh. Our members' faces and energy seemed to be saying, "Hey, we work at night. We're good!"

At the end of those 27 hours, we won a great contract—the largest percentage wage increases negotiated by any janitors union in the country that year. While proud of that accomplishment, what I love to remember and think about is that night and that packed room—because that space was filled with so much unbridled joy. It reminds me that, in essence, it is what we do when we work in the labor movement or in any social justice movement—we are working to maximize joy in people's lives. Yes, the raises and benefits are important, but they're important because if you make so little that you have to have two jobs, chances are you do not have time to do the things that bring you real joy—spend time with your kids, sleep in, read a book, enjoy the breeze on a beach. The joy in that room that night, in community and in laughter, that's what it's all about.

And I am proud that the union, now under the capable leadership of others, embodies the spirit of that night in its vision statement, which includes our deeply held conviction: "We All Deserve to Live Lives of Joy."

ENDNOTE

1. I am grateful to Steve Payne for introducing this exercise to the union and, of course, to all of the leaders and staff who put their *all* into all of our work.

REFERENCES

Greenhouse, Steven, and Louise Story. 2010. "Unions Make Strides as They Attack Banks." *New York Times*. March 24. https://nyti.ms/3q034z2.

Lerner, Stephen, and Jono Shaffer. 2015. "25 Years Later: Lessons from the Organizers of Justice for Janitors." Talk Poverty. June 16. https://bit.ly/3KBzqYL.

St. Anthony, Neal. 2010. "Janitor Asks CEO for Mortgage Help." *Minneapolis Star Tribune*. March 4, 2010.

CHAPTER 14

Building Worker Power
Through Strategic Education:
A Conversation on Racial Capitalism with
Valery Alzaga and Harmony Goldberg

VALERY ALZAGA
Global Labor Justice–International Labor Rights Forum

HARMONY GOLDBERG
Grassroots Policy Project

MODERATED BY MAITE TAPIA
Michigan State University

Abstract

In this conversation, Valery Alzaga and Harmony Goldberg engage in a discussion around the importance of using the framework of racial capitalism as part of the political education for labor and community organizations. They talk about how we can build organizations that are not race exclusive, that are not race neutral, but that are built on real solidarity and describe how we create a transformational space, where members of unions and other organizations don't just become better critics but better organizers and activists.

PARTICIPANTS

Valery Alzaga is a labor and migrant rights campaigner and organizer with more than 20 years of organizing experience across a range of different sectors, including property services, care, transport, health, retail, IT, renewable energies, and auto manufacturing. She is currently the deputy director of Global Labor Justice–International Labor Rights Forum. She started as an organizer with the Justice for Janitors campaign before becoming the property service director at Local 105 in Denver, where she also was the president of the Colorado Immigrant Rights Coalition. She then worked for SEIU's global department helping win and implement breakthrough global cleaning and security organizing agreements (ISS, Securitas, G4S). From 2008 to 2015, she was the European organizing coordinator with the Change to Win European Organizing Centre (CTW–EOC) based in Amsterdam, working with many European unions and sectors to help them develop their own strategic organizing campaigns and programs. Since 2015, she has worked in UK public sector unions organizing anti-privatization and EU and non-EU migrant rights campaigns. From 2018 to 2021, Valery was a field campaign strategist and advisor to Barcelona and Catalunya en Comú in Spain (in collaboration with the Working Families Party) and to Mijente, a political Latinx organization seeking racial, economic, gender, and climate justice in the United States. Valery has also been a trainer and collaborator with the Grassroots Policy Project, where she has co-led racial capitalism political education courses for various US unions.

Harmony Goldberg is a political educator and facilitator at the Grassroots Policy Project (GPP). She has worked closely with social movements around the United States for more than 20 years. She was a founder and former co-director of SOUL—the School Of Unity and Liberation (www.schoolofunityandliberation.org), a social justice movement training center based in Oakland, California. She has provided political education, strategic facilitation, and writing support for a number of local organizations and national organizing networks, including the National Domestic Workers Alliance, Social Justice Leadership, the Right to the City Alliance, and, most recently, with People's Action. She worked closely with the Bertha Foundation for several years, which exposed her to models of political education used by social movements in the Global South. Harmony is a founding editor of Organizing Upgrade (www.organizingupgrade.com), an online strategy journal for Left organizers in the United States. In 2015, she completed her Ph.D. in cultural anthropology at the City University of New York's Graduate Center. Her research focused on organizing among domestic workers in New York City, focusing on the work of Domestic Workers United.

Maite Tapia is an associate professor at the School of Human Resources and Labor Relations at Michigan State University. Her research focuses on worker voice within the workplace, as well as worker organizing and movement building within the broader society, paying specific attention to workers' social identities and to structural racism.

The following is based on a recorded conversation over Zoom in December 2021. The Zoom meeting was attended by Valery Alzaga, Harmony Goldberg, and Maite Tapia (co-editor of this volume). The text has been edited to fit within this volume.

Maite: Thank you both so much for being here. You both use the framework of racial capitalism as part of a political education for a range of labor and community organizations. Valery, to start off, you have taught classes on racial capitalism for union members through the Grassroots Policy Project, or GPP?

Valery: Yes, GPP is doing an important intervention in this field with lots of organizations, as well as an experimentation with unions. For unions, it is about figuring out how to bring that kind of conversation to their members, how it affects the work they do in the workplace, the work with others in the broader movement, and then work within themselves. This has important implications, as leaders and members will need to think through the organizational changes that need to be made. It has implications on campaigning, on demands, and on staff and leadership development within the unions. Harmony can talk about this from the perspective of the GPP because that is the political house that makes this experimentation possible.

Harmony: At GPP, we do a lot of political education. In my earlier years, I saw political education as something that would make people better critics. We would help people to understand the nature of the system so we know what we're up against and what a thorough level of change that we need. That still matters. But I have come to see that as deeply insufficient. I think that approach can produce people who are good critics but not necessarily good organizers or strategists. In contrast, our racial capitalism curriculum actually starts with the strategic intervention that we want to make: We need to build a deeper approach to class solidarity that has race at its center. That's the shift that we want to achieve. So the training work, in fact, works backwards from there. At GPP, we actually use the phrase "strategic education" instead of "political education" because when people use "political education," they tend to default into this notion of understanding the system so that we can say the right thing—rather than knowing what to actually do about it.

Valery: Yes, and it is important for the strategy to understand the roots, the structural reasons as to why we are where we are and not just work with cosmetics.

Harmony: Yes, it works both ways. The strategy must understand the root causes, but also the way we talk about the systems, and the root causes are shaped by the strategic outcomes that we want to achieve.

Maite: So what is racial capitalism and how did this become part of the curriculum?

Harmony: It came to GPP through our work with People's Action, which is a community organization that was created in 2016 as a result of a merger of a number of different organizations. At People's Action, we found that "racial capitalism" was a helpful framework for people from across these different organizations to overcome the ways in which they were missing each other because they came out of different languages and histories. What became clear was that we needed a framework that helped to walk people through why we actually have shared interests in this fight. We needed a deeper kind of shared interest than "we are all poor and working people, and we need to fight the rich people." That level of shared interest is, of course, true. But, to build a multiracial movement of poor and working people in this country, we will not be able to fundamentally transform the economic structure without going deeply into race. Why? Race has profoundly shaped the way that class has been structured and experienced in this country. So the framework of racial capitalism allows us to look at the way that race has shaped the economic structure, how it shapes the workplace, how it shapes things like extraction and dispossession, how it shapes ideology and politics. We use "DNA" as a metaphor to show how these things are inextricably linked. So we try to encourage organizations to develop a more integrated way of thinking about race, class, and gender—to see race as both a structural reality and as a strategy that has been used to divide us.

Maite: Okay, so how does the labor movement come into play?

Harmony: The labor movement has historically been strong in articulating class issues but has been much weaker in articulating struggles around race and gender. The unions we were working with wanted to develop a more integrative approach. A number of these organizers felt like their members were good on class and economic justice, but they wanted to bring them to a deeper level: to really understand neoliberalism as a political project and to understand capitalism as a system. So they asked us [GPP] to come in and do some trainings. We have done training for staff and senior leaders that cuts across labor organizations, as well as for members of specific unions.

Valery: We are also in a heightened moment with Black Lives Matter and the unions saying, "Hey, we need this," but at the same time, they might not be as prepared to think about their own practice—so we notice a friction there.

Importantly, there is a desperate need for us [trade unionists] to understand that just because we're organized, it doesn't mean we have the ideological stamina and density to really keep our movement antifascist and progressive. I think for us, trade unionists, by not doing political education, by not doing ideological work, it means we have a shifting ground that is becoming quite fascist.

Harmony: This has become even more urgent as Trumpism has made inroads within the membership of unions. When that happens, it is tempting to say, "These 'social' issues are distracting us. Let's just focus on economic issues that unite us. Let's just go back to the economic bread-and-butter issues." But—if we don't take them on—these divisions will hamstring us in the end. So we're trying to help some unions to figure out how to work with the political reality so their members understand that we can't fight these Trumpist ideas in a race-silent way, even though that's tempting. There has been some important work—done through the race–class narrative project—about how to articulate race and class together in ways that build different unity. We are layering on that work to add in the analytical work to help worker–leaders understand the systems and histories that created this context and to learn from the history of multiracial solidarity in the labor movement to help them build a different kind of unionism today. This framework of racial capitalism is very helpful as it helps to think through this complicated project of how to build multiracial class solidarity. That doesn't mean silencing difference but working through difference.

Valery: Yeah, working with the unions on racial capitalism has been a process of both learning and adjusting and also adapting it to every union and every sector and the needs that they internally have. So we have definitely been looking at class and gender. But, for example, we also have had migration as part of this conversation, specifically around healthcare and Filipino membership and leadership. We talked about what the global division of labor is in this sector, the historic colonial relationships that are modernized and how those are used to set up our current neoliberal systems. So what is really interesting is that the methodology is able to be nimble and adapt.

Let me describe our courses for you, briefly: The course is structured to understand how neoliberalism, capitalism, patriarchy, and white supremacy have organized the economy and our ideology against our collective interests. We do this course either in a three-day intensive when we can meet face-to-face, or we do it virtually in about ten two-hour sessions. We create a container that allows us to share, learn, and think together. The methodology has lectures, but it also draws from people's own lived experiences. We do simulations, including, for example, exercises to explore the various ways we are exploited. We reflect on our own workplaces to understand concepts like the "racial division of labor." Worker–leaders go on "gallery walks" to learn about history, whether it's about the tension between working-class power and racial exclusion in the New Deal era or the historical connection between racial slavery and policing today. We contrast and compare; we interrogate the outcomes of policies and laws, and we think of past and current strategies that allow us to see and develop long-term organizing goals.

Maite: Right, that sounds like a great course! I would love to take it!

In any case, last time we spoke you mentioned this video on Filipino nurses [reader—check it out! "Why the US has so many Filipino nurses" available on vox. com, https://bit.ly/3tswXJV], which shows how the Philippines have been grappling with a severe shortage of nurses during the COVID-19 pandemic, while at the same time, the country produces an extraordinary number of nurses each year, highlighting its colonial history. Do you have another example?

Valery: Yes, we have worked with a union on LGBTQ rights. So it is not just about class and gender or class and race but the intersections. For example, we specifically talked about the AIDS crisis and how the narrative of that was being used by the conservative southern political class. And how then the crisis also helped to attack these communities, and particularly the way in which there was no action around this particular virus. We made a parallel with COVID and talked about the implications and how white that fight was and how people of color could have been included and how in some ways an indication of who gets left out, who continues to have problems is still latent.

So in this case, it's about a healthcare union facing COVID, but that is now also thinking through who has been excluded. So interestingly, while that union is very much committed to win, for example, healthcare for all, they might not have seen that fight in terms of racial justice. And I think, through this course, we very much center race as a part of this fight—that is, a fight for racial justice is a fight for healthcare for all. And it's not just thinking how the struggle itself is organized or who is excluded and who is included, but it's also important on how to strategize so that the inclusion is actually embedded in the very way you fight. Not only who speaks but also where we organize, who has the access to the resources, how that is done, how as a multiplicity of groups you fight together. So by design, you have to think about who is most affected by it, and you need to center that as part of your strategy.

Maite: Absolutely! So can you give me a more concrete example of how that then works? How are these courses used to strategize on the ground?

Valery: I think that the intervention, the course itself, makes organizations look at their own practices. I mean, it's like a mirror. In some cases, the controversy around these courses has been because it makes the organizations look at how they run their own work. And how their staff should reflect the shop floor, how to invest in staff of color, the leaders of color, the members of color; thinking about the agency of these particular workers, and the demands that would dramatically improve conditions in their workplace as well. So, for example, the idea that you can ask for more money for cleaners, but if cleaners don't have a pathway to get out of these divisions of labor, you need to not just increase the most precarious salaries but also address the fact that the underlying conditions are bad because of the jobs themselves, the sectors themselves and how these are undervalued. They are undervalued because reproductive and care labor is taken for granted, while ironically being essential to run the economy.

For example, we have worked with Bargaining for the Common Good in Scotland. And they talked about centering racial justice in their strategy. And that led the union leadership in Scotland to think about what the intervention is in COVID when a disproportionate amount of people dying are workers of color. There had to be a Black worker committee to push for higher demands of protection, higher PPE, higher monitoring of where and how these workers are being deployed because it is the job that put them at risk. To me, these are the moments in which you understand the impact and think through the strategy in a way that centers things that otherwise would have been completely left out.

We cannot tell the unions what the strategy should be, but we can only bring the conversation that makes them think about what their strategies need to be: where are we failing, what kind of research do we need to do, what data are we asking from employers, what are we missing, what are our blind spots, how can we think in a different way about our bargaining.

Maite: Right, and you have worked on interesting cases early on in your career, right?

Valery: Yes, in the US with the janitors, [who] are mostly migrant workers. So are we blaming migrants or not? Do we have a solidarity, ideological view of the world? Do we want to create a just multiracial world? And so part of the conversation where I think this shows up, as a trade unionist myself, is, for example, the way in which this organization will invest or not in organizing these mostly migrant workers, right? They occupy very different jobs. So the union had to say, "Yes, politically it is the right thing to do, to invest in this, even though many of our core members are in a better position, this is an important fight. We will use funding for this fight." So as a union, we can decide to organize some of the most precarious sectors that are occupied by people of color and women. And this is important because it's about building a broader movement that understands precisely that the precarious conditions of one is actually the beginning of the undoing of everyone.

Maite: Right—so is this the reason why unions and other organizations are taking these courses—to not just become better critics but become better organizers and activists?

Harmony: A challenge with these courses is that even when staff organizers are hungry to support their members to develop deeper analyses, they aren't always clear what strategic shifts they want to make. In an ideal world, we would not just equip them with the analysis, but they would land concrete things they can do with their union to build deeper solidarity. But it's not that straightforward.

Political education alone is not going to solve this problem that the labor movement is facing. There will need to be organizing interventions to shift the practices of unions, like building deep canvas programs that enable worker–leaders to have deep conversations with their co-workers that will actually move them to deeper solidarity rather than division. But those worker–leaders need to understand—in their bones—why they are taking on such a challenging political project. With that deep commitment, they aren't just picking up a phone and going through a script. They are working to build the kind of union they want to see, not a race exclusion, not a race neutral, but one that is built on real solidarity. We get there through a deep understanding of labor history, through a deep understanding of why labor history and why solidarity is core to worker power, that race is an incredibly powerful tool that has been used against us and that when we are silent on race, it will continue to be used to tear us apart.

Valery: Right, and one of the powerful aspects of this course is that it puts labor in relationship to other struggles as well. It opens up the space to talk about how housing rights, poverty and how capitalism extracts value from every layer of our lives. So it's not just labor. For example, in the course, historically, we look at the Great Depression, the civil rights movement, and we think it's a wonderful thing that happened. But then when you look at the layers of who was excluded and how housing rights were acquired, you understand how wealth was divided by race. And who couldn't build wealth and how that is playing out today. I think for a lot of the workers in this course, it was like a shocking understanding of why it is that Black folks might not own homes and why many white people do. And how those housing policies have a very racialized outcome. I think it invited them to understand why Black Lives Matter made sense and why these activists are angry and why there doesn't seem to be another alternative but to take the streets. From the reactions of the white members, this was really a reckoning—a reckoning of how they and their families fitted into a process that benefited from particular policies or particular unions, whereas if you were a Black farm worker or domestic worker, you were denied … that.

Maite: Absolutely, and more recently, we can think of the role of the police …

Valery: Yes, exactly, and we talk about the violence or the policing in these courses. We talk about the brute force and how that violence is historic, colonial. You can talk about the history of policing from slavery forward. Being able to connect what is happening today to slavery and how white vigilante and police force was used throughout history has been so important. I think a lot of these union leaders initially didn't understand why people are challenging the police as an institution, but through the course, they do, even if they don't necessarily agree with specifics of the demands. So I could see a shift in their considerations. And to me, those are the moments where I think it's not just the history or the intellectual side, but these courses allow you to be able to connect to an emotional space of where we are in this country. We have to continue to center things that keep slipping backwards, right? Because there is a push back, there's always a right-wing attack. So this is a pendulum, and we are part of that. It's not just committing to your next election but committing to class and racial justice and that understanding that what is upon you is bigger than your union membership, bigger than your own organization. I think it has all that raw material and it can go deep in so many directions.

Maite: It seems that teaching these courses had a big impact on yourself as well, Valery.

Valery: Oh yes, it just creates shifts in people, including in myself. I always thought, "Oh, my God, I'm so progressive," and then I learn about this and poof—"You thought you were progressive?!" It's a very transformational space. It's also about understanding that you don't come in, you campaign, and then you leave. You invest in something long term. So the companionship model of GPP is an amazing opportunity to think this through not just in one course but in a relationship that transforms an organization. You can't credit one course for immense change, but you have to keep doing it.

Maite: Just to conclude, as activists/unionists within this space, what are your recommendations going forward? What are big challenges laying ahead, and how do we address those?

Valery: Obviously, I think unions need to do more of this work, and they need to do it in a way that is not cosmetic—just because there is a course, we take it. But it is about changing the conversation, putting yourself in relationship to different considerations. I mean, I think one of the powerful things about this course is that it also lays out exploitation, dispossession, racial and gender division of labor, and a good analysis of capitalism. In my view, that is missing explicitly in a lot of the work we do. The depth of how we understand it is at stake. And I also think we're shifting. We need to not only talk about race or gender but also climate change. And these kinds of conversations allow us to layer different strands of knowledge. I do think that members and workers know that in their bodies. So it's also about the methodology of bringing it out of them rather than us needing to tell them.

We can then think about the implications for bargaining—how to create internal change within our structure, how do we develop people of color within our branch? So it's not just, "Oh, yeah, the token person." But we have leaders of color because they lead—they have a very lived experience of the system and a lived experience of how to challenge it. So ideally, as a person of color myself in labor, the relationship to the global, to colonialism, unions need to revisit this or actually just visit this. All of that to me is of fundamental importance.

So my recommendation is that we have to experiment, we have to be humble. And we know that we might also create friction. Because when you look at racism, you have to be looking at yourself as well. That means that a lot of unions have to cope with what, what this means for them, for their future and the resources. So it takes courage. It takes audacious courage to really do this.

Harmony: I want to really echo the importance of this kind of deep investment in worker leadership. As GPP, we are new enough to the labor movement that I am reluctant to make major suggestions on the future of the labor movement. I do want to lift up Bargaining for the Common Good [BCG] as a well-articulated strategic intervention that reflects the analysis that we have been articulating and that is gaining real traction in the labor movement. BCG speaks to many of these issues, such as building a more inclusive labor movement and integrating race, gender, and other community struggles into the workplace. It would be amazing to see more strategic interventions with that level of sophistication and reach emerge, and we are here to support them as they do.

Valery: Sure, and if enough unions do this, then it becomes more like the norm. I think we're at the beginning of that—very humbly. We'll keep trying to keep moving, but it's also about capacity and political will.

Maite: Yeah, absolutely. Thanks to both of you for all the work that you have been doing with the movements, labor, and community organizations. It's been really impressive.

CHAPTER 15

Conclusion

SHERI DAVIS-FAULKNER
Rutgers University
Center for Innovation in Worker Organization
and Department of Labor Studies and Employment Relations

TAMARA L. LEE
Rutgers University
Department of Labor Studies and Employment Relations

NAOMI R WILLIAMS
Rutgers University
Department of Labor Studies and Employment Relations

MAITE TAPIA
Michigan State University
School of Human Resources and Labor Relations

I think he's [Jean-Michel Basquiat] going to be the Big Black Painter ... [but] how many screaming Negroes can you do?

—Andy Warhol (Warhol and Hackett 1991)

One of the heavy burdens borne by scholar-activists of color is that when we create works about justice, our white allies wonder how many "screaming Negroes" we can do to establish our intellectual presence in the canons of theory and praxis. This is a misunderstanding of our work, a reduction of our contributions normalized by structural racism. We are not merely screaming. We are deeply examining the systems and structures that make us shout. We are offering alternative frameworks for understanding the social problems that concern us all, breaking through the unconscious biases in our existing theories that falsely mitigate systemic racism with color-blindness and good intent, even collegiality. When we center the voices of people of color in our work, we must resist tendencies to narrow the scope of their lens or the value of their analysis. It is common in industrial relations to interpret calls for deep, socio-structural problematization and intentional focus on the voices of the most marginalized as important merely for understanding the conditions of BIPOC workers. However, critical theories about race and racism are explanations in the main about the social construction and consequences of whiteness as property (Harris 1993) and the laws and institutions that shape the lives and conditions of *all* workers.

We are mindful that the voices who have stepped onto our platform are far from exhaustive. Diversity as merely an end was never our intent. Rather we present each voice as it was given—as a gift to our knowledge and curiosity, a challenge to our privileges and power, a call for reparative justice over descriptive performance. Forsaking traditional color-blind conceptualizations of the working class and its labor movements, we have offered this *identity-conscious* (Lee and Tapia 2021) collection of stories as a path forward to a more unified and inclusive approach to labor and employment storytelling. Although not all labor history is critical, we advocate for a family reunification of sorts—a deeper relationship and a shared academic home for siblings theoretically separated over the decades. Here, we can learn from each other conceptually, avoid asking questions already answered, and imagine the future of work in coalition. It is our hope that this volume is received as a blueprint for the field's "movement power brokers" to speak truth to power in both theory and praxis.

SPECIAL NOTES AND CALLS TO ACTION

The building of this volume represents a series of radical conversations by the editors, each of us bringing all of our identities, experiences, and networks into the room. In our editorial capacities, we reached out to the institutions for untraditional means of support in academic settings. For example, it was important for us to operate under a reparative justice model for contributors who would not only compensate contributors of color for their written submissions but also for their emotional labor—which has been too often exploited in the name of diversity. We are thankful that LERA used its power to answer that call without hesitance.

In the midst of an escalating pandemic in 2020, this volume emerged from a global uprising for racial justice and concludes in the aftermath of anti-Taiwanese violence in California and the white supremacist murder of ten Black people in Buffalo, New York. There is war in Ukraine, the result of Russian aggression, where Ukraine, the victim of aggression, is simultaneously denying Black and brown people safe passage across the border based on skin color. The media discusses this war on the European continent as somehow uniquely egregious and different from western white-dominant military aggression that remains constant on the continents of Africa including the Middle East, as well as Asia and Latin America. We speak to this issue of systemic racism in labor and employment relations; however, this is simply a reflection of the global crisis of white supremacy that led to an insurrection in the United States in 2021 and the continuation of racial terror that permeates systems and structures worldwide. We are calling the question: What is labor/what are we prepared and willing to do?

Finally, any time we present our work or talk about our scholar-activism, we receive the question as to what our academic institutions could do better. Through CRT/I, we know it is not surprising that so few women and nonbinary folks of color are in leadership positions (e.g., tenured faculty) in our field. At the same time, our institutions pretend to be stuck when it comes to overhauling or drastically changing tenure requirements. This is a fallacy, of course. Changes can be made at any time if there is enough political will or perceived urgency. For example, many institutions have granted their faculty an extra year to go up for tenure because of COVID-19. Along similar lines, many institutions did not hesitate to have their faculty switch overnight to an online teaching system during the pandemic. It is possible to change.

Our one-size-fits-all requirement for tenure has long been deplored by faculty of color (see, e.g., Matthew 2016; for a recent discussion on white privilege within physics, see Mervis 2022). This system does not consider, for example, that for many students of color, faculty of color are a critical resource on campus. As a result, faculty of color tend to engage to a much greater extent in mentoring, role modeling, and counseling, especially—but not only—around issues of race and racism. Furthermore, faculty of color regularly navigate micro-aggressions at work and "[feel] a need to work harder than their colleagues to be seen as legitimate scholars" (Gutiérrez y Muhs, Niemann, González, and Harris 2012; Rucks-Ahidiana 2019). Any type of activism or movement building that is not meant to further academic publications will be discouraged and dismissed because it does not fit within the traditional, white-dominant rules of tenure requirements. At the same time, faculty of color are quite often asked to speak on panels, be part of committees, or be on boards to "diversify" the setting—also referred to as the "Black tax" (Cleveland, Sailes, Gilliam, and Watts 2018). Along similar lines, putting together this LERA volume in which a community of contributors has been created across academic lines and into practitioners' and artists' spaces in which we all peer-reviewed our work will be given no attention because it is now classified as "just" an edited volume. Acknowledging, therefore, the invisible labor and increased demands but also the critical role for students of many faculty of color would be at least a first step toward reparative justice.

We are going to fight for the kind of education that not only black folks should be aware of, but whites as well. Because you have been conditioned into the system too. I know you don't agree, maybe, with what I'm saying, but there is one thing for sure: you got a feeling it's the truth.

—Fannie Lou Hamer (Parker Brooks and Houck 2010)

REFERENCES

Cleveland, Roger, JaDora Sailes, Erin Gilliam, and Jillian Watts. 2018. "A Theoretical Focus on Cultural Taxation: Who Pays for It in Higher Education." *Advances in Social Sciences Research Journal* 5 (10): 95–98.

Gutiérrez y Muhs, Gabriella, Yolanda Flores Niemann, Carmen G. González, and Angela P. Harris. 2012. *Presumed Incompetent: The Intersections of Race and Class for Women in Academia.* Boulder: University Press of Colorado.

Harris, Cheryl. 1993. "Whiteness as Property." *Harvard Law Review* 106 (8): 1707–1791.

Lee, Tamara L., and Maite Tapia. 2021. "Confronting Race and Other Social Identity Erasures: The Case for Critical Industrial Relations Theory." *ILR Review* 74 (3): 637–662.

Matthew, Patricia A., ed. 2016. *Written/Unwritten: Diversity and the Hidden Truths of Tenure.* Chapel Hill: University of North Carolina Press.

Mervis, Jeffrey. 2022. "The Toll of White Privilege: How the Dominant Culture in Physics Has Discouraged Diversity." *Science* 375 (6584): 952–955.

Parker Brooks, Maegan, and Davis W. Houck. 2010. *The Speeches of Fannie Lou Hamer: To Tell It Like It Is.* Jackson: University Press of Mississippi.

Rucks-Ahidiana, Zawadi. 2019. "The Inequities of the Tenure-Track System." Inside Higher Ed. June 7. https://bit.ly/3tpcENT

Warhol, Andy, and Pat Hackett. 1991. *The Andy Warhol Diaries*, 1st ed. New York: Grand Central Publishing.

About the Contributors

VOLUME EDITORS

Tamara L. Lee, Esq., is an assistant professor of labor studies at Rutgers University, where her research confronts the intersection of labor and racial justice, cross-movement solidarity building, and the impact of radical adult education on workplace democracy in Cuba and the United States. She is the co-founder of Haven, a collective of Black, Indigenous, and women and nonbinary folks of color committed to building a safe space for storytelling, free from white supremacy and its systems.

Sheri Davis-Faulkner is the associate director of the Center for Innovation in Worker Organization. She is also an assistant professor of professional practice in the Labor Studies and Employment Relations Department of the School of Management and Labor Relations at Rutgers University. She co-directs the WILL (Women Innovating Labor Leadership) Empower program. Davis-Faulkner has been a member of the Crunk Feminist Collective since 2009 and currently serves as board chair of the National Black Worker Center. She is a steering committee member with the Advancing Black Strategist initiative and for the fledgling Philadelphia Black Worker Center.

Naomi R Williams received a Ph.D. in US history from the University of Wisconsin–Madison. An assistant professor at Rutgers University's School of Management and Labor Relations, Williams's primary research areas include US working-class history and politics. Their research examines the ways working people impact local and national political economies and the ways workers participate in collaborative social justice movements. Williams engages working-class history in urban settings, looking at low-wage service work, industrial employment, and workers in higher education. They are currently revising a book manuscript, *Workers United: Race, Labor, and Coalition Building in Deindustrialized America*, on the transformation of class identity and politics in the late 20th century.

Maite Tapia is an associate professor at the School of Human Resources and Labor Relations at Michigan State University. Her research focuses on worker voice within the workplace, as well as worker organizing and movement building within the broader society, paying specific attention to workers' social identities and structural racism.

CONTRIBUTORS

Valery Alzaga is a labor and migrant rights campaigner and organizer with more than 20 years of organizing experience across a range of different sectors. She is currently the deputy director of the Global Labor Justice–International Labor Rights Forum. She started as an organizer with the Justice for Janitors campaign before becoming the property service director at Local 105 in Denver, where she also was the president of the Colorado Immigrant Rights Coalition. She then worked for SEIU's global department helping win and implement breakthrough global cleaning and security organizing agreements. From 2008 through 2015, she was the European organizing coordinator with the Change to Win European Organizing Centre (CTW–EOC), working with many European unions and sectors to help them develop their own strategic organizing campaigns and programs. Since 2015, she has worked in UK public sector unions organizing anti-privatization and EU and non-EU migrant rights campaigns. From 2018 through 2021, Alzaga was a field campaign strategist and advisor to Barcelona and Catalunya en Comú in Spain and to Mijente—a political Latinx organization seeking racial, economic, gender and climate justice in the United States.

Tahira Benjamin is a storyteller, creator, and entrepreneur creating and supporting purpose-based businesses through inclusive storytelling and marketing solutions. At Haven Media, she facilitates marketing for their email and social media platforms that push us closer to abolition, liberation, and healing.

Nicole Burrowes is an assistant professor in the department of history at Rutgers University, New Brunswick. Her research and teaching interests include social justice movements, comparative histories, Black internationalism, and the politics of solidarity, with a focus on the African diaspora in the Caribbean and the United States. Her current book project, *Seeds of Solidarity: African–Indian Relations and the 1935 Labor Rebellions in British Guiana*, explores the historical possibility of a movement forged by those at the edges of empire in the midst of economic, environmental, and political crises. Beyond the academy, Burrowes has a lengthy track record of working with communities for transformative justice.

J. Mijin Cha is an assistant professor of urban and environmental policy at Occidental College and a fellow at the Worker Institute, Cornell University. Cha's research focuses on labor–climate coalitions and just transitions. She is a part of the Just Transition Listening Project research team, convened by the Labor Network for Sustainability, which was the first effort of its kind to interview over 100 individuals on their experience with industrial transition. Along with her colleague, Manuel Pastor, she developed a novel framework for developing just-transition policies and conducted a four-state study of what is needed for a just transition and how to build progressive power at the state level. She is also a member of the Labor Leading on Climate initiative at Cornell University's Worker Institute supporting several state-based climate jobs efforts.

Ella Dior is an 18-year-old Black, Queer, and nonbinary activist from Brooklyn, New York. They have organized on-the-ground actions to amplify the voices of Black people.

Ren Fernandez-Kim is a nonbinary, Korean, and Peruvian American artist, anthropologist and educator.

Kristina Gisors, French Caribbean who has lived many lives, finds liberation in literature and shares her passion for Black authors through her book club.

Harmony Goldberg is a political educator and facilitator at the Grassroots Policy Project. She has worked closely with social movements around the United States for more than 20 years. She was a founder and former co-director of SOUL: the School Of Unity and Liberation, a social justice movement training center based in Oakland, California. She has provided political education, strategic facilitation, and writing support for a number of local organizations and national organizing networks, including the National Domestic Workers Alliance, Social Justice Leadership, the Right to the City Alliance and, most recently, with People's Action. She worked closely with the Bertha Foundation for several years, which exposed her to models of political education used by social movements in the global South. Harmony is a founding editor of Organizing Upgrade, an online strategy journal for Left organizers in the United States.

Ericka Hart is a black queer femme activist, writer, highly acclaimed speaker and award-winning sexuality educator with a master's of education in human sexuality from Widener University.

Haven Media is a collective of BIWOC and nonbinary-identifying folks rooted in abolition, liberation, and healing through art and storytelling. Haven created a safe space for its collective to allow the freedom to develop the systems and communities that work for the collective.

Austin McCoy is a historian and assistant professor at West Virginia University. His research and teaching interests focus on African American history, the US Left, labor, and social movements.

Javier Morillo joined the Center for Innovation in Worker Organization as a Fellow with the Bargaining for the Common Good program in June 2019, after stepping down from his role as president of SEIU Local 26 in Minnesota. Under his leadership, Local 26 has earned a national reputation as a creative and risk-taking force for raising standards for low-wage workers, especially immigrants and people of color. As an artist, Morillo was a featured storyteller in a Moth Mainstage production in 2013 and is a repeat winner of the Twin Cities Moth Story Slam. His Moth Mainstage story "Handcuffed in Houston," was later part of a Minnesota Fringe Festival show, "Louder Than Words: Tales of Extreme Action," which was named one of the Top 10 Fringe Newbies of 2014.

Alejandra Pablos is a social justice community organizer, strategist, storyteller, and writer, at the intersections of mass incarceration and immigration.

Jamie Pandit is a South Asian woman and content creator who shares beauty, fashion, and her experiences living openly as a transgender woman, all with a bit of humor and sass.

Danielle T. Phillips-Cunningham is an associate professor and program director of Multicultural Women's and Gender Studies at Texas Woman's University. She teaches courses about women's labors and migrations, feminist thought, and transdisciplinary research methods. She is also a recipient of the Sara A. Whaley Book Prize of the National Women's Studies Association for her book, *Putting Their Hands on Race: Irish Immigrant and Southern Black Domestic Workers* (Rutgers University Press, 2020).

Sanjay Pinto is a Fellow at the Rutgers School of Management and Labor Relations and the Worker Institute at Cornell ILR. He has an M.Sc. in development studies from the London School of Economics and a Ph.D. in sociology and social policy from Harvard. His current work focuses on efforts to promote equity within care systems, responses to workplace sexual harassment and violence, the use of digital tools to advance worker power, and the confrontation between democracy and racial capitalism.

Salil R. Sapre is a Ph.D. candidate in the School of Human Resources and Labor Relations at Michigan State University. His research focuses on the international political economy of global supply chains; intersectional identities and positionalities of the modern workforce; industrial democracy, worker movements, unionism; and critical race theory.

Erica Smiley is the executive director of Jobs With Justice. A long-time organizer and movement leader, she has been spearheading strategic organizing and policy interventions for Jobs With Justice for nearly 15 years. Before taking up her current position with the organization, Smiley served as organizing director for Jobs With Justice developing campaigns that resulted in transformative changes to how working people organize and are civically engaged at their workplaces and in their communities. Smiley has been instrumental in developing the strategic vision of Jobs With Justice to build power for impacted working people through expanding their collective bargaining power as one way to redefine and claim their democracy, while addressing issues of inequality and poverty. This includes founding the Advancing Black Strategists Initiative and co-convening a national strategy for essential workers.

Danielle St. Luce is a noprofit finance and fundraising professional with a bachelor of science in industrial and labor relations from Cornell University.

Larry Williams Jr. is founder of UnionBase.org and co-founder of Progressive Workers Union (PWU). UnionBase is the first secure social networking and education platform for unions and union workers. UnionBase is regarded by Forbes and Fast Company as the leading digital platform for a new generation of workers. PWU is a growing and powerful national union for nonprofit employees that was started at the Sierra Club, America's largest environmental organization.

WILL (Women Innovating Labor Leadership) Empower is a bold and ambitious initiative to identify, nurture, train, and convene a new generation of women labor leaders. WILL Empower employs a broad, multipronged approach that interfaces with women on multiple levels and through interwoven programs. WILL Empower is a national program, jointly housed at Rutgers University's Center for Innovation in Worker Organization in the School of Management and Labor Relations in New Jersey and Georgetown University's Kalmanovitz Initiative for Labor and the Working Poor in Washington, D.C.

LERA Executive Board Members 2022–23

President
Paul F. Clark, Pennsylvania State University

President-Elect
William E. Spriggs, AFL-CIO

Past President
Wilma Liebman, Former Chair, NLRB

Secretary–Treasurer
Andrew Weaver, University of Illinois Urbana-Champaign

Editor-in-Chief
J. Ryan Lamare, University of Illinois at Urbana-Champaign

National Chapter Advisory Council Chair
William Canak, Middle Tennessee State University (ret.)

Legal Counsel
Steven B. Rynecki

Executive Board Members
Peter Berg, Michigan State University
Robert Chiaravalli, Strategic Labor and HR, LLC
Julie Farb, AFL-CIO
Janet Gillman, Oregon Employment Relations Board
Shannon Gleeson, Cornell University
Beverly Harrison, Arbitrator/Mediator
Quinton Herbert, City of Baltimore
Tamara Lee, Rutgers University
Kevin Legel, Ford Motor Company
Glenard Middleton, AFSCME Maryland Council 67
Deborah Moore-Carter, City of Baltimore
Deborah Mueller, CSEA Local 1000, AFSCME
Dionne Pohler, University of Toronto
Jim Pruitt, Kaiser Permanente
Javier Ramirez, Federal Mediation and Conciliation Service
Christine Riordan, University of Illinois at Urbana Champaign
Sean Rogers, University of Rhode Island
Marc Weinstein, Florida International University

DIVERSITY
IS OUR STRENGTH!

In Solidarity,

International Union, UAW

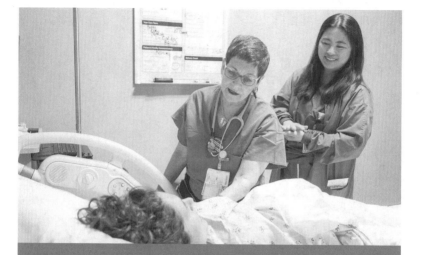

A Better WAY TO →→→→→→→→ WORK

Kaiser Permanente and the Alliance of Health Care Unions thank all our managers, physicians and employees — including more than 50,000 union-represented workers — for 24 years of partnership.

Affordable, quality care. It started in California's shipyards and steel mills in World War II; today we continue that tradition across the country. Kaiser Permanente is America's largest non-profit health care delivery organization. Kaiser Permanente and the Alliance of Health Care Unions are proud to work together to ensure Kaiser Permanente is the best place to work and the best place to receive care.

In 2021, we affirmed our Labor Management Partnership in a new four-year agreement, which includes important new provisions committing to joint work on staffing, racial justice, and promoting the affordability of health care. The new national agreement covers more than 50,000 members of AFSCME, AFT, IBT, ILWU, IUOE, KPNAA, UFCW, UNITE HERE, and USW, in every market where Kaiser Permanente operates.

 KAISER PERMANENTE.

 ALLIANCE OF HEALTH CARE UNIONS

UAW-Ford Labor Management Committee Trust

Powered By Our People

ILR
AND LERA

A Long-Standing Partnership

COLLABORATING SINCE 1947
ilr.cornell.edu

Cornell's ILR School is transforming the future of work, employment and labor through our teaching, research and outreach to the community. As a leader in all aspects of labor and employment relations, ILR is a proud partner with LERA. ILR faculty and students are deeply engaged in this collaboration sharing ideas, contributing papers, chairing sessions and presenting on panels. Together, we've been at the heart of extraordinary changes in the workplace and in the lives of workers. We embrace multiple and diverse perspectives, encourage principled debate and collaborate across disciplines. And, we operate in the real world, drawing on the richness of the LERA community to drive positive impact for people and society, today and in the future.

Leading the Way with LERA

Rutgers School of Management and Labor Relations (SMLR) is proud to partner with LERA through an established tradition of leadership and service to the association across executive, editorial and committee roles. Through our academic programs, research initiatives, and outreach programs, Rutgers SMLR is a leading source of expertise on the world of work, building effective and sustainable organizations, and the changing employment relationship.

Rutgers SMLR is pleased to continue our collaboration with LERA to offer a unique lens to explore the evolution of work and the Future of Work(ers).

RUTGERS

School of Management
and Labor Relations

smlr.rutgers.edu